EUROPEAN BANKS AND THE AMERICAN CHALLENGE

European Banks and the American Challenge

Competition and Cooperation in International Banking under Bretton Woods

Edited by

STEFANO BATTILOSSI
YOUSSEF CASSIS

OXFORD
UNIVERSITY PRESS

OXFORD
UNIVERSITY PRESS

Great Clarendon Street, Oxford OX2 6DP

Oxford University Press is a department of the University of Oxford.
It furthers the University's objective of excellence in research, scholarship,
and education by publishing worldwide in

Oxford New York

Auckland Bangkok Buenos Aires Cape Town Chennai
Dar es Salaam Delhi Hong Kong Istanbul Karachi Kolkata
Kuala Lumpur Madrid Melbourne Mexico City Mumbai Nairobi
São Paulo Shanghai Singapore Taipei Tokyo Toronto

with an associated company in Berlin

Oxford is a registered trade mark of Oxford University Press
in the UK and in certain other countries

Published in the United States
by Oxford University Press Inc., New York

British Library Cataloguing in Publication Data

Data available

Library of Congress Cataloging in Publication Data

European banks and the American challenge : competition and cooperation in
international banking under Bretton Woods / edited by Stefano Battilossi, Youssef Cassis.
p. cm.
Includes bibliographical references and index.
1. Banks and banking, European—History—20th century. 2. Banks and banking,
International—History—20th century. 3. Banks and banking, American—History—20th
century. I. Battilossi, Stefano, 1961- II. Cassis, Youssef.
HG2974 .E9 2002 332.1'5'094—dc21 2001055719

ISBN 0-19-925027-8

1 3 5 7 9 10 8 6 4 2

Typeset by Newgen Imaging Systems (P) Ltd., Chennai, India
Printed in Great Britain
on acid-free paper by
T.J. International Ltd., Padstow, Cornwall

Preface

This book is the outcome of a one-day conference held at the London School of Economics on 25 March 1999 at the initiative of the Business History Unit. The event was made possible thanks to the generous support of our sponsors: the Bank of England and the European Association for Banking History. We owe a great debt of gratitude to them. Besides the quality of the papers presented, the conference benefited enormously from the input of all participants, in the first place the chairs and commentators. Our sincere thanks go to Forrest Capie, Marcello de Cecco, Michael Collins, Philip Cottrell, Steven I. Davis, Terry Gourvish, Leslie Hannah, Geoffrey Jones, and Richard Roberts.

The object of this volume is to discuss a new and important subject which has so far been neglected by historians: the internationalization of banking in industrialized countries and the rise of a new global financial order, with both its potentials for economic welfare and its dangers of economic instability. The roots of this new order date back to the 1950s, with the emergence of the Eurocurrency markets and the relaxation of exchange and capital controls inherited from the inter-war period and the post-war reconstruction. Throughout the 1960s—the high noon of the European Golden Age—market forces flourished despite the reintroduction of new controls and were able to exploit the many asymmetries of the regulatory framework of the Western world. International, and especially American, banks were leading actors of such transformation. They promoted financial innovations and created new markets to service the expansion of world trade and foreign direct investments, and the rising financing needs of multinational corporations, governments, and international institutions. In the process, they deeply transformed their techniques and cultures to design new global strategies. The early 1970s marked the beginning of a new phase, which brought to banks many new challenges. The end of the fixed exchanges regime instituted at Bretton Woods and the transition to floating rates implied the privatization of foreign exchange risk. The oil shock and the recycling of petrodollars gave a new, unprecedented dimension to the international banking business, where European banks were now able to play a substantial role, having somewhat taken up the American challenge of the previous decade. The end of the Golden Age of high and stable economic growth paved the way to a new era of instability and volatility in growth, prices, and foreign exchanges. In the turmoil, attitude of the governments to international finance oscillated between liberalization and controls. Eventually the former prevailed, at different dates, in core countries such as the USA, West Germany, and the UK, although others—such as France and Italy—had to wait until the 1990s.

This, however, is another story, which will have to be told in other books. Our volume instead focuses on the period that encompassed the rise of international banking since the late 1950s and its first setback in the early 1970s. In fact there exists a huge literature on the international expansion of American banks and the response of European banks. However, it has mostly been written by contemporaries of the events—economists, financial analysts, and journalists. The question has not yet been approached from a historical perspective, i.e. not only with the benefit of hindsight, but also with the rigorous use of the archival material now available. Ultimately, only such an approach can get to the heart of the matter and help us draw from those years lessons that are still relevant today.

S.B.
Y.C.

London
April 2001

Contents

List of Figures

List of Tables

Notes on Contributors

STEFANO BATTILOSSI is Visiting Professor at the Department of Economic History, Universidad Carlos III, Madrid, and Visiting Fellow at the Business History Unit, London School of Economics.

ERIC BUSSIÈRE is Jean Monnet Chair of History of the European Construction at the University of Paris IV.

YOUSSEF CASSIS is Professor at the Department of Economic and Social History, University of Grenoble II, and Visiting Fellow at the Business History Unit, London School of Economics.

HAROLD JAMES is Professor at the Department of History, Princeton University.

ULRICH RAMM is Chief Economist and Executive Vice President at Commerzbank AG, Frankfurt am Main.

DUNCAN M. ROSS is Senior Lecturer at the Department of Economic and Social History, University of Glasgow.

CATHERINE R. SCHENK is Senior Lecturer at the Department of Economic and Social History, University of Glasgow.

RICHARD SYLLA is Henry Kaufman Professor of the History of Financial Institutions and Markets, and Professor of Economics at the Stern School of Business, New York University.

1

Introduction: International Banking and the American Challenge in Historical Perspective

STEFANO BATTILOSSI

Until quite recently, American banks in Europe were largely diplomatic and social outposts for the home concern. They evolved in the early 1900s as courtesy stations where rich aunts could get their checks cashed or have a trust officer help keep an eye on investments. Their nephews and nieces on European tours used the bank, and so did a few vacationing businessmen. Even during a short flurry of business activity in the 1920s a faint aura of afternoon tea and evening dinner-jacket languor clung to these way stations. It did not completely disperse till well into the 1950s. Towards the end of that decade, as American companies swarmed overseas, the soft sleep ended; the banks added new staff, new services, and a new dynamism. (E. A. McCreary, *The Americanization of Europe: The Impact of Americans and American Business on the Uncommon Market* (Garden City, NY: Doubleday, 1964), 46)

This volume deals fundamentally with the rise—indeed, a resurgence—of international banking in the post-war Golden Age of Western capitalism. International banking had been a major engine and a product at one time of the first wave of globalization which ran from the late nineteenth century up to the systemic crisis of 1931. After almost three decades of dormancy, its awakening coincided with the full coming into its own of the international monetary regime known as the Bretton Woods System (1958–73). Rapid internationalization of banking and finance then came again to be a fundamental factor affecting economic growth and monetary conditions of Western countries, as well as their international economic relations. In fact, it was far more than a mere re-emergence. The period was marked by the rise of a radically innovative kind of international banking—the so-called Eurocurrency banking. It witnessed the breathtaking expansion of two distinguished though interrelated institutions, both based mainly in the City of London but with wide ramifications that encompassed all major financial centres in Europe and beyond: an international wholesale money and credit market (the Eurocurrency and Eurocredit market) and an international capital market (the Eurobond market). Indeed, since then the growth of Eurocurrency banking largely outpaced that of both world production and international trade in goods and services.[1] Moreover, the rise of Eurocurrency banking provided the groundwork for the global financial revolution that characterized the world economy in the last three decades of the twentieth century. Consequently, the 1960s can legitimately be considered the cradle of structural changes bound to transform not only Western banking, but also and more broadly the political economy of international relations.

Indeed, Euromarkets, and the revival of London's fortunes as an international financial centre that they brought about, are the pivotal issues of this volume. It addresses a time period stretching, quite flexibly, from the mid-1950s (the prologue to convertibility and banking internationalization) to the mid-1970s (the starting-point of a new international financial regime, marked by the transition to floating exchange rates and the explosion of international lending). However, the focus is very much on the period of Bretton Woods convertibility (1958–73). As suggested in the title, a peculiar perspective is proposed: that of the 'American challenge'. The concept became popular in Europe in the second half of the 1960s, as US multinationals swarmed overseas and US foreign direct investment in Europe, triggered by the launching of the European Economic Community, gained momentum. This was regarded in some European countries not merely as a challenge to prospective fortunes of national champions but even as a threat to national independence. France, the standard-bearer of sentiments opposed to Americanization since the Marshall Plan era,[2] took the lead—in fact, J. J. Servan-Schreiber's *Le Défi américaine* became a European best-seller—but others joined in. Across the Channel, public outrage was nurtured by the alleged American takeover of Britain. In West Germany debates over excessive foreign influence on national industries flourished.[3] Clearly, both economic and political arguments interwove in contemporaries' perceptions. Since 1964 the massive landing of American banks in Europe, as followers or escorts of US multinationals, raised similar complaints. As this volume will illustrate at length, American banks reached an undisputed dominant position in the Eurocurrency (mostly Eurodollar) market, and aggressively competed with European banks in the Eurocredit and Eurobond markets. The response of European banks was mainly defensive in the 1960s, then more aggressive and successful in the 1970s. However, it was not only a story of competition and conflicts, but also of collaboration. On many occasions American and European banks cooperated in international syndicates and jointly ventured into emerging markets.

The American dynamism was not entirely a post-war novelty—in fact US–European competition in international banking ran parallel to the rise of the USA as the world's leading economic and financial power from the beginnings of the twentieth century. Neither was the challenge the mere outcome of competition between market forces. The aim of this introduction is therefore to put the 'American challenge' and the European response in historical perspective, as well as to frame post-war developments within their broader economic and political context. For this purpose four issues will be addressed: the rise and rapid waning of a first American challenge after the First World War; the emergence of a potential European challenge to American dominance in international banking in the 1950s and early 1960s; the Americanization of international money and financial markets located in Europe in the 1960s–70s and the response of the European banks; and finally the role of competition in international banking as a facet of a broader Euro-American cross-challenge for international economic hegemony.

1. The First American Challenge? The Rise of US Banks in Pre-war International Banking

Financial globalization from the late nineteenth century to the collapse of the gold exchange standard in 1931 was characterized by the development of a global network of interbank relations and periodical upsurges of international lending (in 1896–1914 and 1923–8). Large commercial and 'universal' banks emerged as important players in the international financial arena and eroded the traditional leadership of *haute banques* in international intermediation. New techniques for financing international trade and modern foreign exchange markets emerged, together with innovative international interbank relations which took the form of international correspondent banking.[4] Against this background, an international wholesale interbank market emerged, based mainly on finance bills (i.e. not related to trade transactions),[5] correspondent deposits and overdrafts, and, after the First World War, on 'swap' transactions that allowed banks to take temporary positions in foreign currencies.[6] International liquidity redistribution, with the London money market in a pivotal role, was mainly driven by arbitrage opportunities arising from interest rate differentials, and occasionally by speculation.[7] At the same time, the rise of large international banking syndicates allowed international circulation of foreign securities, issued in main financial centres by corporate and sovereign borrowers.[8] Financial globalization flourished also with the expansion of banks' multinational activities from 'core' industrialized countries towards peripheral and semi-peripheral areas such as Eastern Europe, the Far East, and Latin America.

International banking in its multiple dimensions gravitated towards London as the centre of a global multilateral payments system, and continued to be largely dominated by British institutions. Something akin to a challenge to their leadership came from mainland Europe—namely from German[9] and French banks[10]—both in trade finance and investment banking, as Paris and Berlin emerged as marginal competitors of London in acceptance business and international issues. However Britain remained by far the main creditor nation in the world, and the City of London provided foreign governments and corporations with a true international capital market.[11] In acceptance business, the pound maintained a dominant role in spite of increased competition from other key currencies such as the French franc and the mark.[12] In Britain new actors emerged, as free-standing overseas banks and amalgamating joint-stock banks challenged the traditional dominance of merchant banks—such as Rothschild, Baring, Kleinwort, Schroeder, Hambros—as international intermediaries, whose market share in acceptance credit and investment banking was progressively eroded.[13] On the contrary, American banks remained quite minor players in international finance until the First World War. Of course, leading New York private bankers, such as Morgan and Kuhn, Loeb, established a solid reputation and a strong network of overseas connections, especially with British counterparts. However, as far as the USA remained a debtor nation and the New York Stock Exchange an overwhelmingly domestic market, whereby only a modest volume of foreign securities were issued and traded, US banks kept focusing on domestic business. Their major international role, together with their partners and agents in London and Paris, was that of intermediaries of foreign (mostly British) capital investments in American railway and industrial securities.[14] US commercial banks were even less internationally oriented. Until 1913, their role was severely bounded by regulations prohibiting nationally chartered institutions to branch abroad. As a consequence only a few trust companies (such as Guaranty Trust Company, later Morgan Guaranty Trust) and international banking corporations established branches in London and Paris. Some were subsequently acquired by New York commercial banks, such as Chase Manhattan and National City Bank, to buy a foothold in European financial centres. However, American business in Europe generally relied on local banks for their international banking services, while US banks' European branches generally limited their business to servicing Americans abroad.[15]

The absence of a central bank and of a discount market for acceptances hindered the development of dollar-based trade finance, so that American foreign trade kept relying almost exclusively on London.[16] American banks also used to resort massively to finance bills on British counterparts as a source of liquidity during domestic rising business cycles and intense stock market activity.[17]

Until 1913 American national banks were also denied the privilege of conducting acceptance business in international transactions, so that foreign banks (together with US private bankers) successfully filled the gap.[18] As in the British case, so also in the USA this was the period of the rise of commercial banks. They established correspondent connections with overseas counterparts, expanded their foreign assets, developed foreign exchange banking, provided international payment services to multinational customers—a business in which the National City Bank (later Citibank) already enjoyed a leading position at the beginning of the century—and gradually stepped into investment banking.[19]

The First World War—from which the USA emerged as the world's main creditor nation—marked a watershed. The oligopolistic structure of pre-1914 international finance collapsed after two of its pillars, Paris and Berlin, saw their international role dramatically diminished by domestic inflation and currency depreciation. Both short-term liquidity and portfolio investments flew from France and Germany towards New York and London.[20] The role of both the dollar and American banks in international finance rapidly increased. For the first time in its history, New York became a truly international financial entrepôt as US foreign lending outstripped that of Britain.[21] In fact the USA accounted for 60 per cent of the outflows from creditor countries (according to the aggregate figures calculated by C. Feinstein and K. Watson for the period 1924–30), while the UK and France together for 30 per cent.[22] At the same time London's international financial intermediation, though somehow revived after the 1925 stabilization, was weakened by an overvalued sterling and increasingly focused on the traditional British area of influence. A new bipolar structure emerged, centred around New York and London as the main international financial centres competing for world hegemony.[23]

American bankers felt that time was ripe for challenging the British leadership. Relaxation of regulatory constraints in the US legal framework—as American authorities adjusted legislation to the international economic leadership conquered by the country—laid the groundwork of American banks' unprecedented international dynamism. The 1913 Federal Reserve Act granted international banking facilities to all national banks; the 1919 Edge Act authorized American banks to form federally incorporated corporations specializing in international banking. Thanks to the creation of the Federal Reserve System, US trade increasingly came to be financed by member banks through dollar acceptances, and the dollar—the only major currency convertible into gold—gained an unprecedented role as an international key currency. As a means to establish the American role in world trade finance, some US banks adopted an aggressive policy of expanding foreign branches and subsidiaries (either individually or through joint ventures). Inroads into

European financial centres remained few, however—even in London, whereby only Bankers Trust Company, Hanover Bank, and the Bank of America established branches in the 1920s. Overseas expansion focused mainly on Latin America and the Far East.[24] The 1920s marked also the rise to dominance of American private investment bankers in international finance, under the undisputed leadership of the House of Morgan. Cooperation between American and British merchant banks, acting mainly as agents of their governments, provided financial assistance which proved fundamental for the success of stabilization plans of European governments and the restoration of a gold exchange standard.[25] The role of the US banks was also crucial in organizing international syndicates that opened up the New York market to foreign corporate and sovereign borrowers and distributed foreign securities both to the American public and, through their cosmopolitan connections, to European investors.

However, the rise of American international banking proved short-lived. Overseas branching led rapidly to overexpansion; many ventures rapidly began to run losses and ended up with failure, because of a lack either of business or of experience. In the USA enthusiasm for foreign securities, initially boosted by aggressive marketing strategies, proved equally a flash in the pan. As Wall Street boomed in 1928, the international lending fever rapidly abated: American investors actually returned to bondsellers at least half of their stock of foreign bonds.[26] In fact, however, the sudden withering of the American capital market during the domestic stock-exchange boom brought a lethal blow to governments in desperate search of further borrowing to service outstanding debts. Some were temporarily bailed out by banks that granted additional liquidity (as was the case regarding the explosive increase of German short-term indebtedness in 1928–9), only to be left to their destiny after Wall Street's crash. Globalization was abruptly brought to an end by the systemic crisis of 1929–31. By then, the grand move of American banks into international finance had already been brought to a 'sick end' (to use Herbert Feis's expression). Direct presence in European financial centres had remained marginal: only six banks had made their entry in London, and even fewer in Paris. The American challenge to British leadership in trade finance and investment banking had fragile foundations. Unregulated, cut-throat competition proved an easy road to unsound banking practices. Moreover, the aggressive competition between New York and London substantially contributed to the spiralling of the international debt crisis of the early 1930s. The boom-and-bust cycle ended up with a complete liquidation of international political indebtedness (war debts and reparations) and a substantial reduction of commercial indebtedness through default, transfer moratoria, or depreciation of creditors' currencies. American investors in foreign securities were left to face a chain of defaults and rescheduling: in many cases settlements could be negotiated only after the Second World War.[27]

International bankers had much for which to blame themselves. In spite of increased politicization of international finance[28] and closer (though reluctant and loosely institutionalized) co-operation among central banks, they enjoyed large autonomy.[29] Both American and British authorities espoused a hands-off policy, though retaining some politically oriented controls on foreign borrowers' access to their capital markets. While London issuing houses seemed generally more prepared to enforce collective monitoring and self-regulation, US banks proved far more incautious. Systemic instability made things worse. The restored gold exchange regime was stunned with unprecedented volatility in interest rates and foreign exchanges, as confidence in the commitment to gold remained weak. Core countries' monetary authorities failed to design a co-operative framework to make the system sustainable, as demonstrated by the frequent use of discount rate actions to attract (and hoard) scarce global gold stocks. International private bankers' orthodox attitude to adjustment contributed to give the system a marked deflationary orientation and imposed recurrent shocks to the economies.[30] With the collapse of the international monetary regime, the widespread imposition of exchange and capital controls and the sharp decline in world trade, banking in both the USA and Western Europe entered a long period of nationalistic retrenchment and extensive national regulation. This was a structural change that international banking would have to face after the war.

2. A European Challenge? The Emergence of the Eurodollar and Eurobond Markets

The inheritance of the pre-war period—in the form of a general reassessment of the deflationary thrust incorporated by orthodox financial thinking of both central and private bankers, as well as of the destabilizing role of short-term capital flows—was evident in the restrictive financial international order designed at Bretton Woods in 1944. Pre-eminence was assigned to autonomy of domestic macroeconomic policy over free capital flows; this represented a major break with the liberal tradition of international finance that had dominated in the past. The official endorsement of capital controls, both unilateral and cooperative ('at both ends'), was an apparent victory of unorthodox, 'embedded liberal' financial culture[31] of both the US and the British Treasury (under the leadership of Henry Morgenthau, Harry Dexter White, and John Maynard Keynes) against New York bankers. In fact Wall Street openly supported a return to complete freedom of capital movements after a short transitional period. In tune with the Federal Reserve of New York, they advocated a quick return to convertibility of the two international key currencies, the dollar and sterling. After having opposed in vain the creation of the IMF (a position shared with the Bank of England), they successfully defended the Bank for International Settlements against plans for its liquidation as a sanctuary of liberal orthodoxy.[32]

However the 1947 events brought a final blow to their residual hopes of a quick return to financial liberalism. As the Anglo-American 'key currency' plan to enforce an untimely sterling convertibility was sunk by massive speculation, Wall Street bankers' ambition to promote New York again as the world's leading financial centre suffered a hard setback. The enforcement by most European governments of extensive exchange and trade controls against the destabilizing effects of trade deficits and substantial flights of capital to the USA—particularly welcomed by Wall Street bankers as a means of strengthening the role of New York as the world's leading financial centre (so much so that they refused to cooperate with European authorities to check capital inflows)—was proof of their unwillingness to sacrifice domestic recovery and employment to the precocious restoration of a liberal order.[33] Finally, the Cold War heavily influenced the attitude of the US government towards the international monetary system. As a matter of fact, the Federal reserve and the US Treasury—whereby the voice of New York bankers' became far more influential under the Truman and Eisenhower administrations—assigned high priority to a rapid return to a liberal regime in international finance. However, the State Department and the Marshall Plan agencies (the Economic Co-operation Administration and its successor, the Mutual Security Agency) proved much more sensitive to the impact of monetary and trade matters on US–European political cohesion and security cooperation within NATO.[34]

During the 1950s therefore international financial relations remained largely inter-governmental and politically motivated. European dependence on Washington for international liquidity and security created the conditions for a substantial harmony in trans-Atlantic economic relationships. Assistance provided by the USA—then enjoying a position of unchallenged hegemony as 'the world factory and the world banker'—through the Marshall Plan allowed European countries gradually to proceed towards the restoration of a multilateral regime of trade and payments within the European Payments Union (EPU)—actually a 'soft area' of multilateral settlements managed by the BIS and based on both a clearing mechanism (using gold and dollars) and sterling.[35] The establishment in 1950 of such a 'soft' currency bloc—a major breach in the Bretton Woods edifice—was accepted by American authorities as a fundamental means of fostering European cooperation. At the same time, both Truman and Eisenhower administrations tolerated infractions to GATT rules-of-the-game, such as exceptions to the trade liberalization code of the OEEC, the maintenance of discriminatory tariffs and quotas on American products and the establishment of the European Economic Community as a discriminatory trading bloc. The rise of the US balance-of-payments deficit, mainly driven by the expansion of US military expenditures abroad and increased net foreign investments, was regarded as beneficial, for it allowed European countries to replenish their reserves and provided international liquidity to the growing world trade.

However, the transition towards current account convertibility proved far slower than had originally been designed. The policy of slow advancement, espoused by European countries with vulnerable external positions, was defended against pressures from both the US Treasury and some European authorities (mainly British and West German) that urged a more rapid return to dollar convertibility of major European currencies.[36] In the course of the process, liberalization of traditional foreign currency banking went hand in hand with the dismantling of exchange controls. A key decision was the gradual reopening of European foreign exchange markets and the re-emergence of multilateral arbitrage in the first half of the 1950s, assumed at the initiative of British authorities.[37] Indeed, since then the Bank of England, whose foreign monetary policy was deeply influenced by the merchant banking community even after the 1946 nationalization, openly supported the restoration of London as an entrepôt financial centre in competition with New York.[38]

Sterling convertibility into dollar and other major foreign currencies was actually reached in 1955, when the Bank of England began to peg sterling's parity by intervening in major foreign exchange markets such as New York and Zurich.[39] By that time, the compromise reached by EPU partners on the European Monetary Agreement (EMA), signed in July of the same year, signalled that European governments were preparing for the final move towards convertibility and market-based multilateral settlements.[40] However, the deterioration of external accounts of the UK and France in 1956–8 created further problems, although cooperation between US and European monetary authorities and the IMF, ill-equipped and with inadequate resources to manage post-war international problems, quickly granted financial assistance and restored confidence in their currencies.[41] Eventually, in 1958, time proved ripe for the restoration of external current account convertibility of Western currencies, thus making possible the merging of the EPU soft currency area into a wider dollar area encompassing the Atlantic economic market place as a whole.[42] Again, the British initiative (whose external accounts' quick recovery was facilitated by IMF and US financial assistance as well as by cooperation with German authorities in reversing the markets' expectation of a sterling devaluation) proved fundamental—together with US open support

and consensus by German authorities—in forcing reluctant European partners (namely France and Italy) to accept the liquidation of the EPU and the
return to external current account convertibility.[43]

In the process, and virtually by default, the dollar conquered a dominant
role as the key currency for international payments and reserves.[44] As US liabilities to foreigners increased by nearly $10 bn. in the period 1949 to 1958, the
post-war dollar gap was bridged and actually turned into a dollar glut.[45] Convertibility and the relaxation of the international repressive system enhanced
the gradual reprivatization of international financial transactions. Even in
the late 1940s, capital flights from Europe to the USA, mainly occurring
through 'leads and lags' in current account payments, had proved substantial.
The outflow continued after the stabilization of the European economies, to
such an extent that the Marshall Plan was regarded as a source of offsetting
financing *vis-à-vis* not only European current account but also capital deficit.
The reactivation of correspondent relationships brought to light the existing loopholes in exchange controls—principally, difficulties in monitoring
short-term capital transactions disguised under current account and interbank dealings—which soon proved the source of substantial leakages.[46] It
was in the transitional period of the second half of the 1950s that interbank
dealings in dollar-denominated, wholesale short-term time deposits—soon
bound to win undying fame as 'Eurodollars'—emerged in Europe. Countries
beyond the Iron Curtain, in order to avoid the risk that their dollar funds
could be frozen by American authorities, used to hold them with 'friendly'
banks in London and Paris, such as the Moscow Narodny Bank and the
Banque Commerciale pour l'Europe du Nord.[47] After the Suez crisis, probably the same habit took oil-exporting Arab countries in the Near East, which
also placed their dollar holdings with banks in Beirut and Switzerland. In
mainland Europe, Italian banks were reported to have been heavy borrowers
of Eurodollars from their European correspondents as well as from international companies in order to finance their national customers' trade. The
Bank for International Settlements was reputed to have injected dollars into
banking systems in continental Europe through deposits and swaps in order
to smooth the functioning of EPU settlements.[48] Swaps were also arranged by
the Deutsche Bundesbank and the Bank of Italy with national banks in the late
1950s as an incentive for them to export short-term funds and offset excess
expansion of the money supply. Demand for Eurodollars however did not gain
momentum before the crisis of September 1957, when the British government
restricted the use of sterling for financing third-party international trade in
order to stem the run on sterling and defend external reserves. Such restriction affected mainly British overseas banks and merchant banks, which found
their traditional source of liquidity (sterling acceptance credits) cut off. They

Introduction: Historical Perspective

strove to keep their business by switching to a dollar basis: indeed Eurodollar deposits were considered to have provided the basis for the emergence of a 'merchant banks' money market'.[49]

As convertibility improved confidence and rates paid on Eurodollar deposits in London and other European centres rose above rate ceilings imposed by the US Federal reserve under Regulation Q—a legacy of the New Deal era analysed by Richard Sylla in Ch. 3—supply of Eurodollar deposits by commercial banks, central banks, and international companies began to mount, for they provided a profitable alternative to low-interest-earning deposits with US banks.[50] The existence in London of experienced brokers and a large volume of foreign exchange interbank dealings (connecting all major financial centres) facilitated the pooling and the circulation of information. Technological innovations in data processing and communications (such as telex) also played a critic role in the process. Low transaction costs made the evolution of trading from bilateral and correspondent to multilateral and transaction banking possible, and eventually led to the establishment of a highly efficient market. In fact, as Catherine Schenk argues in Ch. 4, the outward-looking and tolerant regulatory policy espoused by British authorities proved fundamental in securing to London a competitive advantage over New York and other European centres in attracting entrepôt business. In spite of concerns that unsecured Eurodollar banking might affect British reserves under unfavourable circumstances, the Bank of England maintained a hands-off posture, thus setting both British and foreign banks free to trade dollar deposits, and relied mainly on the City's ability to self-regulate.[51]

In fact, the emergence of the Eurodollar market was a potential challenge brought by European to American banks on the ground of the very source of their post-war international hegemony—their ability to intermediate world-wide dollar liquidity. The same was to prove true for the emergence of the Eurobond market. During the 1950s international investment banking—indeed the very brand of the pre-war globalization—recovered slowly. As the ability of capital markets in Europe to service foreign borrowers emerged seriously impaired from the Second World War, raising international capital proved difficult. High government borrowing absorbed an increasing proportion of available capital resources. Capital outflows were generally seen as a major threat to external payments and foreign exchange stability. As a consequence, issues of foreign securities were generally discouraged, officially regulated and subject to heavy taxation. The change in attitude was particularly visible in London. Britain suffered from serious balance-of-payments weakness and recurrent crisis of confidence in sterling. However British authorities continued to guarantee free access to the London capital market to sterling area countries as a quid pro quo for holding sterling balances;

the ensuing capital outflows proved an additional source of strain on British external payments. Large sterling balances held by foreign governments were permanently exposed to the risk of conversion into dollars, thus turning into a major trigger of private speculation against the pound.[52] In France, plagued by external deficits, political unrest, and periodical crises of confidence in the franc, a virtually complete ban on foreign issues was enforced and maintained even after the successful recovery of the early 1960s; limited exceptions were made only in favour of countries of the franc area and a few international organizations. Some larger leeway was left to foreign borrowers by Belgian and Dutch authorities. On the other hand, in West Germany—a country with a rapidly growing current account surplus and monetary authorities devoted to favouring capital exports as a means of checking domestic liquidity and sterilizing inflationary sources—since 1957 foreign issues were completely free of restrictions and even enjoyed fiscal privileges not extended to domestic issues. However, relatively high interest rates and widespread expectations of D-mark revaluation (emergent already in 1957 and again in 1960; the D-mark was indeed revalued in 1961) proved a major curb. In fact, Switzerland was to prove the only capital market in Europe open to international issues, thanks also to its low interest rates. Here Federal monetary authorities allowed foreign governments (mainly European), international institutions, and American companies to raise loans until 1961, when a sudden deterioration of external accounts induced them to close the market to foreign borrowers.[53]

As a matter of fact, international capital raising regained momentum only towards the end of the 1950s. International bonds, however, were issued almost exclusively by European governments and international institutions— among which the World Bank and the European Coal and Steel Community (ECSC) were by far pre-eminent. Issues concentrated mainly in New York, which then re-emerged as the world's main international capital market. Interest of Americans for foreign issues, however, was modest, not only because the pre-war losses were still fresh in US investors' minds. American investment banks—which had undergone both consolidation and incorporation, and were now subject to tight regulation and disclosure requirements set by the Securities and Exchange Commission—dealt mainly with the rapidly growing domestic business of underwriting and distributing corporate bonds and stocks.[54] However they also managed issues of 'Yankee bonds' (as dollar-denominated bonds issued in New York by foreign borrowers were nicknamed) on behalf of the World Bank, the ECSC, foreign governments, and a bunch of Western European and Japanese companies. From 1955 to 1962, the volume of foreign issues placed in New York reached US$4.2 bn.—for the sake of comparison, in the same period total corporate, state, and municipal bonds offered in the USA amounted to US$126.5 bn. Foreign issues in European financial centres as a whole reached US\$2.9 bn., 36 per cent of which was accounted for by London, 30 per cent by Zurich and other Swiss markets, and 24 per cent jointly by Brussels and Amsterdam.[55]

Potential demand for international securities, however, was rising quickly. In spite of the maintenance of extensive capital controls on portfolio investments (under the Foreign Exchange Control Act of 1947, for example, British investors were not allowed to purchase foreign currency denominated securities unless they used 'investment dollars'),[56] gradual though asymmetric relaxation occurred in mainland Europe. By 1957–8 West Germany, Switzerland, and Belgium had liberalized virtually all resident and non-resident capital transactions.[57] In fact, Swiss investment trusts played a fundamental role, managing the funds of wealth holders from Europe, the Near East, and Latin America. In other major countries such as the UK, France, Italy, and the Netherlands, residents' purchases of foreign securities required special authorization, as well as non-resident imports and exports of capital, but the general attitude of governments was moderately in favour of a higher degree of freedom—especially in view of the substantial and illegal flight of capital out of their countries—and made limited and selective allowance for purchases of foreign securities officially quoted at major stock exchanges.[58] Though laboriously, relaxation of capital controls not only proceeded, but was also consolidated at EEC level by two directives on the liberalization of intra-community movements of capital of May 1960 and December 1962.[59]

It was against this background that a bunch of ingenious merchant bankers in London detected the possibility of competing with their American counterparts in attracting international business. After all, Europeans were by far the heaviest borrowers in New York. As a matter of fact, a substantial part of their American issues was placed by international syndicates with European investors—a pattern already emerging in the 1920s. Moreover, in New York regulation of capital issues was tight, and American bankers earned fat fees and commissions while European members of underwriting syndicates could get only modest rewards from bearing most of the burden of distributing bonds overseas. The Kennedy administration provided further indirect incentive, as in 1962 Douglas Dillon, the US Treasury secretary, vigorously campaigned with European governments in order to convince them to relieve pressure on New York—hence on the US balance of payments—and raise capital at home. London quite naturally loomed large to enjoy substantial competitive advantages over any other European centre as a prospective hub of European capital markets. The attitude of public authorities proved crucial, however. While political divisions frustrated the EEC Commission's attempts to prepare the move towards liberalization of foreign issues in national capital markets—which would foreshadow the establishment of a unified European capital market—the Bank of England officially declared its support to the restoration of London as an international entrepôt financial hub.[60] That was enough to urge London-based banks, either British or foreign, towards the prospectively lucrative business of intermediation between foreign borrowers and lenders in foreign currency denominated securities. Time looked ripe for an attempt to Europeanize the raising of international capital by Europeans. Pioneers of early Eurobond issues, launched first in 1963, were London-based issuing houses such as S. G. Warburg and traders such as Strauss Turnbull, supported by a group of European allies—namely, Deutsche Bank, Banque de Bruxelles, and Rotterdamsche Bank (one of the leading Dutch banks, later merged with Amsterdamsche Bank to form AMRO). Further stimulus came from the ECSC, then considered a most sophisticated international borrower, obviously interested in valuable European alternatives to New York.[61] Once again, however, a crucial boost to the market came from Washington. In 1963 the Kennedy administration, concerned that large capital outflows further contributed to the deterioration of US external accounts announced the introduction of an Interest Equalization Tax (IET) which would increase the cost of capital raised by foreign companies and institutions in the US financial market. This issue is extensively addressed by Richard Sylla and Catherine Schenk in Chs. 3 and 4. Passed in 1964 and subsequently extended to cover also mid-term loans abroad (by which US banks tried to circumvent the regulation), IET effectively barred Europeans from borrowing in New York, probably even beyond the intentions of the US authorities.[62]

3. The Second American Challenge: the Americanization of International Banking and the European Response

The events of the late 1950s and early 1960s were a prologue to the rapid rise of Euromarkets and the full-blown emergence of Euro-American competition—indeed the core subject of this book. Table 1.1 gives a quantitative representation of the Euromarkets' relative size and growth. It shows that Eurocurrency markets (in fact Eurodollars for 70–80%) within a decade reached a gross volume equal to twenty-four times their initial size (more than sixteen times when interbank transactions are netted out)—a striking performance, just unthinkable at its beginnings. In the same time-span Eurobonds replaced traditional foreign bonds (mostly Yankee bonds—i.e. dollar bonds issued in the USA by international borrowers—and Swiss franc bonds) as main sources of international finance. Both were outweighed by international syndicated loans, which boomed especially in 1973–4.

Table 1.1. *Euromarkets size, 1964–1975 ($ bn. equivalent)*

	Eurocurrency market's size		Syndicated Eurocredits[c]	Eurobonds[d]	Foreign bonds[e]
	Gross[a]	Net[b]			
1964	20	14		0.7	1.4
1965	24	17		0.8	1.7
1966	29	21		1.3	1.7
1967	36	25		1.8	2.1
1968	50	34		3.1	3.1
1969	85	50		2.9	2.7
1970	110	65	4.7	2.8	1.7
1971	150	85	4.0	3.3	2.8
1972	205	110	6.8	5.5	3.6
1973	310	160	21.9	3.7	3.7
1974	390	215	29.2	1.9	4.8
1975	480	250	21.0	7.3	11.6

Notes:
[a] Estimated gross size of the Eurocurrency market (foreign currency liabilities of banks from BIS reporting countries *vis-à-vis* non-residents, including interbank positions). Year-end volume outstanding. Data from BIS.
[b] Estimated net size of the Eurocurrency market (excluding interbank and other positions). Year-end volume outstanding. Data from BIS.
[c] Publicly advertised syndicated Eurocredits. Data from Euromoney. Data prior to 1970 not available.
[d] Volume of Eurobonds' annual issues. Data assembled from a variety of sources, not always consistent.
[e] Volume of foreign bonds' annual issues. Data assembled from a variety of sources, not always consistent.
Source: F. G. Fisher, *Eurobonds* (London: Euromoney, 1988), 8–9, 26–7.

There is some irony in the fact that the potential threat of Europeanization of international banking in Europe led eventually to its heavy Americanization. Already in the early 1960s US banks proved able to exploit fully their competitive advantages as dollar-based institutions to establish a strong leadership in the Eurodollar money market. As branching abroad turned into a rush to London—branches based in the City went up from ten in 1958 to fifty-five in 1974[63]—and other European financial centres, the US banks' dominance in the market became hard to contest. In fact, as Richard Sylla explains in Ch. 3, massive landing in Europe was as much an invasion as an escape from the constraining American domestic system, whereby new capital controls on banks' foreign investments and loans came on top of regulatory devices inherited from the 1930s. Indeed, the challenge to US banks' international leadership came as much from European competitors as from

Washington authorities. The programme launched in 1965 by the Johnson administration to reduce the growing external deficit of the USA and defend the dollar advocated a 'voluntary' slowdown of commercial banks' lending abroad. In spite of the president's call for 'a constructive partnership' and his appeal to businessmen's patriotism, bankers lobbied against it throughout the whole life of the programme (though actively involved in its adminis-tration), reluctantly adhered to its letter, and quite happily circumvented its constraints. Shifting international transactions to rapidly growing overseas branch networks proved a most successful strategy.[64] As a matter of fact, the regulatory shock brought by American authorities to their banks' inter-national interests turned out to be in the end a major incentive to innovation and overseas expansion.

American authorities largely tolerated this strategy. In fact, their attitude towards US banks' activities abroad can be regarded as a quid pro quo for over-regulating their home-based business. The Federal Reserve, to which the US legal framework on banks' foreign activities left large discretionary leeway, espoused a very permissive approach. Foreign expansion was accommo-dated, if not actively encouraged, as a means of promoting American foreign trade. As a consequence, foreign branching and investments in overseas sub-sidiaries and affiliates were generally permitted; banks were authorized to open branches or subsidiaries not only in London and other major financial centres in Western Europe and Asia, but also in offshore tax havens such as Nassau and the Bahamas. Whereas in 1964 only eleven US banks had 181 overseas branches (with assets of US$6.9 bn.), in 1973 banks had become 125 and branches 699, with US$118 bn. assets. US overseas branching got increasingly focused on Western Europe: European branches, representing 18 per cent of total overseas branches at the mid-1960s, accounted for 24 per cent ten years later. London—the hub of the Eurodollar market, which provided a huge liquidity reservoir from which banks could draw funds for financ-ing their international activities—maintained its leadership (17 branches in 1965, 55 in 1975) though its relative share declined from 53 to 33 per cent; West Germany (30 branches in 1975) was the only Continental country in which the American 'invasion' reached comparable dimensions, and by a wide margin. The Fed also abstained from constraining US banks' foreign activities. In contrast to heavy domestic regulation, mainly motivated by concerns as to competition and concentration, the Fed's purpose concern-ing US banks' international activity was to enhance their competitiveness in foreign and international markets. US commercial banks were there-fore permitted to engage abroad, through foreign subsidiaries and affiliates, in investment banking activities, domestically forbidden under the Glass-Steagall Act. The banks' ability to compete in international markets was also regarded as having beneficial consequences on competition at home, since foreign expansion of banks from Chicago or California challenged the traditional monopoly enjoyed by New York money centre giants—such as Citibank and Chase Manhattan—in providing international banking services.[65] Therefore the activities of US banks' foreign branches were not subject to capital controls: indeed offshore dollar loans were exempted from the 'voluntary' credit restraint programme and (since 1967) from the IET, as a means of supporting the financing of US direct investments in Europe and assisting US multinationals' expansion abroad.[66]

Overseas branches of the US banks proved successfully instrumental in intercepting a large portion of world dollar liquidity, both official and private, which otherwise could be intermediated by non-American banks. They usually channelled these funds back to headquarters in the USA, especially as a means of circumventing restrictive monetary policy. This came particularly true during the credit crunches of 1966 and 1968–9, which recorded an explosive growth of the Eurodollar market (the Eurocurrency market's estimated gross size, i.e. including interbank dealings, rose from $24 bn. to $110 bn. equivalent in 1965–70, with Eurodollars accounting for 80–84% of it). In both occasions, resorting to the Eurodollar market allowed banks to partially offset the liquidity strain domestically enforced by the Federal Reserve.[67] Such developments were mirrored in the structure of the Eurodollar market. London's banks—including US and other foreign banks—were in fact permanent net borrowers *vis-à-vis* the Continent (mainly Switzerland), Canada, and, in the late 1960s, peripheral areas such as the Middle East and Latin America. In continental Europe, Swiss banks themselves acted as entrepôt intermediaries that recycled funds borrowed from the Middle East and other non-European areas to lend to the USA, London, and other European countries. Banks from EEC countries, whose Eurocurrency business was generally regulated by national monetary authorities (whether through administrative or market-oriented instruments) for monetary policy purposes,[68] were generally net lenders. As a whole, at the end of the 1960s the Eurodollar market had turned into a powerful magnet attracting dollar liquidity from Europe (mainly through continental banks) and oil producing countries (mainly through Swiss banks) and channeling such funds towards the USA, mainly through London's intermediation.[69]

Americans rapidly conquered a strong position in the Eurobond market as well. In the first decade of Eurobonds' life (1963–73), dollar-denominated issues largely prevailed (62% against 23% denominated in DM). Also borrowing in the market became substantially Americanized: time and again, a major boost came from Washington. In 1965 a Foreign Direct Investment Program (FDIP) was enforced which required multinationals to 'voluntarily' reduce capital exports by 20 per cent; it became 'mandatory' in 1968, when the compliance of US companies proved less than satisfactory. As a consequence, the US multinationals' demand for medium- and long-term funds to finance foreign investments was shifted overseas. In fact, initially the Eurobond market was largely a market for corporate borrowing, as straight and convertible bonds issued by private companies and state-owned concerns accounted for three-quarters of total issues. North American borrowers—quite exclusively corporate—accounted for 38 per cent of total Eurobonds issued in the period 1968–73 (30% in 1963–7); in comparison, Europeans (including all types of borrowers) accounted for 40 per cent in both periods. Quite naturally, therefore, this was a golden age for major American investment bankers, as shown in Table 1.2. Firms such as Morgan et Cie, Kuhn Loeb, White Weld, and Lehman Brothers became top-list Eurobond managers/co-managers; they accounted for 25 per cent of overall issues placed in the market from 1963 to 1972 (measured by amount of the issues), but the overall 'American' share was well over 30 per cent when other relatively minor players—such as First Boston, Smith Barney, and Kidder Peabody—were included. Only the big German *universalbanken*, both individually and collectively—Deutsche Bank (by far the market's leader), Dresdner Bank, Westdeutsche Landesbank, and Commerzbank—and a bunch of London merchant bankers, such as S. G. Warburg and N. M. Rothschild, stood up successfully against the American hegemony.[70] Other large European commercial banks, such as AMRO, Kredietbank, and ABN from the Netherlands and Banca commerciale italiana from Italy, played a relevant role in assisting national borrowers in the market. French banks—with the exceptions of Paribas and, in the late 1970s, Crédit Lyonnais—were mostly conspicuous for their absence. Even Swiss banks made quite a late entry as Eurobond managers: UBS emerged as a major player only in the mid-1970s, while Crédit Suisse benefited from its acquisition of White Weld and First Boston to form CSFB.[71] In fact, the role of most European commercial banks in the Eurobond market was to prove fundamental not so much in the capacity of managers or co-managers as in that of participants in selling syndicates—often ponderous international arrangements encompassing up to 200 banks—to allocate Eurobonds to wealthy investors through their vast nationwide branch networks.[72]

What was the impact of the American challenge on European banking? This is the issue addressed by most of the contributors to this book. They give fresh evidence and open new perspectives on the response of the European banks. In fact, US institutions brought an unprecedented edge of competition into international business. Far from limiting their activity to servicing US companies, they established extensive branch networks connecting world's major financial centres, courted European multinationals, promoted financial

Table 1.2. *Top 20 Eurobond managers and co-managers, 1963–1972 and 1973–1977*

	1963–72		1973–77		Rank
	Issues	Amount[a] ($ mln)	Issues	Amount[b] ($ mln)	
1. Deutsche Bank	93	2,828	94	6,505	1
2. Morgan et Cie	71	2,121	76	2,876	4
3. S. G. Warburg	62	1,319	72	3,104	3
4. Kuhn Loeb	51	1,219	16	1,435	11
5. White Weld[c]	56	1,156	59	3,378	2
6. Dresdner Bank	42	974	44	2,008	7
7. Lehman Brothers	41	919			
8. N. M. Rothschild	29	829			
9. Westdeutsche LB	27	742	68	2,571	5
10. AMRO	35	697	44	1,105	13
11. Commerzbank	26	668	34	1,469	10
12. Banca commerciale italiana	24	647			
13. First Boston	28	618	34	1,470	9
14. Kredietbank	39	580	30	802	16
15. ABN	29	514	27	718	18
16. Dillon, Read	19	460			
17. Goldman Sachs	17	399			
18. Hambros	25	369	17	790	17
19. Smith Barney	21	367			
20. Paribas	19	365	27	1,480	8
New entrants					
UBS			25	2,113	6
Morgan Stanley			18	1,375	12
Orion			18	956	14
Kidder Peabody			25	881	15

Notes:
  [a] Managers take the entire amount of issues managed.
  [b] Managers take proportional amount of issues managed.
  [c] Crédit Suisse White Weld.

Source: I. Kerr, *A History of the Eurobond Market: The First 21 Years* (London: Euromoney, 1984), 29–31, 53.

innovations in both commercial and investment banking,[73] and gave a crucial boost to the growth of Eurobond and Eurocredit markets. Although
traditional business, such as retail banking, remained virtually unaffected as
the preserve of domestic commercial banks, in international wholesale and
investment banking American dominance was perceived as an actual threat.
Europeans' response was mainly defensive at the beginnings. As Youssef Cassis
argues (Ch. 2), on the eve of the American invasion, there already existed a gap
between top American and European banks in terms of size—though major

British clearing groups, such as Barclays and Lloyds, stood up to comparison with their American counterparts—as well as managerial resources and propensity to innovation. Moreover, British and French banks' long-dated experience in multinational banking and their extensive overseas networks were to prove not particularly well suited to adjust to the emerging Eurobanking business, due to their mostly 'imperial' character. Indeed, due to the concentration of American banks in London, British banks found themselves in the front line of the 'challenge', and even more so as some major US banks began to compete successfully with local institutions in sterling wholesale and corporate banking. The response of British clearing banks to the international challenge—an issue addressed by Stefano Battilossi in Ch. 5 and by Duncan Ross in Ch. 6—was initially hampered by institutional and regulatory constraints. It gained momentum in the early 1970s, when Competition and Credit Control removed many binding regulations. This allowed them rapidly to catch up with American competitors and gain the status of true international players.

In mainland Europe, the establishment of the EEC had already encouraged international cooperation among commercial and investment bankers in view of a possible forthcoming *Europe bancaire*. But it was the American invasion that gave them a critical boost. Traditional correspondent relationships were redesigned and turned into prospective partnerships. However, loose arrangements such as banking clubs—among which European Advisory Committee (EAC) and Europartners were prominent—failed to pave the way towards true strategic alliances among member banks, as both Duncan Ross and Eric Bussière demonstrate in Chs. 6 and 7.[74] More structured international joint ventures such as consortium banks, with clearer business focus, proved far more successful in making their way in the Eurodollar and Eurocredit markets. In many cases they were the outcome of cooperative strategies between American and European banks. In the mid-term, however, they also proved flawed institutions. Consortium banking—Ross argues—was the outcome of a safety-first strategy for establishing a presence in international banking while minimizing both costs and risks. As shareholder banks developed their individual expertise and competitive capabilities, duplication of activities and conflicts of interest arose between the consortium and its partners: in fact such alliances proved shooting stars in international finance and were generally disbanded in the 1970s. Major European banks, such as the German Big Three—whose case is illustrated by Ulrich Ramm in Ch. 8—soon abandoned their previous 'cooperative' attitudes and individually pursued strategies of global expansion, by extending their foreign branch and subsidiary networks to all major world financial centres, including the USA, where the presence of foreign banks increased dramatically throughout the

Table 1.3. *Internationalization of main OECD banking systems, 1960–1980*

	1960		1973		1980	
	b	s/a	b	s/a	b	s/a
Foreign branches (b) and subsidiaries/affiliates (s/a) of banks from:						
UK	2,676	8	1,149	65	1,280[a]	68[a]
France	—	—	15	49	22[b]	58[b]
West Germany	3	—	23	27[c]	74	52[c]
Italy	13	—	29	—	50	5
Belgium[d]	1	19	1	47	13[e]	65[e]
The Netherlands	—	—	—	74	68[e]	104[e]
Switzerland	9[f]		32[f]		71[f]	
USA	131	39[g]	699	300[h]	787	943
Japan	31	5[c]	82	14[c]	139	74[c]
Branches (b) and subsidiaries/affiliates (s/a) of foreign banks in:						
UK	51[f]		129[f]		243[f]	
France	19	14[c]	60	76[c]	67[b]	116[b,c]
West Germany	21	3[c]	72	—	103[b,c]	46[b,c]
Italy	1	3	14	5	34	7
Belgium	7	7	18	20	25	28
The Netherlands	—	—	14	25	24	25
Switzerland[i]	8/15	—	15/27	84/120	15/27	81/121[b]
USA[j]	—	—	94	27[c]	328	44[c]
Japan	34		58		85	

Notes:
—: data not available.
[a] 1982.
[b] 1979.
[c] Subsidiaries only.
[d] 1960 and 1973, three 'big' banks only.
[e] 1981.
[f] Branches and subsidiaries.
[g] 1964.
[h] Estimate.
[i] Number of banks/offices.
[j] Excluded Edge or Agreement Corp. and New York State Investment Co.

Source: R. M. Pecchioli, *The Internationalization of Banking* (Paris: OECD, 1982), 154–83.

1970s. As shown in Table 1.3, which gives some rough indications of the process of the internationalization of banking, it was in fact in the 1970s that banking systems of major OECD countries rapidly expanded their foreign ramifications and opened up their frontiers to foreign penetration. Against this background and in spite of the remarkable progress of the European banks

the American dominance in international banking remained strong up to the
end of the decade.

4. International Banking and International Political Economy: The Euro-American Cross-Challenge

American successes and European responses in the challenge for supremacy
in international banking have also to be evaluated against the background of
changing balance in international economic relations. The rise of Eurocurrency and Eurobond markets was fundamentally a manifestation of growing
interdependence within the Atlantic economy. The implementation of an
international liberal regime based on free trade and free currency convertibility, as shaped by the Bretton Woods-GATT regime, was fostered by the gradual
removal of tariff and non-tariff barriers, relaxation of exchange and capital
controls, sustained growth of international trade, the boom of foreign direct
investments, improvements in communication technologies, and the waning
of information barriers.[75] Along with the benefits of freer international flows
of goods, services, and capital, however, increased interdependence implied
also new political constraints. Interdependence undermined the autonomy of
national authorities by embedding each country into a matrix of constraints
that required an increased degree of policy coordination in order to make
domestic and foreign economic policies compatible.[76]

The impact of such a matrix of constraints, however, depended very much
on existing asymmetries in the distribution of economic power (i.e. the ability to structure and modify the principles and procedures of the international
economic regime) and economic strength. In both respects the USA enjoyed
a privileged position. In the post-war period, Washington had set up the basic
norms and rules that shaped the international economic regime and promoted multilateral interdependence. At the same time, thanks to their largely
self-sufficient economy and a small ratio of external accounts to national economic activity, American authorities suffered virtually no external constraints
and could retain a large autonomy in the management of the domestic economy. The role of the dollar as an international vehicle and reserve currency
allowed them to run large balance-of-payments deficits (stemming mainly
from massive governmental aid programmes abroad), as they were financed
by mounting international holdings of dollars, both official and private, without having to enforce any restrictive policy to adjust domestic economy to the
balance of payments. On the contrary, external constraint was far more binding for European countries, which found their autonomy in the conduct of
domestic economic policy seriously affected by international developments

and could not afford to run payments deficits or surpluses for prolonged periods without having to resort to some kind of adjustment. Indeed a further asymmetry of the Bretton Woods System was that surplus countries could postpone adjustment indefinitely, in so far as monetary policy or capital controls allowed them to prevent increased reserves from affecting domestic price level and monetary conditions. As a consequence of such double asymmetry—one in favour of the USA as the main reserve-currency centre, the other one in favour of surplus countries—the Bretton Woods System penalized minor deficit countries by shifting the burden of adjustment onto them.[77]

These asymmetries were sources of conflict over the rules of the game of the international economic regime during the period of the Bretton Woods convertibility (1958–71). In fact, the American balance-of-payments deficit proved a major wedge that undermined the cohesion of the Atlantic partnership, as European governments began to complain about the international transmission of inflationary pressures stemming from the undisciplined economic policy of US authorities.[78] As a matter of fact, governments in Europe proved increasingly reluctant to accumulate indefinitely dollar reserves that, under the fixed exchange rates with convertibility regime, were bound to have a permanent expansionary impact on national money supply, thus undermining national authorities' control over domestic monetary and credit conditions.[79] At the same time, American administrations under presidents Kennedy, Johnson, and Nixon periodically used their hegemonic position as a means of pressing Europeans to renegotiate some rules of the Bretton Woods-GATT system. Americans also took unilateral actions in order to relax external constraints and maintain their autonomy in domestic economic policy, increasingly geared towards full employment, expansion of welfare programmes, and the financing of the Vietnam War.

In fact, serious rifts emerged between Americans and Europeans as to how to deal with the US payments imbalances. Washington authorities insisted on further liberalization of trans-Atlantic trade relations and a redistribution of the financial burden of US troops in Western Europe.[80] In their turn, Europeans proved determined to resist the American pressure. France successfully vetoed the extension of the EEC to the UK, warmly supported by the USA. Similarly, the new round of GATT negotiations on further liberalization of both manufactures and agricultural trade (the Kennedy Round), urged by Americans, actually was allowed to start only after EEC partners had reached a compromise on the Common Agricultural Policy. More importantly, the US proved unable to control the final outcome of multilateral negotiations and found themselves increasingly trapped into the principle of reciprocity traditionally championed by American officials. The USA succeeded in forcing EEC countries to make tariff concessions (not least, by arm twisting, threatening a trade war)[81] and industrial tariff reductions averaged 35–40 per cent, but progress towards liberalization of agricultural trade was minimal. Europeans proved able not only to defend their commercial interests, but also to benefit from trade liberalization far more than the American themselves. As critical industries in the USA came to be threatened by European (and Japanese) competition, a shift in attitude towards *ad hoc* protectionism, aiming at protecting particularly distressed sectors (such as textiles, steel, and chemicals) became manifest in US trade policy from the late 1960s.[82]

In fact, Europeans increasingly called for reform of the international monetary system as a means of inducing the USA to give up part of their privileges stemming from the international role of the dollar. As a matter of fact the international monetary system suffered virtually continuous strain throughout the whole decade. The deterioration of US external accounts and the ensuing decline of American gold reserves came to erode confidence in the dollar as soon as external convertibility of European currencies was restored. The first post-war dollar crisis in 1960 paved the way for incremental reforms aimed at propping up the creaking Bretton Woods System. In the first half of the decade, in spite of French and West German opposition to any substantial reform that would expand international liquidity, US authorities, backed by the British as a manifestation of the Anglo-American 'special relationship', won European consensus to design new cooperative schemes aimed both at strengthening confidence in the dollar and at financing temporary payments imbalances through mutual borrowing.[83] 'Multilateral management under US leadership'[84] led to the creation of a number of outer perimeter defences. These included the Gold Pool (to stabilize the price of gold on international markets at $35 an ounce), a network of bilateral swap lines between the Federal Reserve and other central banks, and the creation of a multilateral currency-pooling scheme at the IMF, called General Arrangements to Borrow (GAB), in order to provide emergency stand-by credit lines in support of countries experiencing sudden losses of reserves and speculative attacks.[85] For the same purpose, the group of central bankers (known as the G-10) that used to meet regularly in Basle at the BIS arranged joint stand-by facilities ('Basle operations'), whose main beneficiary proved to be the UK in 1961, 1963–4, and again in 1966–8.[86]

However, serious conflicts emerged from 1963–4 as the USA proved increasingly reluctant to pursue any serious policy of structural adjustment, while Europeans vainly called for greater discipline in the management of US external accounts. Indeed the joint economic consequences of the Great Society welfare programmes and the escalation of US involvement in the Vietnam War—a weakening dollar, increased military expenses abroad, growing strain on the federal budget, and rising inflationary pressures—produced a shift in the attitude of Washington authorities from cooperation towards unilateral actions as a means of preventing further deterioration of the payments deficit and strengthening the international role of the dollar.[87] Further strain came from the increasing reluctance of Europeans to accommodate to US inflationary policy, totally inappropriate for a key-currency country. France, after the austerity programmes of the early 1960s, succeeded in strengthening external accounts and restoring confidence in the franc, used foreign economic and monetary policy to promote its role as an international power and challenge the American economic and political leadership. Affected by unwanted large capital inflows with inflationary consequences, French authorities advocated a return to the Gold Standard and pressed the US Treasury with massive requests for conversions of dollars into gold. As a result, French government not only actively undermined the stability of the international monetary system, but also found itself often isolated from EEC partners.[88] Quite differently, West Germany, another surplus country also affected by mounting dollar reserves and even more massive capital inflows due to a strong Deutschmark, showed a stronger commitment to the fixed exchange regime and a much more cooperative attitude by volunteering not to convert dollars into gold. In turn, however, the Germans' resistance to adjustment through revaluation from 1961 to 1969, allowed by capital controls that successfully sterilized the expansionary impact of money flows, demonstrated their reluctance to give up the competitive advantage secured to German trade by an undervalued DM.[89]

Against this background of rising unilateralism, the imposition of IET and capital controls in the USA were actions that aimed to defend US autonomy in domestic economic management. In fact, far from solving American problems, they exported them to Europe.[90] The growth of Euromarkets and their increasing Americanization proved instrumental therefore to the preservation of American privileges. The existence of the Eurodollar market was a strong incentive to foreign private and official institutions to hold dollars instead of converting them into gold. Through their overseas branches, US banks were allowed to offset disintermediation caused by US regulation. In the Eurocredit and Eurobond market, US multinationals found an efficient substitute for domestic borrowing to finance overseas expansion. It is little surprise therefore that the US authorities resisted any attempt made by Europeans to bring the expansion of Euromarkets under a system of cooperative controls, as they turned into a magnification factor of international speculation. This emerged clearly during the financial turmoil of the late 1960s (sterling devaluation in 1967, gold and dollar crisis in 1968, French franc devaluation, and DM revaluation in 1969), which led to the final collapse of the fixed exchange system in 1971–3.[91] In fact, since 1968, after the dismissal of the Gold Pool, the USA succeeded in giving up the obligation assumed at Bretton Woods and put the world on a *de facto* dollar standard, while Europeans no longer had the benefit of any effective instrument to impose discipline on the USA. US choice was tantamount to threatening the possibility of a more radical step: the unilateral suspension of dollar convertibility into gold. This policy of financial deterrent, coupled with passive acceptance of balance-of-payments deficit (or 'benign neglect', as it came to be known), meant also that the USA shifted abroad the burden of facing speculation against a weak dollar, as foreign monetary authorities were left with the alternative of either losing control over dollar reserves (hence of domestic liquidity) to defend the exchange parity, or accepting adjustment in the form of a currency revaluation which would improve the US foreign trade position.

Subsequent events leading to the final crisis of the fixed exchange rates regime—the peak of US unilateralism, when the Nixon administration closed the official Gold window in August 1971—were a logical consequence of this choice. By putting the world on an actual dollar standard, US authorities lifted the last external constraint that limited their freedom of action. At the same time, they openly supported the shift towards a liberal order in international finance as a means of capitalizing on its dominance; capital controls were in fact rapidly relaxed and eventually lifted in 1974. As Eric Helleiner has argued, in the US authorities' view 'market pressures would achieve what direct negotiations could not ... it was clear that a non-negotiated, market-oriented system would preserve America's dominant position in international finance'.[92] The American challenge in international banking was therefore a crucial facet of a wider challenge for world hegemony. As Harold James illustrates in Ch. 9, however, unleashed market forces soon became a source of concern, especially after the 1973 oil shock, the explosion of petrodollar recycling through the Euromarkets, and the mounting international debt of developing countries. International private bankers, however, opposed any attempt made by the IMF to bring international lending under control throughout the 1970s. It was only after the debt crisis of the early 1980s that the IMF was brought to the centre of the international financial system and prudential regulation of international banking eventually emerged as a fundamental issue of systemic relevance.

5. Conclusion

One main point emerges from this historical excursion: the American challenge to Europe's supremacy in world finance was indeed a post-1945 novelty. In the interwar years, in spite of the emergence of the USA as a world economic power, the rise of US international banking (as well as of New York as an international financial centre) was a short-lived and geographically limited phenomenon. With only few though outstanding exceptions, US banks played a role of marginal competitors at best. British banks (occasionally paralleled by their French counterparts) maintained their dominance on a worldwide scale, from Latin America to Africa to the Near and Far East. Europe itself remained a virtually impenetrable fortress, dominated by mercantilistic attitudes. It was only in the post-war period that an epoch-making breakthrough occurred. The war and its consequences marked a clear discontinuity in the path-dependent trend which had guaranteed the survival of Europe's hegemony so far. While traditional areas of political and economic influence began to fade, American banks boosted their international fortunes by rapidly building on positive externalities created by the widespread presence of American troops abroad, the launch of the Marshall Plan and other foreign aid programmes, the emergence of the dollar as the world key currency, the rise to leadership of the USA among trading nations, and the overwhelming expansion of Yankee multinationals. The turnover in international financial leadership gained momentum in the late 1950s and early 1960s, when the transition to a more liberal international order, both in trade and finance, eventually came of age. The success of the American challenge became manifest first outside Europe, but eventually crept onto the Old Continent too, affecting not only international but in some cases also domestic business of national champions. In fact US banks turned isolated financial innovations such as Eurocurrency trading and Eurobond issues—originally designed and promoted by European institutions—into the very source of their worldwide dominance. Their stronghold on the emerging Euromarkets remained uncontested until the late 1970s, in spite of the new—indeed successful in a number of cases—dynamism showed by European banks. Finally, such financial supremacy drove a wedge into US-European solidarity, inducing US authorities increasingly to resort to unilateral actions and pursue policies of liberalization and deregulation. It would not be an exaggeration to argue that the Bretton Woods years should be regarded in a number of respects as the cradle of the global financial order that eventually emerged in the two final decades of the last century. The roots and foundations of this order are thoroughly explored in the chapters of this volume.

NOTES

1. See R. Bryant, *International Financial Intermediation* (Washington, DC: The Brookings Institution, 1987), 19–30.

2. R. F. Kuysel, *Seducing the French: The Dilemma of Americanisation* (Berkeley, Calif.: University of California Press, 1993).

3. From 1960 to 1971 the estimated stock of foreign direct investments (on an outflow basis) of the USA grew from $65 billion to $165 billion and accounted for half of the total foreign direct investment of developed countries: data in W. F. Sheperd, *International Financial Integration: History, Theory and Applications in OECD Countries* (Aldershot: Ashgate, 1994), 44–5. For a reaction to the invasion of American multinationals, see J. J. Servan-Schreiber, *Le Défi Américain* (Paris: Denôel, 1967).

4. S. Battilossi, 'Financial Innovation and the Golden Ages of International Banking: 1890–1931 and 1958–81', *Financial History Review*, 7 (2000), 147–54.

5. S. Nishimura, *The Decline of Inland Bills of Exchange in the London Money Market 1855–1913* (Cambridge: Cambridge University Press, 1971), 70–1.

6. A swap consists of a simultaneous purchase and sale of a specified amount of foreign exchange for two different value dates. For a technical description see P. Isard, *Exchange Rate Economics* (Cambridge: Cambridge University Press, 1995), 19–21. Historical cases are illustrated by P. Einzig, A *Dynamic Theory of Forward Exchange* (London: Macmillan, 1967). See also P. Cottrell (with C. J. Stone), 'Credits, and Deposits to Finance Credits', in P. Cottrell *et al.* (eds.), *European Industry and Banking Between the Wars* (Leicester: University of Leicester Press, 1992).

7. A classic reference text is A. Bloomfield, 'Short-Term Capital Movements under the Pre-1914 Gold Standard', *Princeton Studies in International Finance*, 11 (1963). See also M. De Cecco, 'Short-Term Capital Movements under the Gold Standard', in J. Braga de Macedo, B. Eichengreen, and J. Reis (eds.), *Currency Convertibility: The Gold Standard and Beyond* (London: Routledge, 1996), 102–12.

8. R. Cameron, 'The Growth of International Banking', in C.-L. Holtfrerich (ed.), *Interactions in the World Economy* (New York: New York University Press, 1990), 204–5; K. E. Born, *International Banking in the 19th and 20th Centuries* (Leamington: Berg, 1983), 115–59.

9. Bloomfield, 'Short-Term Capital Movements', 77–9; R. Tilly, 'International Aspects of the Development of German Banking', in R. Cameron and V. I. Bovykin (eds.), *International Banking 1870–1914* (Oxford: Oxford University Press, 1991), 108–110; S. Chapman, *The Rise of Merchant Banking* (London: Allen & Unwin, 1984), 121–5.

10. Cameron, 'The Growth of International Banking', 210–11; and H. Bonin, 'The Case of the French Banks', in Cameron and Bovykin (eds.), *International Banking*, 73–80.

11. R. Michie, *The London and New York Stock Exchanges 1850–1914* (London: Allen & Unwin, 1987), 271.

12. P. Lindert, 'Key Currencies and Gold 1900–1913', *Princeton Studies in International Finance*, 24 (1969).

13. S. Chapman, *The Rise of Merchant Banking*, 104–8; and P. Cottrell, 'Great Britain', in Cameron and Bovykin (eds.), *International Banking 1870–1914*

(Oxford: Oxford University Press, 1991), 31–6. On British overseas banks, see G. Jones, *British Multinational Banking 1830–1990* (Oxford: Oxford University Press, 1993); and idem, 'British Overseas Banks as Free-Standing Companies, 1830–1996', in M. Wilkins and H. Schröter (eds.), *The Free-Standing Company in the World Economy 1830–1996* (Oxford: Oxford University Press, 1996).

14. V. P. Carosso and R. Sylla, 'U.S. Banks in International Finance', in Cameron and Bovykin (eds.), *International Banking*, 55–67.

15. J. Kelly, *Bankers and Borders. The Case of American Banks in Britain* (Cambridge, Mass.: Ballinger, 1977), 3–6.

16. Bloomfield, 'Short-Term Capital Movements', 34–7.

17. C. Goodhart, *The New York Money Market and the Finance of Trade, 1900–1913* (Cambridge, Mass.: Harvard University Press, 1969), 54–9.

18. M. Wilkins, 'Foreign Banks and Foreign Investments in the United States', in Cameron and Bovykin (eds.), *International Banking*, 241–51.

19. Carosso and Sylla, 'U.S. Banks in International Finance', 67–70.

20. United Nations, Department of Economic Affairs, *International Capital Movements during the Inter-War Period* (New York: United Nations, 1949), 21–3; and P. Einzig, *The Fight for Financial Supremacy* (London: Macmillan, 1931), 94–101.

21. M. Wilkins, 'Cosmopolitan Finance in the 1920s: New York's Emergence as an International Financial Centre', in R. Sylla *et al.* (eds.), *The State, the Financial System and Economic Modernisation* (Cambridge: Cambridge University Press, 1999).

22. C. H. Feinstein and K. Watson, 'Private International Capital Flows in the Interwar Period', in C. H. Feinstein (ed.), *Banking, Currency, and Finance in Europe between the Wars* (Oxford: Oxford University Press, 1995), 94–130.

23. Einzig, *The Fight*, 39–82.

24. Kelly, *Bankers and Borders*, 6–11.

25. See H. Feis, *The Diplomacy of the Dollar: First Era 1919–1932* (Baltimore: Johns Hopkins Press, 1950).

26. Often foreign bonds found their way back from New York to Europe, whereby investors regarded them as attractive due to low prices and high (potential) return.

27. See A. Fishlow, 'Lessons from the Past: Capital Markets During the Nineteenth Century and the Interwar Period', *International Organisation*, 39 (1985); and B. Eichengreen, 'The U.S. Capital Market and Foreign Lending, 1920–1955', in J. D. Sachs (ed.), *Developing Country Debt and Economic Performance* (Chicago: The University of Chicago Press, 1989), 107–55.

28. The 1920s were 'perhaps the high-noon of politicised international finance': M. De Cecco, 'The International Debt Problem in the Interwar Period', *EUI Working Paper*, 103 (1984).

29. Einzig, *The Fight*, 41–2; J. M. Atkin, 'Official Regulation of British Overseas Investment, 1914–1931', *Economic History Review*, 23 (1970), 324–35; and Wilkins, 'Cosmopolitan finance', 280–3.

30. B. Eichengreen, 'International Policy Coordination in Historical Perspective: A View from the Interwar Years', in idem, *Elusive Stability. Essays in the History*

of International Finance, 1919–1939 (Cambridge: Cambridge University Press, 1993): 113–52.

31. On the concept of embedded liberalism, see J. G. Ruggie, 'International Regimes, Transactions and Change: Embedded Liberalism in the Postwar Economic Order', *International Organisation*, 36 (1982), 379–415.

32. The literature on the origins of Bretton Woods is enormous. For an account centred on the issue of capital controls see E. Helleiner, *States and the Reemergence of Global Finance. From Bretton Woods to the 1990s* (Ithaca, NY: Cornell University Press, 1994), ch. 2.

33. Helleiner, *States and the Reemergence of Global Finance*, 51–8. On the 1947 crisis as a watershed in postwar history, see A. S. Milward, *The Reconstruction of Western Europe, 1945–51* (London: Methuen, 1984), ch. 1. On international short-term capital flows in the late 1940s, see A. Bloomfield, *Speculative and Flight Movements of Capital in Postwar International Finance* (Princeton, NJ: Princeton University Press, 1954).

34. See A. S. Milward, 'Motives for Currency Convertibility: The Pound and the Deutsche Mark, 1950–59', in Holtfrerich (ed.), *Interactions in the World*, 273.

35. On the EPU, see J. Kaplan and G. Schleiminger, *The European Payments Union: Financial Diplomacy in the 1950s* (Oxford: Clarendon Press, 1989).

36. Kaplan and Schleiminger, *The European Payments*, chs. 10–11. Telling insights are provided by Milward, 'Motives for currency', 267–74; and Helleiner, *States and the Reemergence of Global Finance*, 68–72.

37. In December 1951 the Bank of England reopened the London foreign exchange market for spot and forward transactions. A further major step came in 1953 when the EPU substituted a simplified, market-oriented mechanism of payments settlement for former complex arrangements. As a consequence, commercial banks from all major European countries (the UK, West Germany, France, Belgium, the Netherlands, Switzerland, Sweden, Norway, Denmark, joined two years later by Italy), were allowed to establish a scheme for multicurrency arbitrage between their respective exchange markets.

38. C. Schenk, 'The Origins of the Eurodollar Market in London: 1955–1963', *Explorations in Economic History*, 35 (1998), 224–9; and G. Burn, 'The State, the City and the Euromarkets', *Review of International Political Economy*, 6 (1999), 239–49.

39. See R. W. Hinshaw, 'Toward European Convertibility', *Essays in International Finance*, 31 (Princeton, NJ: Princeton University, 1958). On previous British plans for sterling convertibility, see Milward, 'Motives for Currency', 261–71; and C. R. Schenk, *Britain and the Sterling Area: From Devaluation to Convertibility in the 1950s* (London: Routledge, 1994), ch. 5.

40. Kaplan and Schleiminger, *The European Payments*, ch. 12; and A. Milward, 'The European Monetary Agreement', in G. Trausch (ed.), *The European Integration from the Schuman Plan to the Treaties of Rome* (Baden-Baden: Nomos Verlag, 1993), 115–28.

41. International assistance and cooperation between British and German authorities succeeded in 1957 in reversing the markets' expectation of sterling devaluation.

France recovered only after the franc was devalued and both a stabilization program and monetary reform was enforced in 1958.

42. See B. Tew, *The Evolution of the International Monetary System 1945–81* (London: Hutchinson University Library, 1982), ch. 2; and H. James, *International Monetary Cooperation since Bretton Woods* (Washington: IMF, and Oxford: Oxford University Press, 1996), ch. 4.

43. Kaplan and Schleiminger, *The European Payments*, 303–21; Milward, 'Motives for Currency', 278–82; S. M. Schwaag, 'Currency Convertibility and European Integration: France, Germany and Britain', in A. Deighton and A. Milward (eds.), *Widening, Deepening and Acceleration: The European Economic Community 1957–1963* (Baden-Baden: Nomos Verlag, 1999), 89–106.

44. From 1949 to 1958, world reserves grew from US$45.6 bn. to US$57.3 bn. Gold's share declined from 73.5% to 65.3%; the foreign exchange component (virtually only US dollar) went up from 22.8% to 30%. In 1958 the USA had 39.2% of total world reserves, *vis-à-vis* 60.8% of the rest of the world; shares were 56.5% and 43.5% respectively in 1949. See V. Argy, *The Postwar International Money Crisis: An Analysis* (London: Allen & Unwin, 1981), 33–4.

45. R. Triffin, *The World Money Maze: National Currencies in International Payments* (New Haven: Yale University Press, 1966), ch. 6.

46. On short-term capital flows through unofficial transactions in the early 1950s, see R. Mikesell, *Foreign Exchange in the Postwar World* (New York: The Twentieth Century Fund, 1954), 190–216.

47. The story goes that the telex address of the Banque Commerciale per l'Europe du Nord—Eurobank—would be the very source of the term 'Eurodollar'. As a consequence, it has often been argued that the emergence of the Eurodollar market was in fact a by-product of the Cold War. This however overemphasizes the actual importance of such deposits.

48. Bank for International Settlements, *27th Annual Report*, 1956–7 (Basle: 1957), 226–8.

49. P. Einzig, *The Eurodollar System: Practice and Theory of International Interest Rates* (London: Macmillan, 1970), 11.

50. Early accounts of the emergence of the Eurodollar market, often based on personal insights and information circulated by financial circles in London and continental Europe, are A. R. Holmes and F. H. Klopstock, 'The Market for Dollar Deposits in Europe', *Federal Reserve Bank of New York, Monthly Review*, November 1960; and O. L. Altman, 'Foreign Markets for Dollars, Sterling, and Other Currencies', *IMF Staff Papers*, 8 (1960–1), 313–52.

51. See the debate over the possible imposition of liquidity ratios on Eurodollar activity in the early 1960s, reported by Schenk, 'The Origins', 233–4, and Burn, 'The State, the City', 240–3.

52. See F. Block, *The Origins of International Economic Disorder: A Study of United States International Monetary Policy from World War II to the Present* (Berkeley, Calif.: University of California Press, 1977), 185–9; and James, *International Monetary Cooperation*, 185–6. The issue of sterling balances as a sword hanging

over the head of British reserves in the 1950s is readdressed by Schenk, *Britain and the Sterling Area*, ch. 2.

53. For a survey, see Chambre de commerce Suisse en France, *Les Principales Places financiéres du monde* (Paris: 1957); and P. Einzig, *Foreign Dollar Loans in Europe* (London: Macmillan, 1965), ch. 4.

54. V. P. Carosso, *Investment Banking in America: A History* (Cambridge, Mass.: Harvard University Press, 1970), 496–509.

55. Data on foreign bonds issued in the USA and Europe from J. Mensbrugghe, 'Foreign Issues in Europe', *IMF Staff Papers*, 11 (1964), 327–35. Data on domestic US bonds from Carosso, *Investment Banking*, 499.

56. Under British exchange control regulation, investment dollars were dollars deposited by UK residents with banks in the USA that could be used only for the acquisition of dollar or other foreign securities; they could never be sold at a discount and in fact were usually at a substantial premium. See Einzig, *Foreign Dollar Loans*, ch. 12.

57. In fact, Belgium segmented capital from current account transactions by imposing a dual exchange rate system. Thus, Belgian capital market was formally free; however, capital transactions were conducted at a different exchange rate.

58. On the policy of European governments in the 1960s, see A. Lamfalussy, 'Changing Attitudes towards Capital Movements', in F. Cairncross (ed.), *Changing Perceptions of Economic Policy* (London: Methuen, 1981), 194–8.

59. A. F. P. Bakker, *The Liberalisation of Capital Movements in Europe: The Monetary Committee and Financial Integration, 1958–1994* (Dordrecht: Kluwer Academic Publishers, 1996), 85–94.

60. See the speech addressed by Lord Cromer, Governor of the Bank of England, to London bankers and merchants, 3 October 1962, quoted by Einzig, *Foreign Dollar Loans*, 42. On political divisions among EEC partners on the grounds of a unified capital market, see Bakker, *The Liberalisation of Capital*, 94–105.

61. I. M. Kerr, *A History of the Eurobond Market: The First 21 Years* (London: Euromoney, 1984), 11–16; and K. Burk (ed.), 'Witness Seminar on the Origins and Early Development of the Eurobond Market', *Contemporary European History*, 1 (1992), 72–87. On the role of the ECSC as an international borrower, see C. R. Geisst, *Raising International Capital: International Bond Markets and the European Institutions* (Westmead: Saxon House, 1980), 85–93.

62. See J. P. Hawley, *Dollars and Borders: U.S. Government Attempts to Restrict Capital Flows, 1960–1980* (Armonk, NY: M. E. Sharpe, 1987), 45–62.

63. Kelly, *Bankers and Borders*, 23.

64. P. Dombrowski, *Policy Responses to the Globalisation of American Banking* (Pittsburgh: University of Pittsburgh Press, 1996), ch. 3; and Hawley, *Dollars and Borders*, 63–81; and J. Conybeare, *U.S. Foreign Economic Policy and the International Capital Markets: the Case of Capital Export Controls, 1963–74* (New York: Garland, 1988).

65. A. F. Brimmer and F. R. Dahl, 'Growth of American International Banking: Implications for Public Policy', *The Journal of Finance*, 30 (1975), 342–4. In the

1970s, Citibank, Bank of America, and Chase Manhattan had the largest foreign deposits/total deposits ratios, ranging from 17% to 11%.

66. The point is raised by Helleiner, *States and the Reemergence of Global Finance*, 84–91. Insights of US authorities' tolerant attitude as to the impact of capital controls on offshore activities of US banks in Hawley, *Dollars and Borders*, 52–3; Conybeare, *U.S. Foreign Economic*, 116–20.

67. E. Chalmers, *International Interest Rate War* (London: Macmillan, 1972), ch. 5; D. R. Kane, *The Eurodollar Market and the Years of Crisis* (London: Croom Helm, 1983); M. De Cecco, 'Inflation and Structural Change in the Eurodollar Market', in M. De Cecco and J. P. Fitoussi (eds.), *Monetary Theory and Economic Institutions* (Basingstoke: Macmillan, 1987), 182–208.

68. See R. H. Mills, 'An Evaluation of Measures to Influence Volatile Capital Flows', in A. Swoboda (ed.), *Capital Movements and Their Control* (Leiden: Sijthoff, 1976), 143–61.

69. K. Friedrich, 'A Quantitative Framework for the Euro-Dollar System', *Princeton Studies in International Finance*, 26 (1970).

70. After an unwelcome boom of DM Eurobond issues, in November 1968 a Subcommittee for Euro-DM Bonds was established by German banks at the initiative of the Ministry of Economics and the Bundesbank, in order to regulate the volume of issues placed with German investors. See H.-C. Donnerstag, 'The Deutschmark Sector', in Kerr, *A History of the Eurobond*, 119–21.

71. Kerr, *A History of the Eurobond*, 29–31, 53. For a breakdown of the market by type and country of borrower, see F. G. Fisher, *Eurobonds* (London: Euromoney, 1988), 58–66.

72. Institutional details of Eurobond syndicates' structure in Y. S. Park, *The Eurobond Market: Function and Structure* (New York: Praeger, 1974), 90–103. For a straightforward survey, see Battilossi, 'Financial Innovation', 165–9.

73. D. Vittas, 'How Far is the US Ahead in Financial Innovation?', *The Banker*, 135 (1985), 711, 47–51.

74. See also D. Ross, 'European Banking Clubs in the 1960s: A Flawed Strategy', *Business and Economic History*, 27 (1998), 353–66.

75. Bryant, *International Financial Intermediation*, 15–57.

76. R. N. Cooper, *The Economics of Interdependence: Economic Policy in the Atlantic Community* (New York: Columbia University Press, 1980), 4.

77. T. L. Ilgen, *Autonomy and Interdependence: U.S.-Western European Monetary and Trade Relations, 1958–1984* (Totowa, NJ: Rowman & Littlefield, 1985), 10–21. On the asymmetric positions of the USA and surplus countries, see also M. D. Bordo, 'The Bretton Woods International Monetary System: An Overview', and M. Obstfeld, 'The Adjustment Mechanism', in M. D. Bordo and B. Eichengreen (eds.), *A Retrospective on the Bretton Woods System: Lessons for International Monetary Reform* (Chicago: University of Chicago Press, 1993), 51–60 and 219–24 respectively.

78. A. C. Stockman, 'International Transmission under Bretton Woods', in Bordo and Eichengreen (eds.), *A Retrospective*, 332–44.

79. R. Bryant, *Money and Monetary Policy in Interdependent Nations* (Washington, DC: The Brookings Institution, 1980), 367–78. See also V. Argy, 'Monetary Policy and Internal and External Balance', *IMF Staff Papers*, 18 (1971), 508–25.

80. Particular attention to interconnections between foreign economic policy and the evolution of the Cold War is paid by Block, *Origins*, 166–74.

81. In 1968 the Johnson administration publicized plans for a tariff surcharge on imports and a tax rebate to support US exports, thus posturing to embark upon a trade war. Plans were dropped after the conclusion of the Kennedy Round.

82. On Dillon and Kennedy Rounds, see Ilgen, *Autonomy and Interdependence*, 38–40, 63–8; Block, *Origins*, 174–7.

83. Indeed defending the pound was the main objective of these efforts. In fact the British currency served not only as a lightning rod for expectations of devaluation and periodical speculative attacks, but also as a bulwark in defence of the dollar, as long as keeping the pound at the $2.80 parity would deflect speculation from focusing on the dollar: Block, *Origins*, 185–9. On the battle for sterling, see B. Eichengreen, *Globalising Capital: A History of the International Monetary System* (Princeton, NJ: Princeton University Press, 1996), 125–8.

84. The expression is used by J. E. Spero, *The Politics of International Economic Relations* (London: Unwin Hyman, 1990), ch. 2.

85. See new archival evidence provided by T. Zoumaras, 'Plugging the Dike: The Kennedy Administration Confronts the Balance-of-Payments Crisis with Europe'; and R. T. Griffiths, ' "Two Souls, One Thought"? The EEC, the United States, and the Management of the International Monetary System', in D. Brinkley and R. T. Griffiths (eds.), *John F. Kennedy and Europe* (Baton Rouge, La.: Louisiana State University Press, 1999), 169–211.

86. Also Italy in 1964 and France in 1968 benefited from international financial assistance. See James, *International Monetary Cooperation*, 159–65; and R. Solomon, *The International Monetary Systems, 1945–76: An Insider's View* (New York: Harper & Row, 1977), ch. 3.

87. The turning point represented by the Johnson administration is stressed by J. S. Odell, *U.S. International Monetary Policy: Markets, Power and Ideas as Sources of Changes* (Princeton: Princeton University Press, 1982), 79–164.

88. See M. D. Bordo, D. Simard, E. N. White, 'France and the Bretton Woods International Monetary System, 1960–68', in J. Reis (ed.), *International Monetary Systems in Historical Perspective* (London: Macmillan, 1995), 160–73.

89. On West Germany, see O. Emminger, 'The D-mark in the Conflict between Internal and External Equilibrium', *Essays in International Finance*, 122 (1977); and C.-L. Holtfrerich, 'Monetary Policy under Fixed Exchange Rates (1948–70)', in Deutsche Bundesbank (ed.), *Fifty Years of the Deutsche Mark: Central Bank and the Currency in Germany since 1948* (Oxford, Oxford University Press, 1999), 307–401.

90. De Cecco, 'Inflation and Structural Change'.

91. See Solomon, *The International Monetary System*, chs. 6–9; and James, *International Monetary Cooperation*, chs. 7–8. Insights are provided by C. A. Coombs, *The Arena of International Finance* (New York: J. Wiley & Sons, 1976), 188–240.

92. Helleiner, *States and the Reemergence of Global Finance*, 112–13.

2

Before the Storm: European Banks in the 1950s

YOUSSEF CASSIS

The aim of this brief chapter is to assess the state of European banks on the eve of the American 'invasion'. How well prepared were they to face the challenge? The conventional wisdom is that they were rather unprepared. Until the 1960s at the very least, European banks have often been described, in a somewhat caricatural way, as sleepy and risk-averse giants, encumbered with state regulation, cosy cartels, and outdated management, in sharp contrast to their lean, fast expanding, and highly innovative American competitors. Is this just a cliché—but all clichés contain a grain of truth—or a fairly accurate picture of the reality? Answering this question should help to understand both the context of the American challenge and the nature of the European response, which will be discussed in the following chapters. But answering this question is no easy task. The history of European banks in the post-Second World War period is still in its infancy; and the issue of competitiveness, which is at the heart of the matter, has not been on top of banking historians' research agendas.

An attempt, however, is well worth trying. This will be done by examining five measures of European banks' overall competitive capabilities: the institutional framework within which they operated; their size; their multinational development; the quality of their management; and their innovative capacity. This survey will take the form of a comparative synthesis, concentrating on the leading banks of the three European countries discussed in this volume: Britain, France, and Germany. For Britain, this means the Big Five, the top merchant banks, and the major overseas banks; for France, both the *banques de dépôts* and the *banques d'affaires*; and for Germany, the big three universal banks.

1. The Institutional Framework

For banks in all countries, the legacy of the war was, as far as their business operations were concerned, a shift from commercial to government lending.

Everywhere, including in former neutral countries, their assets became dominated by government securities. In Britain, for example, by August 1945, government paper and cash amounted to 82 per cent of the deposits of the London clearing banks. However, these were but temporary effects, even though banks did not return to fully normal business conditions until the early 1950s. More fundamental changes were to affect German and French banks.

In Germany, the Allies' determination to decentralize the German economy led to the decision to divide each of the three big banks (Deutsche, Dresdner, and Commerz) into regional banks on a *Land* basis.[1] The Deutsche Bank, for example, was succeeded in 1948 by ten separate institutions. The largest was the Rheinisch-Westfälische Bank, with head office in Düsseldorf (total assets DM 891m. in 1950), well ahead of its immediate follower, the Südwestbank (DM 327m.), whose head office was in Stuttgart/Mannheim.[2] Such measures, inspired by American banking legislation, were clearly at odds with German, and more generally European banking traditions. They met with resistance from the German business community, which immediately set about working towards reunification. As early as 1949 bank representatives made proposals for a first regrouping on a wider regional basis, taking advantage of Britain's disagreement with the decentralization project and the favourable conditions presented by the Cold War. The number of successor banks had already been reduced to three by 1952—the Norddeutsche Bank AG, the Rheinisch–Westfälische Bank AG, and the Süddeutsche Bank AG in the case of the Deutsche Bank. Complete reunification took place in 1957 for Deutsche Bank and Dresdner Bank, and the following year for Commerzbank. Deutsche and Dresdner chose Frankfurt as their head office (Commerz opted for Düsseldorf, and only moved to Frankfurt in later decades), a choice largely determined by the Allies' decision in 1948 to set up the Bank deutscher Länder—the forerunner of the Bundesbank—in the city on the Main.[3] Interestingly, the years of fragmentation were prosperous ones for the German big banks: they enjoyed extremely rapid growth as a result of high demand for their specific services, namely the financing of industrial investment and foreign trade. By the end of 1951, their share of the country's total banks' balance-sheets had reached a historical 19.5 per cent, as against 10.4 per cent in 1936, and around 10 per cent again by 1963. The reunited banks thus lost market share, despite a significant growth of their business activities, their assets more than doubling in real terms between 1952 and 1958. They also returned to their traditional business practices, in particular their close links with large industrial companies, through both advances and interlocking directorships.

In France, the main transformation was the complete control established by the state over the mechanism of credit. The Banque de France and the four major deposit banks (Crédit Lyonnais, Société Générale, Comptoir National d'Escompte de Paris, and Banque Nationale pour le Commerce et l'Industrie) were nationalized in 1945, adding to a public sector already including the Caisse des dépôts et consignations (the recipient of most of the assets of the savings banks). However, the nationalized banks did not lose their corporate identity, while the investment banks, the so-called *banques d'affaires* (Banque de Paris et des Pays-Bas, Banque de l'Indochine, Banque de l'Union Parisienne, and others) remained in private hands, thus maintaining a certain degree of institutional continuity. The nationalized banks played only a modest role in the country's economic reconstruction and modernization. With the state now in the driving seat, it was the Treasury that financed the first Economic Plans and the Caisse des dépôts that financed local communities. The large commercial banks, though fairly autonomous, contented themselves with collecting short-term deposits and supporting Treasury issues.[4]

In Britain, only the Bank of England was nationalized in 1946, though the Big Five (Barclays Bank, Lloyds Bank, Midland Bank, National Provincial Bank, and Westminster Bank) remained under strict official control.[5] They received precise instructions from the Treasury concerning not only their liquidity but also their lending priorities, especially as far as manufacturing investment and the support of exports were concerned. As Keynes had reflected, they hardly needed to be nationalized. The British clearing banks remained within the strict limits of deposit banking. However, they did retain a significant degree of autonomy, and differences in individual performances reflected different strategic choices. Midland's cautious and conservative policies, for example, contrasted with Barclays' more dynamic approach, resulting in the former losing its leading position to the benefit of the latter. Merchant banks remained a major component of the English banking system, despite being dwarfed, in terms of size, by the clearing banks and retaining a private family structure of ownership. The most famous of them (N. M. Rothschild & Sons, Baring Brothers & Co., Morgan Grenfell & Co., J. Henry Schröder & Co., Kleinwort, Sons & Co., Hambros Bank) had dominated the City's major international financial operations since the nineteenth century. However, the economic environment was much less congenial in the post-war years: New York had become the world's undisputed financial centre, the dollar was the main trading and reserve currency, and the pound suffered from not being fully convertible on current account until 1958.[6] A third category of banks was to face the American challenge: the British overseas banks.[7] They were British, in the sense that their capital and management was British, and their head office in London; but their main fields of operation were abroad, usually in a specific area of the British formal or informal empire. Though smaller than the Big Five, the largest among them (Standard Bank of South Africa; Australia and New Zealand Bank; Chartered Bank of India, Australia and China; Hong Kong and Shanghai Banking Corporation) had reached respectable sizes by international standards. However, as will be discussed later, they were facing problems of their own, deriving from the declining position of the United Kingdom in the world economy.

2. Size

Can size be considered as a measure of a bank's competitive performance? The answer is yes, though only to a certain extent, and more so at national than international level. With the exception of Commerzbank and Banque Nationale pour le Commerce et l'Industrie (BNCI), the banks considered here were already at the top of their country's ranking by the turn of the century.[8] Most had reached a dominant position virtually from the moment of their foundation in the early days of joint stock banking. They were the first movers, to use the Chandlerian terminology: National Provincial Bank and Westminster Bank in England (founded respectively in 1833 and 1834), Comptoir National d'Escompte de Paris (CNEP), Crédit Lyonnais and Société Générale in France (1848, 1862, and 1864), Deutsche Bank and Dresdner Bank in Germany (1870 and 1872). However, a few challengers, especially in England, were able to expand in later years by pursuing a more dynamic policy, usually in the field of mergers and acqusitions. Lloyds Bank and Midland Bank are unique examples of provincial banks (both originating from Birmingham) rising to the top through a systematic amalgamation policy; Barclays Bank was founded in 1896 through the simultaneous mergers of twenty private banks whose partners were all linked by family ties. By 1918 they had become the country's three largest banks. Commerzbank was founded in 1870 in Hamburg, but did not reach a leading position before its mergers with Mitteldeutsche Privat-Bank in 1920, and then with Mitteldeutsche Credit-bank in 1929; even so, it remained the smallest of the German Big Three credit banks. BNCI was founded in 1913 (as Banque Nationale de Crédit) and expanded rapidly before being forced into liquidation in 1931 and reorganized the following year under its new name; by the 1950s it had overtaken CNEP as France's third largest bank. However, the room to manœuvre to upset the established hierarchy was fairly limited, especially after 1918, given the restrictions on competition imposed by cartel agreements and state intervention, which utlimately ensured that a large deposit bank could not go under. This became apparent during the depression of the 1930s, with the rescue of such major banks as the Darmstädter und National Bank (which suspended payments in July 1931) and the very weakened Dresdner Bank (the two were merged in 1932 as part of the government measures to resolve the banking crisis) in Germany; or the Banque Nationale de Crédit (referred to above); and the Banque de l'Union Parisienne in France.

In the early 1950s, the leading European banks were significantly smaller than their American counterparts. However, there were equally significant differences between European banks, with the British banks well ahead of their European rivals (Table 2.1). In 1953, the smallest of the Big Five (National Provincial) was twice as large, in terms of total assets, as Deutsche Bank[9] or Crédit Lyonnais. Taken as a group (i.e. including Barclays Bank DCO), Barclays was nearly five times as large. There was thus a clear international hierarchy consisting of several layers, with a difference in total balance sheet of about one to two billion dollars between each of them. At the top were the three leading American banks (Bank of America, Citibank, Chase Manhattan); they were followed by the three largest British clearing banks (Barclays, Midland, Lloyds)—though, considered as a group, Barclays would feature alongside the top American banks. Then came a group comprising the two smaller British clearers (Westminster and National Provincial) and a number of second-tier American banks (Continental Illinois, First of Chicago, Manufacturers Trust). The world's top ten banks were thus all unmistakably 'Anglo-Saxon'. A fourth layer included the largest French and German banks (Crédit Lyonnais, Société Générale, BNCI, Deutsche Bank), the largest British overseas banks (Standard, ANZ), and several third-tier American banks (Hanover, Chemical, First of Boston, Bankers Trust); and a fifth the smaller of the large European banks (CNEP, Dresdner, Commerz) and British overseas banks (Chartered, Hongkong and Shanghai). As can be seen from Table 2.1, this hierarchy was not fundamentally altered during the 1950s. If anything, the gap between American and European banks widened, while the difference between British and Continental banks remained basically unchanged. As they launched their invasion of Britain, and especially the City of London, American banks were thus challenging their closest foreign rivals.

International rankings of banks have been permanently changing in the course of the twentieth century. In the inter-war years, British banks were the largest in the world, from the 1950s through to the 1970s, it was the turn of the American banks, then came the French and even more the Japanese banks, which at some stage in the 1980s occupied the top ten positions, and the field has become more open again since the 1990s. The significance of a top international ranking, and more generally of a very large size, must therefore be put in perspective. Banks were mainly operating within domestic markets, sheltered from foreign competition, and their size was to a large extent determined by the nature of this domestic market. American banks, discussed by Richard Sylla in Ch. 3, are a case in point. Yet this is not to say that differences in size were meaningless, if not objectively, at least subjectively. There

Table 2.1. *Total assets of the major European and American banks*
($ m.)

	1953	1960
Barclays Bank	4,142/ 6,064[a]	5,182/7,463[a]
Lloyds Bank	3,745	5,033
Midland Bank	4,264	5,103
National Provincial Bank	2,592	3,069
Westminster Bank	2,641	3,809
ANZ Bank	933	1,307
BOLSA	379	739
Chartered Bank	525	1,020
Hongkong and Shangai	621	1,250
Standard Bank of South Africa	1,023	1,161
Crédit Lyonnais	1,243	2,616
Société Générale	1,068	2,285
BNCI	1,041[b]	1,730
CNEP	641	1,180
Deutsche Bank	1,295	2,690
Commerzbank	381[c]	1,640
Bank of America	7,022[d]	11,200
Citibank	6,026	8,160
Chase	5,574	8,420
Manufacturers' Trust	2,581[d]	5,860
Continental Illinois	2,554[d]	2,595
First of Chicago	2,252[d]	2,950
Bankers' Trusts	1,973[d]	3,140
Chemical Bank	1,764[d]	4,130

Notes:
[a] Including Barclays Bank (DCO).
[b] 1954.
[c] 1952.
[d] 1951.

Sources: *Banking Almanac*; G. Jones, *British Multinational Banking*
(Oxford, 1993); Service des Archives historiques, Crédit Lyonnais; L. Gall
et al., *The Deutsche Bank 1870–1995* (London, 1995); H. van B. Cleveland
and T. Huertas, *Citibank 1812–1970* (Cambridge, Mass., 1985);
J. D. Wilson, *The Chase* (Boston, 1986).

were at least two reasons why Continental banks could have been worried
about the distance separating them from the leading Anglo-Saxon, especially
American, banks. The first is that, irrespective of ranking, the size of business
is a measure of its economic power, and this power appeared to have shrunk

considerably since 1914. The second reason is the circumstances surrounding this loss of economic power. On the eve of the First World War, the top
French and German banks, together with their British counterparts, were the
largest in the world. Their weakening in the following decades was the result
of the severe difficulties they encountered during the 'Thirty Years War' of the
twentieth century. More than during any other period, diverging sizes were a
reflection of diverging macro-economic conditions.

3. Multinational Development

In the field of multinational banking, European banks were far more experienced than their American counterparts. The latter hardly expanded overseas
before the 1960s. In 1913, six American banks had a total of twenty-six
foreign branches,[10] as against 1,387 for the British banks[11] and some 500
for the French and German banks. By 1955, there were as many as 3,612
foreign branches of British banks[12] as against 131 for American banks in
1960, seventy of which for the sole First National City Bank that had been
pursuing a global strategy since the beginning of the century.[13] The figures are
less precise for French banks, but the number of their foreign branches must
have remained more or less the same as in the pre-1914 days, while German
banks were stripped of their foreign assets after the War. These figures do
not include private international bankers—Rothschild, Morgan, Lazard, and
many others—in both Europe and America who from an early stage had been
represented in several financial centres, usually through networks of family
relationships. Within the context of the American challenge, the question
is whether this greater international experience gave European banks some
kind of competitive advantage. The answer is probably no, though there were
important variations not only between countries, but also between individual
banks.

   Multinational banking, understood in the sense of a bank owning at least
one branch in a foreign country, traces its origins to the first British overseas banks founded in the early nineteenth century. Until the mid-twentieth
century, such banks operated primarily in colonial empires and developing
countries. The situation changed radically during the 1960s. Multinational
banks shifted their attention from developing countries to the world's major
financial centres. These banks were much more involved in wholesale banking than in retail banking. And the leading players, at least until the
mid-1970s, were American banks. British and—to a lesser extent—French
multinational banks had thus to undergo a profound restructuring, while
German banks started to move abroad only in the 1970s and did not form
major multinational banking groups before the globalization of the 1980s.

The particularity of British multinational banks was, to use Mira Wilkins's concept, their 'free standing' character. In other words, most of them were founded with the purpose of operating abroad, their only link with the home country being their administrative headquarters in London. Mainly for regulatory reasons, in the first place the opposition from the Bank of England, the integration between overseas banks and domestic banks had proceeded very slowly.[14] The exception was Barclays Bank, which had established Barclays Bank DCO (Dominion, Colonial, and Overseas) in 1925 to merge the banks it had acquired in South Africa, Egypt, and the West Indies. Another clearer, Lloyds, held a controlling interest in a number of overseas banks, including the Bank of London and South America, without, however, exerting any real managerial control. During the 1950s, consolidation took place at a regional level, around such banks as the Australia and New Zealand Bank, the Bank of London and South America, the Standard Bank of South Africa, the Hong Kong Bank, and the Chartered Bank of India, Australia and China. As we have seen, these were all sizeable banks. However, they remained locked in areas of slow economic growth, the most notable exception being South East Asia. As Geoff Jones put it, 'the competitive advantage of being a British bank was . . . in danger of becoming a competitive disadvantage'.[15] Nevertheless, in terms of growth and profitability, they fared well in the 1950s and 1960s.

French banks were in different position in the sense that integration between domestic and overseas banking had existed from the very start. Unlike their British counterparts, the major French commercial banks had started to build a network of foreign branches in the late nineteenth century. Crédit Lyonnais, for example, had branches in London, Geneva, and Brussels, as well as in several cities in Egypt, Spain, Russia, the Ottoman Empire, and Algeria, Tunisia, and Morocco, part of the French colonial empire.[16] The Banque de Paris et des Pays-Bas, an investment bank, was present from its early days in Amsterdam, Brussels, and Geneva. There were, to be sure, a number of banks operating specifically in the empire (the largest of them being the Banque de l'Indochine), though they tended to be subsidiaries of the major metropolitan banks.[17] The downside was that, like their British counterparts, French multinational banks were mainly established in the Third World, not only for historical reasons, but also as a result of the strong expansionary wave following the Second World War, and mainly directed towards Africa.

In the end, only three banks worldwide could be considered as multinational banks in the modern sense of the word, i.e. with a strong metropolitan basis and a geographically diversified overseas presence. One was American, one was British, and one was French. The American bank was First National City Bank (Citibank), with its headquarters in New York City and 76 foreign branches in 1959, most of them in Latin America. From a business culture point of view, Citibank saw itself as a global bank and had consistently worked towards achieving this status.[18] The British Bank was Barclays, with its head office in London and over 1000 foreign branches in 1955. On this measure, Barclays was thus by far the largest multinational bank in the world. The bulk of this branch network (997) was provided by its subsidiary, Barclays Bank DCO, which had already become the largest British overseas bank by the 1930s. Like Citibank, Barclays' foreign branches were unevenly spread across the world, with half DCO's branches operating in South Africa.[19] The French bank was Crédit Lyonnais, with its head office in Paris and nearly 200 foreign branches in 1962 (85 directly and 113 through subsidiaries and associated banks). Most of these branches had been created after 1945, even though Crédit Lyonnais was the first of the three banks to expand overseas. Its network was also more evenly spread than that of the two Anglo-Saxon banks, with branches in Africa, Latin America, the Middle East, and Western Europe.[20] Besides these three banks, a few others got close to this multinational model: the major French commercial banks (BNCI had 56 foreign branches, Société Générale 35, Comptoir d'Escompte 26), the leading British overseas banks, and Lloyds Bank, with its numerous stakes in overseas banks. The advent of the Euromarkets was to test their capacity to adapt to the New World of international finance.

4. Management

Assessing the managerial capabilities of European banks, as compared with their American competitors, appears particularly difficult in the current dearth of historical studies of the subject. However, a few lessons can be drawn by looking at their governance structures and, in a little more detail, at their top executives (chairmen and managing directors).

The functions of the boards of directors had not been fundamentally altered since the mid-nineteenth century. The origins of the single board, prevailing in Britain and France, and the two-tier board, prevailing in Germany, went back to the company laws of the 1860s and 1870s, which freed the way for the growth of joint stock companies. The most important changes had taken place in France. In the first place, the 1940 company law rendered mandatory the merger of the functions of chairman and general manager, thus creating a new all-powerful executive, the *PDG*, or *président directeur général*. Whatever the origins of this new law,[21] it clearly resulted in an increased professionalization of the French business leadership, though at the cost of an excessive concentration of power in the hands of a single person. Nevertheless, throughout the 1950s several bank chairmen (for example at Crédit Lyonnais and Banque de Paris et des Pays-Bas) appear to have delegated a

great deal of authority to their chief executives.[22] Secondly, the nationalization of the deposit banks led to a reconstruction of their board of directors,
which now included representatives—eight in total—of the various economic
interests (industry, commerce, agriculture, trade unions) appointed by the
government on the advice of interest groups; as well as four nominees (two
representing the Bank of France) of the Minister of Finance.[23] The effects of
these measures on bank management remain to be properly assessed.

In Germany, the main change concerned the membership of supervisory
boards, which included employees' representatives in accordance with the
principle of codetermination first introduced in 1951. During the first part of
the 1950s, the management of the Big Three credit banks was of course divided
between three separate institutions, each with its executive and supervisory
boards. Whether this resulted in a waste of managerial resources appears
unlikely. In the case of Deutsche Bank, for example, the *Vorstand* of the
reconstituted bank in 1957 included 11 of the 12 executive directors of the
three successor institutions. The remaining one—Oswald Rösler, spokesman
of Deutsche Bank's *Vorstand* between 1943 and 1945—became chairman of
the supervisory board.[24]

In Britain, boards of directors remained unchanged, whether in their
statutory functions or in their composition. The gap between directors and
managers—who as a rule were not board members—remained far wider than
in continental Europe and, apart from a few exceptions, did not start to narrow
before the 1960s. As for the merchant banks, they retained their traditional
private family form despite the wave of conversion into private limited companies that seized the industry in the early post-war years, with eight major
banks converting between 1945 and 1950. This is usually seen as a managerial weakness, though it remained to be properly ascertained. Merchant banks'
governance structures were in fact highly flexible. For more than a century, the
most successful (including Barings, Lazard, Morgan Grenfell, and Schröder)
had offered partnerships to bright outsiders in order to compensate for lack of
family resources. And what was the exception became the rule in the increasingly competitive environment of the 1960s. In any case, British private banks
were not far behind their American counterparts in opening their ranks to
meritocratic elements.

The analysis of a small sample of 20 leading bankers[25] in 1954 reveals,
not surprisingly, that they were not young men: their average age was 62,
the median 61. At 74, Edouard Escarra, chairman of Crédit Lyonnais, was the
oldest, followed by Lord Balfour of Burleigh, 71, in his last year as chairman of
Lloyds Bank; Escarra was to retire the following year. The youngest was David
Robarts, 48, who had just been elected chairman of the National Provincial
and was to stay in office until 1976—from 1968 as chairman of National

Westminster Bank following the merger of the two venerable institutions. Other 'young' executives included Hermann Abs, 53, managing director of Süddeutsche Bank and from 1957 spokesman of the *Vorstand* of Deutsche Bank; Jean Reyre, 55, general manager of Paribas; and Maurice Lorain and Antony William Tuke, respectively general manager of Société Générale and chairman of Barclays Bank, both aged 57. Chairmen were on whole older than managing directors, leaving the latter with an average age of just under 60, a far from excessively advanced age given the hierarchical structure of large corporations.

Educational levels reflected the business traditions prevailing in each country:[26] a very high level of formal education in France (*all* chairmen and general managers were university educated, with degrees in law, usually combined with politics and economics); the continuing prevalence of the banking apprenticeship in Germany (about half the cases, including the biggest names in the profession, such as Hermann Abs, though he did attend university lectures for a year or so);[27] and the traditional separation between 'gentlemen' and 'players' in Britain (major public school most often followed by Oxford or Cambridge for the directors, training on the job after leaving school at 16 for the managers).

The significance of education to the training of business leaders should not be overestimated: it basically conformed to the traditions shaping the paths to élite positions in their respective country. Career patterns played a more important role. And here, despite differences, a high degree of professionalism can be perceived in all three countries. The overwhelming majority (75%) of the top executives of Europe's leading banks made their entire career in banking. About half of them spent the whole of their working life within the same institution. Some started as apprentices at 16 or 18 years of age (the chief general managers of the British banks such as William Edington of Midland, Cecil Ellerton of Barclays, Arthur Ensor of Lloyds), others after a university degree (for example Jean Reyre, general manager of the Banque de Paris et des Pays-Bas); in one case (Anthony William Tuke, chairman of Barclays), it still actually meant entering the family firm. A minority changed bank in mid-career: Hermann Abs was promised a partnership in a private bank, but in 1937, aged only 35, he preferred the *Vorstand* of the Deutsche Bank; Carl Goetz was 'transferred' from the *Vorstand* of Commerzbank to that of the ailing Dresdner as part of the Reich's rescue package in 1932.[28] And in Britain, the chairmen of two of the Big Five (Lord Aldenham of Westminster and David John Robarts of National Provincial) were also partners in private banking firms (respectively A. Gibbs & Sons and Robert Fleming & Co.). Outside banking, a few chairmen were recruited within the higher echelons of the public service: Emmanuel Monick, chairman of Paribas, had been a

Governor of the Banque de France between 1944 and 1950; at the Société Générale, Pierre de Moüy was a former senior civil servant in the Ministry of Finance. In Britain, Midland Bank and Lloyds Bank chose a succession of public figures as their chairmen after 1945: at Midland, Lord Harlech, High Commissioner in South Africa, succeeded in 1952 the Marquis of Linlithgow, a former Viceroy and Governor-General of India; at Lloyds, Sir Oliver Franks, a disinguished academic and civil servant, and former British ambassador in Washington, succeeded in 1954 Lord Balfour of Burleigh.

It is difficult to generalize about the quality of the top management of European banks in the mid-1950s. As noted above, the path to banking remained deeply rooted in the traditions prevailing in each country. On the other hand, with the 'dynastic factor' playing a much smaller role in their appointment than a quarter of a century earlier,[29] Europe's top bankers had become a fully managerial élite. Overall, it is unlikely that the quality of bank management could have been significantly better. However, despite the weight of regulation and cartelization, there were differences between banks, which were ultimately reflected in their performance.

5. Innovative Capacity

The early post-war years are not known as an era of great innovative spurt for European banks. The British banks, which took the brunt of the American challenge, have been particularly criticized in this respect. There is no doubt that the institutional framework discussed above, with its cartel agreements and tight government controls, was not particularly conducive to dynamic, risk-taking, or entrepreneurial behaviour. For Lord Franks, chairman of Lloyds Bank and a former academic and civil servant, 'it was like driving a powerful car at 20 miles an hour. The banks were anaesthetised—it was a kind of dream world'.[30] While the view that clearing banks were rather sleepy in the 1950s is certainly correct, two points should be borne in mind. The first is that the banks' innovative edge had started to erode since the 1920s, if not earlier, as a result of both the long-term process of financial sophistication in the United Kingdom and greater cartelization of retail banking.[31] The clearing banks were content to concentrate on their speciality—deposit banking—and leave to other institutions, such as building societies and insurance funds, the provision of new and faster-growing financial services. The second point is that the British clearing banks were not entirely apathetic. There was a degree of non-price competition amongst the banks, through opening new branches, launching new products, or taking a stakes in companies involved in new financial activities. Barclays was clearly the most active

of the Big Five. It was the first to venture into hire purchase finance, by buying 25 per cent of United Dominion Trust in 1958, after being permitted
by the Bank of England. As we have seen, it had also considerably extended
its overseas expansion through Barclays DCO; and it offered some merchant
banking services, such as underwriting British Commonwealth stock, though
the bank remained highly conservative and opposed to hostile takeover bids,
which were first introduced at the time.[32] Midland, which was overtaken
by Barclays as the country's largest bank in the 1950s, reacted by setting up
a Business Development Committee in 1956, strengthening its branch network, and decentralizing the bank's management structure; it also entered
the hire purchase business in 1958 by acquiring the Forward Trust, jointly
with the Clydesdale Bank. Midland was the first British bank to advertise its
services on television.[33] Moreover, by attracting dollar deposits to fund its
own operations as early as 1955, the Midland Bank was at the origins of the
most important financial innovation of the period, the Eurodollar market.[34]

British merchant banks have also been described as highly conservative,
mainly as a result of their private family structure discussed above. Nevertheless, they were successful in expanding, and for some in rebuilding, their
business: the volume of their operations quickly surpassed its pre-war level,
at both current and constant prices. In fact, for most houses acceptance credit
remained the principal activity well into the 1960s if not the 1970s. In the issuing business, merchant banks continued to turn their attention to domestic
companies, a move that had started in the 1920s. The field, however, was
changing and becoming what is now known as corporate finance, that is the
provision of advice to companies, especially in connection with mergers and
acquisitions. Here the leading player and innovator was a newcomer, S. G.
Warburg & Co., a bank founded in 1934 by Siegmund Warburg, a scion of the
famous Hamburg banking dynasty. Warburg radically transformed the field
of corporate finance by popularizing the hostile takeover bid, following his
victory in the 'Great Aluminium War' in 1958–9.[35] This is not the place to discuss this well-known City episode.[36] Much has been made of the significance
of this battle: its outcome has been seen as a victory of the dynamic outsider
against a conservative establishment, a triumph of a new, more professional,
if also more ruthless business approach over an old-fashioned amateurish and
cliquish way of dealing. There is of course some truth in this. However, all
the leading merchant banks had already started to build highly professional
teams; they adapted fairly easily to the new rules of the game introduced by
Warburg and maintained their hold over corporate finance in the following
decades. As far as the American challenge is concerned, it is also significant that merchant banks were among the initiators of the Euromarkets. The
first dealings in Eurodollars in 1957–8 were carried out by London merchant

banks (Samuel Montagu, Kleinwort, Warburg) and overseas banks (Bank of London and South America at the instigation of its chairman, Sir George Bolton). Siegmund Warburg was responsible for the first Eurobond issue in 1963 (on behalf of Autostrade Italiane), though 'the idea [had] evolved over time with the participation of dozens of individuals'.[37]

In France, with the domestic market controlled by the big national-ized banks, privately owned banks had to prove innovative in order to remain competitive. The Banque de Paris et des Pays-Bas, the leading *banque d'affaires*, is a case in point. In the early post-war years, in the midst of the dollar gap, it launched a medium-term financing scheme in the shape of export-credits: rather than lending the foreign buyer dollars, the bank would grant a French franc loan to the French manufacturer, who would gradually repay his loan as he was himself repaid by the foreign buyer. Paribas remained the leader in this field well into the 1960s. In the same way, as domestic issues for French companies were the preserve of the cartel of nationalized banks, Paribas specialized in foreign issues on behalf of both French and foreign firms.[38] As in Britain, investment banks appear to have been more dynamic than deposit banks and thus readier to face the American challenge. How-ever, competition from American banks was mainly confined to international banking operations, the natural domain of investment banks.

6. Conclusion

To what extent can banks alter the economic environment in which they are working, and to what extent are they straitjacketed by this environment? All the major debates in banking history have ultimately revolved around this question. Answering that the two interact on each other is not a truism, though it must be admitted that one aspect can temporarily be dominant, depending on varying sets of circumstances—economic, social, political, or entrepreneurial. Banks' competitiveness must thus be assessed on a long-run perspective. Taken in isolation, the 1950s were not a particularly propitious time for European banks. Despite significant differences between countries and even individual institutions, they looked ill-prepared to face successfully the onslaught of American banks. That a gap between American and European banks should have existed in the 1950s is hardly surprising. It only reflected the overwhelming dominance of the American economy over the rest of the world, not only in terms of size and levels of income and productivity, but also in terms of dynamism and innovative capacity.

The picture looks different over the longer term. European countries had deep-rooted banking traditions and a longer experience of international banking than their American counterparts which, to a certain extent, were forced to move to Europe. As in other sectors of the economy, the catch-up factor could be at work and European banks soon regained their international positions: the number of American banks amongst the world's top ten dropped from five to two between 1970 and 1980, while that of European banks increased from three to eight.[39] However, this was not entirely the result of European banks' new competitiveness. The American challenge had a limited impact. For one thing, it was mainly concentrated on the City of London and for another domestic banking, for both regulatory and cultural reasons, remained on the whole impenetrable to foreigners, whether American or European.

NOTES

1. For details see C.-L. Holtfrerich, 'The Deutsche Bank 1945–1957: War, Military Rule and Reconstruction', in L. Gall, G. D. Feldman, H. James, C.-L. Holtfrerich, and H. E. Büschgen, *The Deutsche Bank 1870–1995* (London: Weidenfeld & Nicolson, 1995), 357–521.

2. Ibid. 429.

3. C.-L. Holtfrerich, *Frankfurt as a Financial Centre: From Medieval Trade to European Banking Centre* (Munich: C. H. Beck, 1999), 222–38, 243–51.

4. See J. S. G. Wilson, *French Banking Structure and Credit Policy* (Oxford: Oxford University Press, 1957).

5. See M. Collins, *Money and Banking in the UK: A History* (London: Croom Helm, 1988).

6. See B. Bramsen and K. Wain, *The Hambros 1779–1979* (London: Michael Joseph, 1979); K. Burk, *Morgan Grenfell 1838–1988: The Biography of a Merchant Bank* (Oxford: Oxford University Press, 1989); R. Roberts, *Schroders: Merchants & Bankers* (London: Macmillan, 1992); J. Wake, *Kleinwort Benson: The History of Two Families in Banking* (Oxford: Oxford University Press, 1997); N. Ferguson, *The World's Banker: The History of the House of Rothschild* (London: Weidenfeld & Nicolson, 1998).

7. See G. Jones, *British Multinational Banking, 1830–1990* (Oxford: Clarendon Press, 1993).

8. See Y. Cassis, 'A Century of Consolidation in European Banking: General Trends', in M. Pohl, T. Tortella, and H. van der Wee (eds.), *A Century of Banking Consolidation in Europe* (Aldershot: Elgar, 2001).

9. The figure refers to the combined balance sheet of the three regional banks making up the Deutsche Bank 'group'; see Holtfrerich, 'The Deutsche Bank', 509.

10. M. Wilkins, 'Banks Over Borders: Some Evidence of their Pre-1914 History', in G. Jones (ed.), *Banks as Multinationals* (London: Routledge, 1990), 232.

11. Jones, *British Multinational Banking*, 397.

12. Ibid. 401.
13. T. Huertas, 'US Multinational Banking: History and Prospects', in Jones (ed.), *Banks as Multinationals*, 253.
14. See Jones, *British Multinational Banking*, 235–9, 272–5.
15. Ibid. 247.
16. M. Mogenet (ed.), *Un Siècle d'Économie Française: 1863–1963* (Paris: s.n.,1963).
17. See H. Bonin, 'L'Outre-mer, Marché pour la Banque Commerciale de 1875 à 1985', in *La France et l'outre-mer: Un siècle de relations monétaires et financières* (Paris: CHEFF, 1998), 437–83.
18. See H. van B. Cleveland and T. H. Huertas, *Citibank 1812–1970* (Cambridge, Mass.: Harvard University Press, 1985).
19. See Jones, *British Multinational Banking*; J. Crossley and J. Blandford, *The DCO Story* (London: Barclays Bank International Ltd., 1975).
20. Mogenet (ed.), *Un siècle d'économie*, 224–7.
21. The 1940 company law was clearly inspired by the German example, set up by the Nazis a few years earlier, which reinforced the authority of the executive board, and especially that of its chairman.
22. See J. Rivoire, *Le Crédit Lyonnais. Histoire d'une Banque* (Paris: Cherche-Midi, 1989), 136–57; E. Bussière, *Paribas. Europe and the World 1872–1992* (Antwerp: Fonds Mercator, 1992), 152–4.
23. Wilson, *French Banking*, 53–4.
24. Holtfrerich, 'The Deutsche Bank', 467; H. Büschgen, 'Deutsche Bank 1957 to the Present', in Gall *et al.*, *Deutsche Bank*, 524.
25. The sample includes the chairmen and general managers of Barclays, Lloyds, and Midland in Britain; Crédit Lyonnais, Société Générale, and Paribas in France; and Deutsche and Dresdner (as for 1957) in Germany; the chairmen of National Provincial and Westminster in Britain, and CNEP in France; and the general manager of Bankverein Westdeutschland/Commerzbank-Bankverein in Germany.
26. See Y. Cassis, *Big Business: The European Experience in the Twentieth Century* (Oxford: Oxford University Press, 1997), 132–42.
27. L. Gall, 'Hermann Josef Abs and the Third Reich: A Man for All Seasons?', *Financial History Review*, 6 (1999), 2, 151–2.
28. C. Kopper, *Zwischen Markwirtschaft und Dirigismus: Bankenpolitik im Dritten Reich 1933–1939* (Bonn: Bouvier, 1995), 62.
29. See Y. Cassis, 'European Bankers in the Inter-War Years', in M. Kasuya (ed.), *Coping with Crisis: Reshaping Financial Institutions in the 1920s and 1930s* (Oxford: Oxford University Press, forthcoming).
30. Quoted in A. Sampson, *The Money Lenders* (London: Hodder & Stoughton, 1981), 121.
31. See Collins, *Money and Banking*, 201–2.
32. M. Ackrill and L. Hannah, *Barclays: The Business of Banking, 1690–1996* (Cambridge: Cambridge University Press, 2001).

33. A. R. Holmes and E. Green, *Midland: 150 Years of Banking Business* (London: B. T. Batsford, 1986).
34. See C. Shenk, 'The Origins of the Eurodollar Market in London: 1955–1963', *Explorations in Economic History*, 35 (1998).
35. Warburg advised the American aluminium company Reynolds Metal in its successful takeover bid (jointly with the Midland engineering group TI, advised by Helbert Wagg and Schröders) for the venerable British Aluminium, advised by two old-established City houses, Hambro and Lazard. For the first time, a company appealed directly to the investing public, against the wish of the incumbent board.
36. See in particular J. Attali, *A Man of Influence: Sir Siegmund Warburg, 1902–1982* (London: Weidenfeld & Nicolson, 1986); R. Chernow, *The Warburgs: A Family Saga* (London: Chatto & Windus, 1993); Roberts, *Schroders.*
37. M. vom Clemm, of Crédit Suisse First Boston, to K. Burk, in K. Burk, 'Witness Seminar on the Origins and Early Development of the Eurobond Market', *Contemporary European History*, 1 (1992), 67.
38. See Bussière, *Paribas.*
39. *The Banker*, June 1971 and June 1981.

3

United States Banks and Europe: Strategy and Attitudes

RICHARD SYLLA

What to Europeans appeared to be a US banking *invasion* from the 1950s to the 1970s was, from the perspective of the American banks, more in the nature of an *escape*. US banking leaders during the 1950s and 1960s were ambitious for their institutions and innovative in their strategies and tactics. Ostensibly, they were in a commanding position to give vent to their ambitions. The US economy was the largest around the world; with only three mild and short-lived recessions, it performed admirably throughout the two decades. The US dollar had already replaced the British pound as the world's international currency, the one the world most desired, especially during the 'dollar shortage' of the late 1940s and the 1950s. The dollar was the anchor of the Bretton Woods world monetary system. Moreover, a freer international trading system largely constructed by US statesmen increased world trade, leading to greater demand for international finance.

In this propitious economic environment, US corporations prospered both at home and around the world. These industrial firms possessed comparative managerial and technological advantages that would have dictated a strategy of worldwide expansion in any case. But that strategy became all the more compelling when European nations—with the blessing of American statesmen for reasons more political than economic—adopted free-trade blocs with common tariffs levied on goods produced outside the blocs. The re-establishment of European currency convertibility in the late 1950s also nudged along the multinational strategies of American corporations.

US economic expansion and the multinationalization strategies of American industrial corporations created increasing demands for banking and other financial services from the financial institutions that had always served them. Foremost among these institutions were the large commercial, 'money-centre' banks of New York City, the US financial centre, as well as a number of large banks in other areas of the United States. American corporations had long been the leading clients of these banks. It was therefore only natural that the banks would try to meet corporate financial needs as the US multinationals implemented their strategies of domestic and international expansion.

As the US money-centre banks tried to meet the growing demands for finance and other services from their corporate clients, and to realize their own ambitions for extending the scale and scope of their activities, they bumped head-on into the craziest patchwork quilt of banking regulations ever devised by the mind of man. The US bank/financial regulatory system of the 1950s was the product of peculiar American attitudes towards concentration of financial power that had been present at the time of the country's founding in the late eighteenth century, as well as from numerous political disputes and compromises that followed from the persistence of that attitude for the next two centuries. The anti-concentration attitude of the US polity towards the banking/financial sector was greatly strengthened in the 1930s, when New Deal financial reforms laid the blame for the debacle of the Great Depression of 1929–33 at the doorstep of bankers, and then proceeded by means of regulatory legislation to further carve up, cartelize, and control the business of banking. A leading example of this was the 1933 Glass-Steagall Act that mandated a separation of commercial and investment banking, forcing banks that had engaged in both activities to choose one or the other.

By the 1950s, the results of US banking regulation were indeed strange. Whereas older American industrial corporations such as Ford, General Electric, and IBM could produce and sell their products throughout the United States and much of the world, and brand-new ones such as McDonald's could be founded to supply America and the world with Big Mac hamburgers, US money-centre banks such as First National City (later Citibank) and Chase Manhattan could not buy another bank, or even open a branch, outside of the confines of New York City. And major non-New York banks such as First National of Chicago and Continental Illinois were restricted to just one office—no branches whatsoever—within the United States. By way of contrast, in booming, growing California, San Francisco-based Bank of America could branch throughout the Golden State to become in 1945 the world largest bank, passing Chase.[1]

Actually, all the US banks just named were among America's and the world's largest banks. But thanks to the size of the US economy (more than a third of the world economy in the 1950s) and the persistent anti-concentration mentality of US banking regulation, even the largest of them individually possessed no more than about 3 per cent of US bank assets. For the big US banks around 1960, hamstrung as they were by draconian regulation at home, Europe was a godsend. Their US corporate clients were directly investing in Europe and could use familiar American banking services from familiar

American banks. European banking regulations were far more reasonable than the ones they faced in the United States. The Europeans were welcoming, particularly the British who were desirous of restoring the status of London as an international financial centre. As one writer put it, 'We can no more speak of the "invasion" of Britain by the international banking community in the 1960s and 1970s than we can speak of the invasion of Britain by the Hanoverian monarchy: both were invited by their hosts.'[2] And in Europe the US banks discovered a small market in Eurodollars, which they would develop into something far greater than it was when the invasion of the 1960s was being launched.

By the mid-1970s, the US banks that led the invasion of Europe would become truly international banks, doing about half their business and earning about half their profits outside the United States. They brought back the international money and capital markets that had flourished before 1914, and to a lesser extent in the 1920s, only to disappear during the Great Depression of the 1930s, the Second World War, and the government-led financial programmes and controls of the post-war years.

In the process of innovating and internationalizing, the banks at first prompted US authorities, in time-honoured fashion, to tighten up on regulatory reach. And then, when the folly of that regulatory tightening for US interests became increasingly apparent to the authorities, the new regulations were relaxed, sometimes eliminated, and world financial markets became more open.

History has its ironies. US history books say that Europeans migrated to America in the seventeenth century and later to pursue economic opportunity in the New World and to escape from oppression at home. In short, pull and push. It appears that US banks migrated to Europe in the 1960s and 1970s for exactly the same reasons. In both migrations, the natives at first were welcoming, then fearful of being overwhelmed, and finally had to make adjustments to the invaders from across the Atlantic with their new ways of doing things.

This chapter documents in more detail the sketch laid out above. The focus is on the strategies that led the US banks to invade Europe, or escape from US banking regulation in the 1960s. It was an invasion/escape led by just a few large banks, although quite a few more followed them. Foremost among leaders, because it was the most innovative and had the most comprehensive global strategy, was First National City Bank (Citibank) of New York. Other leaders, based more on size than strategy or innovation, were Morgan Guaranty (J. P. Morgan) and Chase Manhattan, both New York based, and Bank of America (San Francisco). Europe was not new to them; they were among the seven US banks having London branches in 1960, and all four of the leaders had maintained those branches for decades before that year. They also had branches outside Europe, far more in fact than they had in Europe. Among the larger followers of the four leaders were Manufacturers Hanover, Bankers Trust, and Chemical of New York; Continental Illinois and First National from Chicago; and First National of Boston. Lesser-sized followers raised the total number of US banks in London from seven in 1960 to about 60 by the mid-1970s.

Preparation for the invasion occurred during the 1950s, when three of the four leaders achieved larger size through major mergers, encountered difficulties in funding their operations because of US banking regulations, and sought innovative ways of circumventing regulatory constraints. Much of the invasion proper took place from 1963 to 1974, when US economic and military policies together with new and restrictive financial regulations made it very difficult for the American banks to pursue strategies of international expansion from their home base. By the mid-1970s the invasion was essentially complete, the leading US banks were fully international financial institutions, and non-US banks hoping to compete with the Americans had to adopt some of the US banks' strategies and tactics.

1. Laying the Groundwork for International Expansion: The 1950s and Early 1960s

For more than a decade after the Second World War, large US banks had no more than a limited interest in international expansion. Conditions were not ripe for it. Restrictions on private capital flows and currency convertibility were drawbacks. Governments, along with quasi-international institutions organized and controlled by governments, directed what financial flows there were, for reasons that were at least as much political as economic.

A few of the banks had international branches. These dated to the last decades of the nineteenth century. The largest commercial banks, namely the nationally chartered banks of New York City, were not allowed to open foreign branches until passage of the Federal Reserve Act in 1913. Only one of them, National City, thereafter developed an extensive international branch system. In the 1920s New York flourished as the world's new financial centre. But the Depression interrupted that development for three decades. National City, the leader, for example had 83 foreign branches in 1930, generating 25 to 30 per cent of its loans, deposits, and earnings, but only 61 such branches in 1955, which generated 11 to 16 per cent of loans, deposits, and earnings. In 1955 National City had only three branches in Europe. None the less, the leading US banks by the 1950s had long experience in international banking.

When further opportunities arose and conditions became more favourable for international expansion, they were in a position to move quickly to exploit them.[3]

Before international opportunities opened up, the leading banks focused in the 1950s on domestic business. Here there were many opportunities, but also threats posed by market developments and banking regulations. The opportunities came from the rapid growth and rising productivity of the US economy, and the expansion of US corporate clients overseas, which as far as banking services were concerned could be financed mainly from domestic resources.

In the decade after the war, the banks had ample resources to take advantage of their opportunities. The war's financial legacy was a bank balance sheet stuffed with US Treasury debt. When loan demand increased during the post-war expansion, the banks could sell off their holdings of government debt to fund their private-sector lending. It was, in the words of the Citibank historians, getting 'back in the business of banking'.[4]

Rising interest rates in the US, especially after the Treasury-Federal Reserve Accord of 1951 released the Federal Bank from its war-engendered obligation to peg interest rates on US Treasury debt at low levels, made getting back to the business of banking profitable. For a time, banking regulation even helped bank profitability. The Federal Bank's Regulation Q, dating from the 1930s New Deal banking reforms, decreed that the banks could not pay interest on demand deposits, and it set ceilings (whose levels tended to be adjusted upwards only with a lag when market and bank-loan interest rates rose) on rates the banks could pay for time deposits. Ceilings on deposit rates kept down the cost of bank funding. US bankers would come to detest the ceilings and call for their removal, but for more than two decades after these were imposed in the 1930s, most bankers thought they were just fine.

During the 1950s a banking innovation that later would provide opportunities for the US banks to exploit in Europe became highly developed at home. This was the term loan, a credit of intermediate maturity that could be tailored to a borrowing client's needs. It was based on a new concept of creditworthiness, namely a forward-looking analysis of the cash flow the borrower could be expected to receive over the life of the loan and have available to pay it, rather than the banker's traditional and essentially backward-looking analysis of the borrower's existing assets that stood behind and might be pledged to secure repayment of the loan. The term loan when it began was viewed as domestic credit, but it quickly assumed an international flavour. National City bankers were among its leading proponents, and their chroniclers tell amusing stories of client Aristotle Onassis dangling shipping charters before them and begging to pledge them as collateral for loans to buy more ships.[5]

Rising interest rates and banking regulations also had their downsides for the big banks. Rising interest rates by the late 1950s caused treasurers of their corporate clients to question why they should leave funds on deposit at the banks for little or no interest when they could invest these funds in higher-yielding money market instruments. Because of Regulation Q, the banks' hands were tied; they could not pay more interest than the regulations allowed, and over the course of the 1950s they began to lose corporate deposits, traditionally a major funding source for large-bank lending.

Given the development of term loans, the timing of the market-oriented innovations in corporate cash management posed a real threat to the banks. Before term loans came in, the banks were like 'clubs of capital' (a term used by US financier Robert Morris as early as the 1780s) in which a bank's customer-clients largely funded themselves, some lodging temporarily surplus funds in the bank while others took them out as traditional short-term bank loans. Term loans, on the other hand, were for extended periods, often several years, and tied up bank funds for the term of the loan. Offsetting seasonal patterns of deposit flows and loan demand were less and less relevant to banks making term loans.

Another problem the large banks faced was that, although they were among the largest banks in the world, their US corporate clients were even larger and, with no or fewer regulatory limits on their expansion, growing faster. Banking regulations dictated lending no more than, say, 10 per cent of a bank's capital to one borrower. Larger clients needed larger loans, but the US banks, because of regulatory limits on lending, were less and less able to supply them. So while some corporate clients were taking their deposits out of banks and investing them in money market instruments such as Treasury bills and commercial paper, others were bypassing the banks when it came to borrowing and instead funding their short- and intermediate-credit needs by issuing commercial paper. The traditional banking clubs were being eroded by money market developments.

By the mid- to late 1950s, therefore, the large US banks were caught in a funding squeeze, the product of rising interest rates and restrictive banking regulations. This was mainly a domestic problem; the banks' international business—mainly trade finance and serving corporate clients overseas—was still a small and traditional sideline for only a few banks. The banks' responses to the funding squeeze, however, were innovative in ways that would prepare them well when the European invasion/escape came in the next decade.

These innovative responses were essentially twofold: the banks became larger, mostly by way of merger and raising new share capital, and they developed new and innovative funding sources. Among the leaders of the later invasion of Europe, in 1955 National City merged with First National of

New York to form First National City Bank; this was a joining of a diversified wholesale-retail bank with the largest international branch network of any US bank (National City) with a once-great wholesale (that is, one that dealt mainly with corporations) bank that had fallen on hard times. In the same year, Chase Manhattan Bank emerged with the merger of Chase National, a wholesale bank, with Bank of the Manhattan Company, a retail bank with a large branch network in New York City. Four years later, J. P. Morgan, a relatively small (by New York standards) but prestigious and internationally well-connected wholesale bank, merged with the much larger Guaranty Trust Company, a wholesale and trust bank, to form Morgan Guaranty.[6] Unlike the other leaders, Morgan Guaranty remained a wholesale bank.

In New York City, there were other bank mergers in the 1950s, including Manufacturers Trust and Hanover to form Manufacturers Hanover, which later became a major player, if not a leader, of the European invasion. Another leader of the invasion, San Francisco's Bank of America, was not involved in a major merger during the 1950s, although it had grown by that route earlier in its history, even attempting without success to become a nationwide bank at the end of the 1920s. Bank of America, thanks to California's liberal (for the United States) allowance of statewide branching and the state's rapid growth in population and resources after the war, did not need a major merger to maintain, even increase, its position as America's largest bank.[7]

Mergers among New York City banks were about the only avenue open to them to grow in the regulatory climate of the 1950s. Under US law, even nationally chartered banks had to follow the banking laws of the states in which they were located. In the funding squeeze of the 1950s and early 1960s the New York City banks made numerous attempts to expand their deposit bases by merging with suburban and, later, upstate New York banks. But these attempts were usually beaten back by regulatory rulings that now, with nationwide banking allowed, seem quaint. The regulators cloaked their rulings in the traditional American rhetoric of preserving competition and preventing concentrations of financial power. What they were really doing, however, was protecting the local positions of the numerous smaller yet politically powerful banks that feared an invasion by the money-centre banks seeking to solve their funding problems. Local banks thus gained protection from competition in regulator-enforced cartels, and the regulators gained from an absence of bank failures in the sheltered local cartels.

During and after their mergers with other New York City institutions, the money-centre banks developed new funding sources. One possibility was rediscounting with the central bank, but the Federal Bank had turned that into at best a temporary relief for a bank experiencing difficulties, not a regular source of funds for expanded lending. An alternative was the federal funds market, a market in which banks with surplus reserves lent them overnight to banks with reserve deficits. The market had been around for decades, but had fallen into abeyance in the 1930s and 1940s when banks generally held surplus reserves. It was revived and expanded in the 1950s, a time when numerous out-of-town banks around the United States still had excess reserves that could be borrowed by the resource-starved money-centre banks. The federal funds market provided some relief for the money-centre funding squeeze. More importantly for the later European invasion, it gave them experience in dealing in a large interbank market.

A related funding source was security repurchase agreements, or repos, in which a bank needing funds would sell securities in its portfolio to another bank, agreeing in advance to buy back the securities at a later date. The Citibank historians note that First National City by 1961 was borrowing $160 m. a day in the federal funds and repos markets, compared to only $26 m. just seven years earlier.[8]

By far the most important of banks' funding innovations of the pre-invasion era was the certificate of deposit or CD, a bank-issued credit instrument stating that a depositor had agreed to leave funds on deposit at the bank for a stated term, at a stated rate of interest. Like federal funds, these had been around for a long time in US banking. The innovation of First National City executives George Moore and Walter Wriston in 1961 was to turn them into a negotiable money-market instrument and expandable source of funding by issuing them in large denominations while creating a secondary trading market to give them liquidity. Interestingly, Wriston at the time was head of First National City's Overseas Division, where lending opportunities were growing faster than in the United States itself. Five years later the CD innovation would be introduced in Europe.

The large-denomination negotiable CD was the main solution to the money-centre banks' funding squeeze, and one that issued in a new era of entrepreneurial banking. Formerly, banks lent out funds placed with them to the extent banking regulations permitted, with federal funds and repos constituting marginal additions to deposits as funding sources. The CD changed all that. Thanks to the CD, if a bank had a profitable loan opportunity it did not have to pass it up merely because it was already loaned up; it could fund it with newly issued CDs, in effect going out to buy the money to fund the loan. The CD thus relaxed a traditional constraint on bank expansion; with it, banks could now manage their liabilities as well as their assets. It was the dawn of 'spread' banking

By 1967, just six years after negotiable CDs were introduced, they surpassed in volume the commercial paper issued by non-bank corporations as a US money market instrument. Corporate deposits that had flowed out of banks and into the commercial paper and Treasury bill markets in the 1950s began to flow back as CDs in the 1960s. The CD surpassed the fondest hopes of the bankers who introduced it. Rather than be beaten by the money market, the banks decided to join it.

Like many financial innovations that are not patentable, and would probably be of less value even to the innovators if they could be patented, the National City Bank CD innovation was quickly used by other banks. Wriston himself, according to his biographer, claimed that the CD saved the Morgan bank, which lacked a retail netword to gather up deposits, as well as the big Chicago banks that were confined to one office.[9] To a considerable extent, the CD overcame the barriers posed to large US banks by the prohibition of interstate banking.

Within the United States, CDs like other deposits were subject to Regulation Q interest rate ceilings and reserve requirements. That was not true of another funding source that US banks began to tap in a small way by the end of the 1950s, Eurodollars. First National City again was a leader, since its London branch accepted deposits both in sterling and in dollars. Late in 1959, the bank used its London branch to attract dollars that were then advanced to New York to alleviate tightness in US money markets. In London the bank could pay more for dollar deposits than allowed by Regulation Q at home, and it could do so profitably because Eurodollar deposits were not subject to Federal Reserve requirements. Initially in this period before the CD innovation, Eurodollars were viewed by the bank as just one more marginal source of funds, akin to the Federal Reserve discount window. That would change in the next decade, when Eurodollars became an important funding source for domestic US lending in credit crunches as well as an important market in their own right.

Two further developments of the 1950s completed preparations for the US banking invasion of Europe in the 1960s. Strategies for expanding the scale and scope of US banking required more and better-educated personnel. The banks therefore began to recruit at leading business schools. Initially, they were rebuffed. Ambitious business-school students viewed banking as a rather stodgy, old-fashioned, and over-regulated business; the action was in cutting-edge manufacturing and marketing businesses, which at the time were becoming increasingly multinational for leading US corporations.

In truth, the students were right. Banking was laden with stuffy traditions and regulatory scleroses that more US bankers loved than detested. Governmentally regulated banking cartels cut down on competition, simplifying and making pleasant the lives of the members.[10] But the leading banks were then developing competitive strategies that would make banking more interesting for bright and ambitious students. These banks already in the 1950s were looking for new markets. They were paying more and more attention to business strategy, product development, marketing, and costs, the stuff of business-school curricula. When the European invasion took place it was staffed with American MBAs prepared to shake up their less ambitious, less well-trained European counterparts.

Finally, the large US money-centre banks began to invest in modern computer technologies and information systems, in the development of which the United States led the world. In time these would help control and cut costs, as well as open up new lines of business and improve the flow of information to management. The results with computers were at first halting and hardly impressive. Such is often the experience of innovators. But it later gave the American banks a leg up on their international competitors.

Innovations such as the CD and liability management also forced the banks to come to grips with the economics of banking. Old-fashioned, over-regulated banks did not always, or even often, have a very good idea of how and where they made their money. The CD and other new funding sources, under the new concept of liability management, caused the banks to pay more attention to concepts such as the marginal costs of funds, which had a heavy bearing on their profitability and growth. As the US banks invaded Europe, such understandings of the economics of modern banking also gave them a leg up on their competitors.

2. The Invasion of/Escape to Europe, 1963–1974

In terms of their long-term strategies, it is hardly an exaggeration to say that leading American banks thought little about Europe before 1963, and thought about little else in the decade thereafter. The most important reasons for the shift in the emphasis of the banks' strategic thinking were a series of US government policy actions that prevented the banks and US money and capital markets from serving their own interests and the world economy from their home bases in the United States.

There were other reasons. The banks' US corporate clients were establishing production and distribution facilities in Europe to avoid having to pay Europe's common tariffs on imports. These moves towards corporate multinationalization were aided by the return of currency convertibility in the late 1950s. European countries, protected by US military forces, were not too opposed to a US banking presence. Britain, not yet in the Common Market, even welcomed it as a way of re-establishing London as an international financial centre as well as of sustaining the special relationship with the United States.

Europe's policies and the spread of US multinational corporations would probably have fostered a gradual expansion of international banking on the part of the leading US institutions. What turned it into an invasion from Europe's point of view, and an escape from the point of view of the US banks, were policy shifts by the US government. On the very day in 1963 that President Kennedy proposed an Interest Equalization Tax to stem the outflow of dollars from the United States, Henry Clay Alexander, head of Morgan Guaranty, presciently told the bank's officers, 'This is a day that you will remember forever. It will change the face of American banking and force all the business off to London. It will take years to get rid of this legislation.'[11]

A year or so later, the US authorities noticed that American banks were becoming active in the still relatively minor Eurodollar markets. Bankers were invited to Washington by Assistant Treasury Secretary Paul Volcker to consider a Johnson administration proposal to stop them from keeping Eurodollar accounts in foreign branches. A Morgan banker later recounted the bankers' reaction: 'We said it was the end of the American banking system. You will throw us out of Europe and Singapore and Japan.' Volcker arranged to have the proposal dropped.[12]

Why were the US officials posing such threats to their country's leading banks? The essential problems were growing conflicts among major US policy goals. These problems were exacerbated rather than alleviated by various measures taken to resolve the conflicts during the 1960s and 1970s. One major goal was to foster the growth of world trade with the Bretton Woods system of fixed exchange rates in which participating countries agreed to maintain the exchange rate of their currencies with the dollar (and therefore with each other) while the United States agreed in official transactions with other countries to exchange dollars for gold at the rate of $35 per ounce of the yellow metal. When Bretton Woods came in, the US government possessed most of the world's monetary gold, and for the next decade or so the post-war dollar shortage posed no threat to the system.

Gradually, and for a number of reasons connected with US policies, the world dollar shortage changed to a dollar surplus outside the United States. The Cold War fought between the Eastern bloc led by the Soviet Union and the Western bloc led by the United States caused US authorities to spend dollars to maintain US military presence throughout the world, and to provide military and non-military dollar aid to friendly and neutral countries. US policy also favoured foreign direct investment by US corporations, leading to another outflow of dollars. And it encouraged freer trade and capital flows. At the same time, banking policies such as Regulation Q continued to keep American interest rates, particularly short-term rates, artificially lower than in other countries. This encouraged foreigners to borrow from Americans, leading to further flows of dollars to other countries.

By the late 1950s and early 1960s, more and more dollars were building up outside the United States than might be converted into the relatively fixed stock of gold that the US held in reserve. The commitment and the ability of the United States to maintain dollar–gold convertibility began to be doubted by foreign leaders. If the Cold War had subsided by the early 1960s, the problem facing American leaders might have gone away. Instead, communist Eastern-bloc threats to the Western alliance increased in Europe, Africa, Latin America, the Middle East, and South-East Asia. All this led to more official US spending in the world. Also, from 1961 to 1969, the US economy had its longest sustained peacetime expansion in history, leading to rising imports and non-official dollar outflows. During this expansion, President Johnson simultaneously sponsored a vast increase in the US military commitment to South-East Asia—mainly the war against communist insurgents in South Vietnam—as well as a broad range of domestic spending programmes labelled 'The Great Society'. More dollars flowed out to the world, and US interest rates and prices experienced upward pressures.

Free-market economics would have called for rising US interest rates to draw overseas dollars back to the United States along with slower US economic growth to stem further outflows—precisely the sort of advice American pol-icymakers and those at the IMF have given to other countries with similar problems in recent times. In the 1960s, however, the Keynesian-type thinking that pervaded the Kennedy, Johnson, and Nixon administrations favoured increased spending, tax cuts, and low interest rates to keep the US economy perking along at full employment. If an unpleasant by-product of the policy mix was a growing world dollar surplus that threatened to undermine Bretton Woods, then the intervention of fine-tuning policymakers of the 1960s would attack it directly, and in the most politically acceptable way by restricting the ability of the leading banks and other Wall Street institutions to mediate dollar outflows.

The Kennedy administration's 1963 interest rate equalization tax was an early measure in this vein. At first, it was a tax on foreign long-term borrowing in the United States, that is, a tax on foreign bond issues in the New York market. There were related fine-tuning measures. Operation Twist was an attempt to raise US short-term interest rates to attract international 'hot money' flows, while keeping long-term interest rates relatively low to sustain US investment and growth. Other measures attempted to discourage overseas spending by US tourists. And foreign official holders of dollars were offered higher yields subsidized by the US on their holdings to encourage them not to redeem dollars for gold.[13]

When these early measures had limited effect, they were expanded and reinforced with additional ones. The interest rate equalization tax (IET), originally placed on Americans' purchases of foreign securities with maturities over three years, simply shifted foreign demands for cheaper American credit to US banks. It did little to help the US balance of payments. The IET was therefore extended in 1965 to cover bank loans to foreigners with maturities of more than one year. Although banks and their customers could avoid the tax by making shorter-term loans and simply rolling them over, the tax did reduce US banks' longer-term claims on foreigners in the later 1960s.[14]

At the same time that IET was extended in 1965 to bank loans, the Johnson administration introduced a Voluntary Foreign Credit Restraint Programme (VFCRP) calling for a limit on foreign bank loans booked in the United States. The limit was 105 per cent of the dollar volume of foreign loans at the end of 1964, raised to 109 per cent of that base in 1966–7. Administered by the Federal Bank, the programme called for the banks to report their foreign lending at the end of each quarter. Chase Manhattan's historian reports that the bank lived within the guidelines, but scrambled at the end of each quarter to bring its foreign loans down to the limit. Chase also made end runs around the programme by booking loans at its London and Nassau branches, funding them with Eurodollars.[15] Noticing such end runs on the part of US banks already having foreign branches, other American banks also began to establish branches.

Still another restriction on capital exports from the US came in 1965. This was the Foreign Direct Investment Program (FDIP) calling for voluntary limits on US corporations' exports of home capital to finance their foreign expansion. The limits became mandatory in 1968. While not directly affecting US banks, the limits had strong indirect effects by raising the needs of US corporations for financing arranged abroad. US corporations and banks, driven from their natural home-based money and capital markets, met up with each other in London and other foreign financial centres. There a growing supply of Eurodollars, intermediated by the banks, was sufficient to finance their foreign expansion free of US-imposed restrictions. If a US bank without European branches had corporate clients expanding overseas, it quickly realized that it had better open such branches or risk losing business to a competitor that did.

Eurodollars proved their usefulness to the banks in other ways. An overheating economy at home bumped into Regulation Q in the credit crunches of 1966 and 1969. Rising interest rates in the US money market unmatched by increases in the Regulation Q ceilings caused an outflow of deposits from banks—disintermediation, it was called—at the same time loan demand was increasing. US banks already operating abroad solved some of their disintermediation problems by raising Eurodollars and placing them at the disposal of their home offices in the United States. Other banks were not so advantaged and again got the message: Go to Europe.

Regulation Q credit crunches were not much of a problem for banks after 1969. In the late 1960s, National City Bank, always the innovator—it had already extended its earlier domestic innovation by introducing Eurodollar CDs in 1966—discovered a loophole in US regulatory law. The loophole allowed a bank to open a one-bank holding company, place itself inside it, and then through the holding company enter businesses and geographic areas of the United States that were prohibited to the bank itself, or ones that a bank would not find attractive for regulatory reasons.

One such activity was issuing commercial paper in the money market, thereby obtaining money—which unlike bank deposits was not subject to Regulation Q or Federal Reserve requirements—that could be used to fund bank lending as well as new ventures of the holding company. Walter Wriston, now head of First National City and soon to rename it Citibank, related commercial paper funding to another of his 1960s innovations: 'The CD funded the world for ten years, more or less, and then commercial paper came in for bank holding companies for another ten years.'[16]

Commercial paper issued by major corporations to avoid having to take out costlier bank loans had been a bane of the money-centre banks in the 1950s. A decade later, via the one-bank holding company, it began to become one of the banks' major funding sources. At roughly the same time, fee income from a variety of financial services began to rival loan interest as a source of bank and holding-company profits.

Overcoming various constraints on its functional, geographical, and funding growth, by the end of the 1960s First National City of New York was well on its way to becoming the global financial services company that had been its ambition from early in the century and its conscious strategy since the 1950s. Other large US banks would imitate some or most of the Citibank/Citicorp initiatives, and would follow it around the world. Another leader, J. P. Morgan, the one-bank holding company to which Morgan Guaranty gave birth in 1969, pursued a less comprehensive strategy. Morgan stayed focused on wholesale commercial banking, as it always had done at home, but used its move to Europe to return to the securities and trading businesses that had been a hallmark of the Morgan bank in the United States until the 1930s New Deal financial reforms had forced it to choose between commercial and investment banking.

By the mid-1970s, the US invasion of Europe was essentially complete. The eight leading US banks had established 113 European branches along with 29 representative offices. London, where the Eurodollar and Eurocurrency markets were centred, alone had a total of 58 US banks present in 1975.

Forty-two of these had arrived since 1967. In numbers they were the largest national contingent of international banks in London, which totalled 243. Foreign banks as a group controlled more than half the total assets (sterling and foreign currency) of the UK banking sector, and nearly half of all the foreign-bank assets were American. Assets of US banks in London were greater than the combined assets of UK clearing banks.[17] Fifteen years earlier, before the invasion began in earnest, the deposits of US banks in London had been only 5 per cent of those of the British clearing banks.

Meanwhile, the US policies that had prompted American banks to escape to Europe were more or less undone. The Nixon administration (1969–74), although it continued many of the ill-conceived domestic policies of its predecessors and added some of its own, can at least be credited with reopening to the world the US banking, money, and capital markets. These markets had been gradually closed to foreigners starting with the interest rate equalization tax in 1963. Also during the Nixon years large CDs became exempt from Regulation Q restrictions.

Nixon's strong suit had always been a keen understanding of international political and economic relations. He and his advisors, some of whom had a free-market bent, realized the inconsistencies of US policies that flooded the world with dollars while committing the country to redeem them with a relatively fixed stock of gold. So they abandoned the dollar–gold link in steps from 1971 to 1973, and the world moved from a fixed to a floating exchange-rate regime.

Floating exchange rates were a boon to the large US banks which, with their international reach and the dollar serving as the world currency, already enjoyed a competitive advantage in international money transfers. They also provided an incentive to stay in London, which had become the centre of the Eurocurrency markets and now would become the centre of foreign-exchange speculation and hedging. Increased interest-rate volatility prompted the US banks to introduce floating-rate lending in Europe, an innovation they would quickly implement in their US domestic lending as well.

Europe continued to offer the US banks opportunities to engage in businesses precluded to them at home. In securities underwriting, and other aspects of corporate finance, J. P. Morgan was the leader. It brought out Eurobond and equity issues throughout the 1960s, sometimes to the consternation of European banks that viewed such operations as their preserve. US bank tactics also disturbed European national authorities who viewed a securities issue in their currency arranged by Americans operating in a different country as a violation of their sovereignty.

Citibank joined the fray in 1972 when it established its own London-based merchant bank, Citicorp International Bank Limited (CIBL). Based on Eurodollar lending and petrodollar recycling after 1973, CIBL would soon become the world leader in organizing syndicated international loans, from which it earned huge fees for parent Citicorp.[18] The scale of the leading US banks' merchant-banking operations would pressure their smaller European competitors to become larger through one route or another, or else be marginalized.

It is evident that the Eurocurrency markets were the main attraction of Europe to US banks, both before 1974 when the US markets were closed because of American regulations, and afterwards when petrodollars swelled the Eurocurrency pool of funds and the Americans controlled the lion's share of them. But entrepreneurial organizations such as Citibank, which had stunned the staid banking world in the early 1970s by announcing its goal of increasing earnings by 15 per cent each year, were on the look-out for any and all opportunities for profit.

The Americans, for example, spotted a gap in the lending menu provided by British banks, one that they could easily fill with term loans. This was intermediate credit. The British menu offered short-term credits from the clearing banks or long-term loans and equity issues arranged by merchant banks, but little in between. The Americans began to cultivate relationships and do business with British firms, shaking up time-honoured traditions of British banking. They also introduced leasing and factoring operations, relatively new in Europe but in which the Americans were experienced at home.

The US banks also noticed that, despite the extensive branch networks of the big UK clearing banks, half the adult British public did not have a bank account. Citibank responded by introducing a string of 'money shops' oriented towards consumer finance, with results at best mixed.[19] Other US banks, as usual, followed Citibank's lead. One was Chase Manhattan. About as large but almost always a follower of the aggressive Citibank, Chase tried a similar strategy in Germany, but its Familienbank experienced even worse results in retail banking than Chase had encountered in Britain.[20] There was some truth in the waggish remark that Citibank's approach to new business was 'Ready ... fire ... aim', while Chase Manhattan's was 'Ready ... aim ... aim.'[21]

However much the US banks' encroachments would upset and challenge European banks, these forays in local retail banking markets were of marginal importance to the Americans compared to what they could accomplish in the wholesale banking of the Eurocurrency markets. To a truly global financial services enterprise such as Citibank, Europe itself, apart from being the location of Eurodollar and later Eurocurrency markets, was not all that important. In the mid-1970s, when Citibank earned half or so of its profits outside the

United States, European earnings *in toto* came to only a quarter of that half, or about an eighth of the bank's global earnings.[22]

For the US banks, Europe was more a convenient place to gather resources to fund global lending free from US banking regulations and a place to engage in investment banking activities proscribed at home by the 1933 Glass-Steagall Act, than it was a source of attractive profit opportunities across a broad range of financial services. J. P. Morgan seemed to understand that from the start, or perhaps it was just a continuation of Morgan's strategy before it expanded its European operations in the 1960s.[23] Citibank tried to provide in Europe every financial service it provided anywhere in the world, but soon discovered that it did not have competitive advantages in many of them. So did those US banks that followed its lead. Invasion did not lead to conquest. Instead it led to assimilation, as both the European and the American banks adapted to the others' presence.

3. Conclusion: Lessons of the Invasion/Escape

The US banks, then, invaded Europe because Europe offered opportunities not available at home—Eurocurrency funding and investment banking are the main examples—and not because they could offer to Europeans banking services their own institutions were incapable of providing. Whatever 'technological' advantages they might have enjoyed because of their earlier innovations in the United States—federal funds, CDs, and other forms of market funding—could be adopted by the European institutions. And they were.

Financial innovations are seldom a source of more than brief competitive advantage. Sometimes they fail to offer any advantage at all, as was the case with the consortium banking that Europeans came up with supposedly as a response to the American invasion.[24] Some of the American banks, Chase Manhattan for example, tried that too. But they discovered, only a little before the Europeans, that in effect they were competing with themselves. They abandoned the approach, which in any case presented a host of managerial problems.

American banking innovations of a more useful nature, negotiable CDs in particular and market funding in general, could be and were adopted by European and other international banks. The Americans seemed not to care at all about the adoption of their innovations by foreign competitors. The more institutions that adopt a financial innovation, the larger is the market, and usually most if not all competitors benefit from larger financial markets.

If the innovations the US banks brought to Europe in the 1960s and 1970s had been more than a source of fleeting competitive advantages, the

Americans would have gone on to dominate world financial markets while their foreign competitors contracted. That did not happen. The US banks led in the recycling of petrodollars in the decade after 1973, but then suffered most during the Less Developed Countries debt crisis of the 1980s. They also had major problems at home, for example, in real estate and US 'oil-patch' lending.

By the start of the 1990s, most of the large US banks had been or were in deep trouble. In the mid-1980s Continental Illinois Bank, one of the followers of the European invasion leaders, went into receivership, and Bank of America, a leader, was forced to contract its global reach. Wall Street in 1990–1, judging by stock prices, had doubts about whether such fabled institutions as Citibank and Chase Manhattan could survive, even if the hotly debated doctrine of 'too big to fail' had been implemented. At the time, only J. P. Morgan among the four leaders of the earlier European invasion was in relatively good shape.

A decade ago, the competitive advantages in world banking that the US banks appeared to have lost seemingly were about to be claimed by Japanese banks. Because of the high saving propensities of the Japanese people and the appreciation of the Japanese yen, these banks by 1990 had become far larger than the leading American and European banks, and had expanded their global reach. American pundits wrote articles and books claiming that the Japanese, who had already triumphed in cutting-edge world manufacturing, were about to do the same in banking and finance. It was a reprise of the earlier US-bank invasion of Europe, with the Americans now the victims of the invaders, as the Europeans had been two to three decades before. We now know, of course, that the Japanese bank invasion of international markets was coming undone just at the time it was being most ballyhooed.

Meanwhile, by the end of the 1990s the US banks that shook up Europe three decades before recovered their earlier lustre. But they were not the same institutions they had been in the years of the European invasion. Bank of America still had its name, but it was in fact taken over by Nations Bank (formerly NCNB or North Carolina National Bank), a US super-regional, and the headquarters of the new Bank of America is now in Charlotte, North Carolina, not San Francisco, California. Chase Manhattan had a similar experience. It was taken over by Chemical, itself the survivor in an earlier merger with Manufacturers Hanover. The Chase Manhattan name survived, but Chemical executives provided most of the top leadership. Citicorp, the Citibank holding company, merged with Travelers, an insurance and Wall Street securities conglomerate, with the new institution, said at the time of the merger to be the largest private financial institution in the world, called Citigroup. Bankers Trust was taken over by Deutsche Bank, which in 1999 could claim, as a result of the merger, that it had become the world's largest bank. And more recently,

J. P. Morgan, having become relatively small compared to the new banking behemoths, sought a merger partner, and ended up being merged into Chase Manhattan, which changed the name to J. P. Morgan Chase. *Sic transit gloria mundi*, but glorious banking names sometimes survived, in whole, in part, or together. It remains to be seen whether the new behemoths, both American imitations of continental Europe's universal banks and European absorptions of American institutions, will justify to customers and stockholders the expectations of the executives who put them together.

Europeans have their own takes on the American invasion. To an American, or at least to this American, its main results were domestic. By invading Europe, the leading US banks demonstrated how misguided in principle and how ineffective in practice were many US banking traditions and regulatory measures handed down from the past. As they did so, the invaders also showed that a bank could do, or try to do, a full banking business throughout the world. These demonstrations led to domestic banking reforms. US bank interest rates became unregulated, except by the market, and the Fed's reserve requirements became both lower and simpler than they were in 1960. In the 1990s, Congress allowed nationwide branch banking and repealed Glass Steagall. As a result, by the end of that decade a US bank at long last could do, or try to do, a full banking business throughout the United States. When the new millenium arrived, US and worldwide banking services were vastly better because Europe a generation ago allowed US banks to invade the Old World and escape from a stifling banking environment in the United States.

NOTES

1. Bank of America was the largest in 1945 according to the bank's biographers: see M. James and B. R. James, *Biography of a Bank: The Story of Bank of America* (New York: Harper & Bro., 1954). It is likely, however, that one or two British banks were actually larger in total assets at the time, although a lack of consolidated balance sheets may have made it difficult to determine actual size. I thank Leslie Hannah for bringing this point to my attention.
2. J. Kelly, *Bankers and Borders: The Case of American Banks in Britain* (Cambridge, Mass.: Ballinger, 1977), 76.
3. On the expansion of US banks internationally to the 1920s, see V. P. Carosso and R. Sylla, 'U.S. Banks in International Finance', in R. Cameron and V. I. Bovykin (eds.), *International Banking, 1870–1914* (New York: Oxford University Press, 1991). On New York as the new international financial capital in the 1920s, see M. Wilkins, 'Cosmopolitan Finance in the 1920s: New York's Emergence as an

International Financial Center', in R. Sylla, R. Tilly, and G. Tortella (eds.), *The State, the Financial System, and Economic Modernization* (Cambridge: Cambridge University Press, 1999). On National City Bank's strategy of internationalization, see H. van B. Cleveland and T. F. Huertas, *Citibank, 1812–1970* (Cambridge, Mass.: Harvard University Press, 1985); the data on its foreign operations in 1930 and 1955 are from pp. 260 ff.

4. Cleveland and Huertas, *Citibank*, ch. 12.
5. Ibid., 230 ff.; and P. L. Zweig, *Wriston: Walter Wriston, Citibank, and the Rise and Fall of American Financial Supremacy* (New York: Crown, 1995), ch. 3, which is entitled 'Planes, Trains, Ships, and Automobiles', an indication of a number of areas in which the term-loan innovation could be applied.
6. For details of these mergers, for First National City see Cleveland and Huertas, *Citibank*, ch. 12; for Chase Manhattan, J. D. Wilson, *The Chase: The Chase Manhattan Bank, N. A., 1945–1985* (Boston: Harvard Business School Press, 1986), ch. 4; and for J. P. Morgan, R. Chernow, *The House of Morgan: An American Banking Dynasty and the Rise of Modern Finance* (New York: Simon & Schuster, 1990), ch. 27.
7. For the story of the rise of Bank of America from its humble 1904 beginnings as San Francisco's Bank of Italy to become the world's largest bank by 1945, see James and James, *Biography of a Bank*. It was the creation of Amadeo Peter Giannini, son of Italian immigrants to California, who has a claim to be called America's greatest banking innovator of the first half of the twentieth century. In the 1990s, more than four decades after his death, Giannini's dream of nationwide banking in the United States at last became possible by a law of Congress. The law brought back nationwide branch banking, which had disappeared from the country when the federal charters of the First and Second Banks of the United States were not renewed in 1811 and 1836.
8. Cleveland and Huertas, *Citibank*, 252.
9. Zweig, *Wriston*, 142.
10. This sort of banking came to have a waggish name, '3-6-3 banking', which meant 'borrow at 3%, lend at 6%, and be on the golf course by 3 p.m.'
11. Quoted by Chernow, *The House of Morgan*, 544.
12. Ibid., 545.
13. Kelly, *Bankers and Borders*, 48–9.
14. Ibid., 106.
15. Wilson, *The Chase*, 124–5.
16. Zweig, *Wriston*, 268. Wriston was probably America's leading banking innovator of the second half of the twentieth century, just as A. P. Giannini of Bank of America was in the first half. Although of very different backgrounds, each made banking history by pressing arcane US banking regulations to their limits, sometimes making them snap, and by adopting the latest in banking technologies.
17. Data in this paragraph come from D. F. Channon, *British Banking Strategy and the International Challenge* (London: Macmillan, 1977), ch. 8.

18. Petrodollars were dollars earned by oil-producing countries from selling petroleum. The sums became huge after the large oil-price increases of 1973 and 1979. As the oil-producing states could not absorb such huge sums in their own economic development programs, they were deposited in large international banks. The banks lent the money, often to other countries for their economic development programs. The sovereign debt crises of the 1980s were rooted in this lending as well as in problems borrowers encountered in repaying the loans on schedule.

19. Kelly, *Bankers and Borders*, 149; Channon, *British Banking*, 161. The 'money shop' experience showed that in Europe, whatever their competitive advantages in other areas of banking, the US banks did not possess one in retail or consumer banking.

20. Wilson, *The Chase*, 236–7.

21. Zweig, *Wriston*, 273. In the same vein, there is a *double entendre*, unintended, in the title of Wilson, *The Chase*; Citibank was the innovator and Chase Manhattan, its rival for decades in New York City, chased after it.

22. Kelly, *Bankers and Borders*, 148.

23. Chernow, *The House of Morgan*, notes that J. P. Morgan's London staff in the early 1970s was nearly as large as the bank's total staff in the 1950s, before the merger with Guaranty Trust.

24. See D. Ross, 'European Banking Clubs in the 1960s: A Flawed Strategy', *Business and Economic History*, 27 (1998), 353–66, and his Ch. 6 in this book. Ross distinguishes two types of consortium banks. The one that best fits the term is a newly organized bank established and capitalized by existing banks of several countries to engage in international banking operations. The other is a 'club' formed by existing banks in different countries to cooperate in international banking without having either a new organization or a direct representation of one of the existing banks in another country.

4

International Financial Centres, 1958–1971: Competitiveness and Complementarity

CATHERINE R. SCHENK

Measuring the competitiveness of international financial centres has proved difficult for economists. Nevertheless, there is a substantial literature that seeks to rank international financial centres either through time or in a single period.[1] The measures include the number of foreign banks, amount of foreign deposits held by financial institutions, and the ranking of financial centres by a sample of bankers and economists.[2] All these approaches assume that one financial centre can be compared with another on the same terms, and then that some judgement can be made on this basis about their relative influence. Some efforts have been made to introduce a functional approach to ranking to account for the differences between financial centres in savings-rich countries compared to importers of capital or offshore centres.[3] Even this, however, does not really allow for the interaction between and among financial centres, which might entail specialization in the services that they offer.[4] They also focus overwhelmingly on banking activity rather than securities, stock markets, insurance, or accountancy services.

Following in this tradition, however, Table 4.1 shows the number of offices of foreign banks in a variety of international financial centres between 1955 and 1980. This shows that foreign banks found the City of London more attractive than New York, and that Hong Kong, with its extremely *laissez-faire* approach to international finance, was the host of more branches of international banks than Paris or New York through the 1960s. To give an indication of the extent of links between financial centres in 1965, Table 4.2 shows the location of banks that had branch offices in at least four of the international financial centres listed.

The rapid multinational expansion of US banks is reflected in the fact that five out of the 11 banks were American. In contrast, only one of these banks is from continental Europe. The greater intensity of branching in Asia compared

Table 4.1. *Number of offices of foreign banks in international financial centres*

	1955	1960	1965	1970	1970A	1980A
London	69(54)	80(59)	97(72)	148(118)	58	72
New York	40(10)	61(16)	67(22)	96(29)	54	80
Paris	24(16)	32(18)	41(17)	52(18)	35	52
Hong Kong	19(19)	27(26)	43(36)	43(27)	24	58
Tokyo	12(11)	16(15)	25(15)	51(17)	45	76
Singapore	15(15)	17(16)	15(15)	28(21)	13	54
Frankfurt/Hamburg	17(9)	23(9)	34(13)	55(24)	39	59
Beirut	12(12)	17(13)	29(13)	42(17)		
Brussels	9(8)	13(10)	14(9)	22(12)	20	29
Amsterdam	6(6)	4(3)	8(6)	10(7)	23	21
Zurich	7(4)	9(3)	17(6)	22(9)	13	24

Note: Number of branches in parentheses.

Source: Years 1955–70 include all banks, from *Bankers Almanac and Yearbook*; 1970A and 1980A include only the world's largest 300 banks, from S.-R. Choi, A. E. Tschoegl, and C.-M. Yu, 'Banks and the World's Major Financial Centres, 1970–1980', *Weltwirtschaftliches Archiv*, 122 (1986), 48–64.

with Europe is also striking, with most banks having offices in Singapore, Hong Kong, and Tokyo. This may reflect the greater relative advantages of London in the European region, while there was no single outstanding centre in Asia. In a framework of integrated financial centres, however, ranking on the basis of any of these measures is static and can be misleading. Few would argue, for example, that Hong Kong was a more important international financial centre than New York, despite the fact that foreign banks were successful at operating branches there.

Measuring foreign assets held by domestic banks is another way to assess international financial centres. The share of such assets held in a variety of centres for 1965 is shown in Table 4.3. Again, however, this can be misleading because the data are only available at a national level, they capture only a small proportion of international financial activity, and reporting practices differed among centres. Nevertheless, Table 4.3 shows the dramatic reduction in the share of foreign assets held by US banks in response to regulatory changes. The table also gives an indication of the greater dispersion of international financial activity as new centres such as the Bahamas, Beirut, Singapore, and Hong Kong expanded.

Given the difficulties in measuring or comparing the activity of international financial centres, a major focus of this chapter is the international monetary environment, which had a profound impact on their performance. The advent of external current account convertibility of most European currencies in December 1958 was supposed to herald the start of the

Table 4.2. *Leading bank branches: location in 1965*

	London	New York	Paris	Hong Kong	Tokyo	Singapore	Frankfurt/Hamburg	Beirut	Brussels	Amsterdam	Zurich
American Express	X	X	X	X	X	X	X		X	X	X
Bank of America	X	X		X	X	X				X	
Chase Manhattan	X		X	X	X	X	X	X			
Citibank	X	X	X	X	X	X	X	X	X	X	
Continental Illinois	X	X			X						X
HSBC	X	X	X	X	X	X	X				
Chartered Bank	X	X		X	X	X	X				
Bank of India	X			X	X	X					
Algemene Bank		X		X	X	X		X		X	
Sanwa	X			X	X						
Bank of Tokyo	X		X	X	X	X	X				

Source: Banks' Almanac and Yearbook, 1965/6.

Table 4.3. *Banks' foreign assets: share in total reporting countries' foreign assets*

	1961	1965	1970
United Kingdom	16.71	17.10	25.10
United States	29.52	23.60	8.58
Japan	5.03	5.70	4.42
France		4.33	6.79
Switzerland	8.71	8.33	9.46
Luxembourg	0.74	0.89	2.48
Bahamas			4.83
Lebanon		1.34	0.43
Bahrein			0.40
Singapore			0.35
Hong Kong	1.16	1.14	0.83

Source: IMF *International Financial Statistics Yearbook*, various issues.

international monetary system as it had been designed during the Second World War. At last, currencies were convertible at fixed exchange rates to allow multilateral trade and payments. Almost immediately, however, persistent US balance of payments deficits in the 1960s challenged this new dawn. By 1962 bilateral talks between the US and the UK sought to solve the liquidity problem of inadequate reliable international reserves, alongside the swelling volume of US dollars.[5] The Gold Pool was established to support the gold value of the dollar, which was the basis of the fixed exchange rate system. Through the rest of the 1960s, negotiations continued within and without the IMF to devise a reserve unit separate from the dollar. This eventually culminated in the issue of Special Drawing Rights in 1967. By this time, however, the dollar-based system was in near collapse. The strains were felt in the dollar gold price and flows of speculative capital which eventually led to the suspension of its convertibility into gold in 1971.

The 1960s should have been the heyday of the Bretton Woods system, when currency convertibility and stability finally delivered multilateral trade and payments. Instead, this decade saw the fumbling collapse of the system punctuated by periodic crises and realignments of exchange rates.[6] A major symptom of this general instability was sharp flows of short-term capital between financial centres that prompted controls on overseas investment in the US and elsewhere. Another result was increased demand from consumers of financial services for ways to deal with this instability.

The supply and demand for international financial services in this period was further increased by the vigorous multinational expansion of

US manufacturers into Britain and Europe. The USA accounted for over 60 per cent of flows of foreign direct investments in the 1960s. This was an especially important factor in encouraging American commercial banks to open branches abroad and for European banks to form consortia. The period 1958–71 also witnessed an explosion of international finance due to increased opportunities and efficiency spurred on by innovation in the supply of products. This dynamism was driven not only by competition among suppliers,[7] but also by the increasing specialization of financial centres that enhanced the services offered to their customers.

1. Sources of Competitiveness of International Financial Centres in the 1960s

The starting premise for any assessment of competition among financial centres in the 1960s is to recognize that they were not all performing the same functions. In this sense they were not competitors but rather parts of an increasingly integrated global financial market. Each had their particular attributes generated by: (1) their historical development, (2) the nature of the domestic economy and geographical location, and (3) the regulatory environment in which they operated. The largest international financial centres in this period were located in London and New York, with the main subsidiary centres located in Paris, Frankfurt, and Tokyo.

London was a genuine entrepôt where financial institutions intermediated between customers abroad and between domestic and foreign customers. This reflected the sophistication of financial services that had been developed over the past century; through the Gold Standard, the subsequent pre-eminence of sterling, and the role of Britain as the world's major trading nation. After 1945 London kept many of the advantages from its long history of international leadership. These included the expertise and critical mass of financial services with which to attract customers. In 1973 the Inter-Bank Research Organization reported that London 'attracts business because of the range of markets and services that it offers and develops new markets and services because of the scale of business it can attract'.[8] The apparent circularity of this argument (London provided a lot of services because London provided a lot of services) reflects the presence of economies of scope in the provision of increasingly complex international financial transactions that required a variety of separate specialist knowledge.

In addition to the remnants of history, post-war exchange controls increased the importance of London for sterling finance. As a result of exchange controls associated with the operation of the sterling area in the

1950s, overseas sterling area countries financed their trade through London, used London as their reserve centre, and received preferred access to London's capital market.[9] In the 1950s the sterling area conducted about half the world's trade, and included all the Commonwealth countries (except for Canada) as well as the colonies and oil-producing states in the Middle East such as Iraq, Kuwait, and the Persian Gulf. The operation of British multinational corporations in the sterling area also focused finance on London. The financial business of these countries and firms explains the persistence and success of branches of British overseas banks located in London in the early 1960s.

The importance of the sterling area to the City of London has usually been denigrated in the literature. Thus, Strange and Kelly have both judged that contemporary British government's claims that the sterling area promoted London as an international financial centre were based on a fundamental confusion over the business that London was doing.[10] Since most of the new business was denominated in dollars, and was increasingly performed through American banks, the sterling link is viewed as insignificant. It must be remembered, however, that the critical mass of services already in London to serve sterling area customers was important in attracting further providers in the 1960s. The location of key commodity markets (such as tea and tin) and global issues by the London stock market all had their roots in the sterling area system. Furthermore, exchange controls made it easier for sterling area customers to use London rather than New York for dollar business as well as sterling commerce. The sterling area also preserved the outward-looking regulatory environment that favoured international finance. While exchange controls on the use of sterling may have affected some British banks adversely, the activities of the City as a whole were not necessarily inhibited.

Along with historical momentum, the regulatory framework in Britain was conducive to international financial activity. After 1958, exchange controls for foreigners were more relaxed than they had been since 1939, and the Bank of England tended to support the activities of the City of London. Partly, this support was due to the desire to maintain the attractiveness of sterling, but as international transactions came increasingly to be denominated in dollars this rationale receded and instead, the City was supported as a net earner for the balance of payments. Figure 4.1 shows estimates of the value of net overseas earnings of the City's financial institutions, although they provide only a minimum guide to the overall value of the City to the balance of payments.[11] Nevertheless, the substantial earnings appear to have justified the support of the British authorities.

Through the 1960s, capital controls continued to operate for British and sterling area residents, and the overseas sterling area benefited from preferential access to the London market. Other foreign issues could be floated

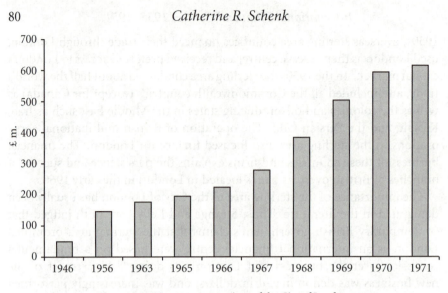

Figure 4.1. *Net overseas earnings of the City of London*
Source: R. Michie, *The City of London* (London: Macmillan, 1992), 26

only if they promised to enhance the UK balance of payments, for example through increased exports. British residents could invest in non-sterling securities only from the existing pool of funds already invested in such securities, which traded as 'security sterling'. These controls on lending to non-residents generated the demand for Eurosterling in Paris and other European centres.

London has benefited from Britain's dominant position as a host for US multinationals, which generated demand for international financial services in London. Geographically and culturally, Britain was the main link between the USA and the rapidly growing European economies. The British economy itself was relatively small and slow growing in this period which emphasized the returns to be made through international transactions.

If the location of financial centres is determined by the financial and economic influence of the home country, then New York should have dominated the post-war period. The USA emerged from the war as the world's creditor, which should have established New York as the world's most important financial centre. In the first few years after 1945 this was certainly the case, as London sought to restore markets and cope with the speculative pressure against sterling in 1947. 'Bankers, economists, industrialists, and government officials in 1946–7 all recognised that New York had emerged from World War II as the world's pre-eminent international financial centre.'[12] By 1960, however, London had resurfaced to rank above New York in most quantity measurements of the provision of financial services.[13]

New York tended to be engaged in net capital export, which reflected the surplus of domestic saving in the US economy after the end of the war and the large size of the domestic market. Like London, New York owed part of its pre-eminence to historical development. As a major port exposed to the European market in the nineteenth century, financial institutions collected there. In the twentieth century, the economic domination of the USA in the world economy lent New York an extra level of importance. Given the size of the American economy, however, the activity of New York was never as prominent as the City of London was in the British economy. The regulatory framework reflected this with successive administrations curtailing the activities of US banks' international operations in order to avoid instability that could threaten national prosperity. In particular, in the 1960s US governments were concerned about the volatility of short-term capital flows and sought to insulate the banking system from the vagaries of the 'hot money' which they believed had exacerbated problems in the inter-war period. Pressure on the dollar from the mid-1960s led to further restrictions.

The pre-eminence of New York in American international finance should not be overemphasized. By the mid-1960s the international activities of US banks were becoming more geographically dispersed. At the end of 1961 there were 10 banks operating Edge Act subsidiaries designed to engage in international banking, and six of these ten had head offices located in New York. By the end of 1964 there were 22 such subsidiaries of which only seven had head offices located in New York.[14] Subsidiaries of banks located outside New York tended to be more involved in short-term lending overseas than the New York banks.[15]

Local economic conditions and historical experience also influenced the role of Paris. In the late nineteenth century, France was the second largest overseas investor in the world after Britain. The focus of its capital market in this period tended to be in Europe, rather than the wider imperial and American focus of most of British investment.[16] The European focus of France's activities was repeated in the post-war role of Paris in the international economy. Paris became the centre of the Eurosterling market, which was by its nature rather smaller than the Eurodollar market located in London.

France's tightly regulated and controlled banking sector was an important determinant of the type of services that Paris could offer. Economic recovery after the war was achieved through deliberate and elaborate central planning and control, which was extended to the banking system. In 1945 the three largest French banks were nationalized and the activities of all French banks were carefully compartmentalized and constrained to ensure the provision of resources for industrial recovery. Paris attracted net capital inflows but their presence as an international financial centre was regional rather than global, developing expertise in smaller European products often in cooperation with London, Brussels, or Frankfurt. The Paris stock exchange was reorganized in 1961 to simplify its organization (combining the Parquet and Coulisse) and to improve state regulation, but the market remained thin, narrow, and dominated by public issues. Special authorization was required for most international capital transactions including issues of foreign companies in France, issues by French companies on foreign markets, all loans and credits not linked with commercial transactions, and short-term investments on the money market.[17] Most of the French banks' positions in foreign currencies were due to the country of issue rather than third parties.

While each of these centres had its own identifying features, the 1960s saw the emergence of a truly global market for finance. There were a variety of factors that encouraged the expansion of international capital flows and, therefore, the demand for international financial services. The advent of external current account convertibility in December 1958 relaxed constraints on some forms of capital flow for third-party participants in financial markets. Convertibility was limited in scope, and controls were usually maintained on short-term capital flows. Nevertheless, the relaxation of exchange controls generated a general rise in activity on international financial markets.

The gradual reduction in controls on capital flows among members of the EEC in the 1960s promoted integration of financial markets. Directives of the European Monetary Committee in 1960 and 1962 required that certain types of international capital flows should be unrestricted.[18] These included direct investment, operations in listed securities, investment in real estate, personal transactions, and short- and medium-term credits linked with commercial transactions or the rendering of services. The OECD Council adopted a similar Code of Liberalization in July 1964.[19] In 1966 a group of experts appointed by the EEC Commission reported favourably about the prospects of establishing a single European capital market as part of the EEC integration process[20] but efforts further to liberalize capital flows were affected by the international payments problems that plagued the 1960s.

Product innovations such as the Eurodollar/Eurocurrency markets, better technology and international clearing systems, and the multinational expansion of banks resulted in a high degree of integration among financial centres. One of the most significant activities of branches of US banks that collected deposits in London, Paris, or Tokyo, was to channel these funds back to their US head offices so these banks might equally be considered part of the US banking system.[21] Banks located in London conferred the benefits of the facilities and regulatory environment of the City on their head offices in New York. To this extent New York and London should not be viewed as competitors or rivals in international finance since both benefited from this business. In the same way, the presence of the Eurosterling market in Paris was not a rival to London since such a market could not exist in London, and offered London-based institutions access to the interest rates available in Paris. Viewed in terms of multinational expansion rather than rivalry, banks were becoming vertically integrated, locating in foreign centres to capture resources for their head office.

Figure 4.2 shows the stock of foreign direct investment in financial services for selected countries as of 1971.[22] The UK, Canada, and the Netherlands enjoyed a net inflow of investment, while the USA and Japan had substantial net outflows. The total foreign direct investment stock in services for these centres in 1971 amounted to US$22.5 bn. of which inflows and outflows from the USA accounted for 54.5 per cent.

The globalization of international financial flows required new types of bank organization that blurred national boundaries. Unlike US banks, European banks tended not to extend branches within Europe because of their relatively small size, legal and technical obstacles, and the relatively small number of European multinational corporations operating in Europe.[23] Instead of branches, more creative responses were instituted that usually required less commitment. One result was the consortium bank, which offered medium-term Eurocurrency loans to their customers, mainly multinational

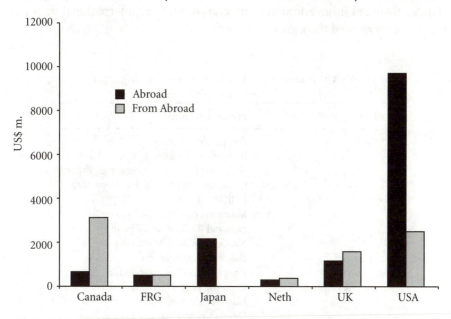

Figure 4.2. *Stock of foreign direct investment in banking and insurance, 1971*

Source: United Nations Centre on Transnational Corporations, *Salient Features and Trends in Foreign Direct Investments* (New York: UN, 1983)

companies. Between 1964 and 1971, 17 such banks were formed from 110 partner institutions of 14 nationalities. The first consortium bank, Midland and International Bank Ltd. (MAIBL), was formed in 1964 by Midland, Toronto Dominion, Standard Bank, and Commercial Bank of Australia. By 1971, three of the 17 consortium banks were located in Paris, one in Brussels, and the rest in London.[24]

Another response by European banks was to try to promote international cooperation through banking groups or clubs. These included European Banks Investments Company (EBIC) formed in 1963 and Orion and Associated Banks of Europe Corporation, both formed in 1971. In the early 1960s European banks and finance houses also cooperated in the operation of unit trusts dealing in EEC shares. In June 1962 the most prominent was Eurosyndicat, which sponsored two unit trusts. The largest, Eurunion, totalled £16 m., of which British residents held about 25 per cent.[25] Finally, national distinctions were overcome by the merger activity that characterized the banking structure in Europe in the 1960s. Table 4.4 shows the minority interests of British banks in foreign banks in 1965. In 1966 US national banks were permitted to invest directly in the stock of foreign banks and by 1971 US banks had bought minority interests in nine British banks.[26]

It is in this environment of international monetary crisis, changing regulation, financial innovation, and integration that the international financial centres experienced their greatest growth.

Table 4.4. *British banks with minority shares in foreign banks,*
November 1965

Bank	Minority interest
Barclays	Banque de Bruxelles
	Banque de Commerce
	Banco del Desarrollo Economico Español
	Canadian Imperial Bank of Commerce
Lloyds	BOLSA
	Mauritius Commercial Bank
	National Bank of New Zealand
	National Bank of Australasia
Westminster	Banco de Financiacion
Hambros	Banca Privata Finanzaria Milan
Hill, Samuel and Co	Banco de Financiacion Industrial
	Harriman Ripley, NY
	Development Finance Corp., Sydney
Samuel Montagu	Guverzeller Zurmont Bank, Zurich

Source: *The Economist*, 20 November 1965, xxxviii.

2. Global Expansion: London, New York, Paris, 1958–1965

The first six years after the re-establishment of external convertibility of most European currencies marked the growth of international capital flows, and a commensurate increase in the activities of international financial centres. It was in these years that the feebleness of the international monetary system was exposed. The patterns of specialization that were described in the previous part of this paper were established and developed in response to the regulatory environment that was developed in response to the crisis. The account in this subsection ends with the presidential declaration on 10 February 1965 restricting US banks' overseas activities. In the same year, British authorities restricted the activities of US banks in London by imposing ceilings on their sterling loans to British residents. This marked the end of Britain's *laissez-faire* attitude to US multinational bank expansion but also coincided with the beginning of the acceleration in the volume of international transactions.

2.1. *Eurodollars and Eurobonds*

The Eurodollar market is widely credited with reviving London as an international financial centre.[27] London banks offered higher returns on wholesale deposits of dollars than were available in New York, as well as hosting the most sophisticated forward exchange market to cover currency swaps. Even at small margins, the volume of business attracted suppliers into the market, particularly US banks which came to dominate.[28] The Eurodollar market in London received official support partly as a defensive gesture and partly because of the invisible earnings it attracted. In addition, the market at least temporarily benefited the balance of payments through capital inflows. In 1963 H. B. Mynors of the Bank of England wrote to a sceptical Sir Charles Hambro:

It is par excellence an example of the kind of business which London ought to be able to do both well and profitably. That is why we, at the Bank, have never seen any reason to place any obstacles in the way of London taking its full and increasing share. If we were to stop the business here, it would move to other centres with a consequent loss of earnings for London.[29]

Similarly, at the beginning of 1963, L. K. O'Brien advised that the Bank for International Settlements (BIS) should be allowed to increase its facility for depositing dollars with UK banks since otherwise the business would merely go elsewhere in Europe. The BIS had Euromarket deposits of $400 m. in Canada, France, Switzerland, Belgium, Scandinavia, and Italy as well as London.[30]

As US balance of payments deficits grew after 1958, European central banks used the Eurodollar market to manage their surpluses. From 1959 the Bundesbank and the Italian central bank engaged in swaps between local currency and dollars at rates that encouraged their banks to place Eurodollar deposits abroad. By September 1960 Japanese banks had obtained Eurodollar deposits in London amounting to more than US$200 m., most of which was converted to yen to finance Japanese industrial expansion. Because of higher perceived risks, Japanese banks offered 2 per cent over the usual rate to obtain the funds but this was still cheaper than borrowing in Japan.[31] The principal use of Eurodollar deposits in London by 1962 was thought to be for the finance of trade, replacing sterling finance, which was either not available or too expensive.[32] Canadian banks tended to re-lend their assets to New York security dealers and brokers, while American banks transferred their assets back to head office in the USA.[33] In 1962 foreign commercial banks were believed to be the main sources of Eurodollar deposits in London, followed by central banks.[34] By 1964 significant depositors were central banks, the BIS, and banks outside the USA (particularly Canadian banks). The largest single source of Eurodollars in 1964 was believed to be US overseas companies.[35] The US Treasury believed that this was due to overseas subsidiaries of US companies depositing ready cash abroad rather than remitting it to the parent company.[36]

Towards the end of 1963, some in the Bank of England became very nervous about the potential volatility of the Eurodollar deposits, especially in the wake of runs on banks in Switzerland and Germany. Preston, a pessimist about the market, noted that 'I am filled with foreboding. There are a number of failures on the international horizon which are mixed up with dishonesty, which remind me all too strongly of the events leading up to the 1931 crisis.'[37] Bridge accepted that Preston's note 'merits attention and reflection' but had more faith in the market, suggesting that recent failures 'may well have shown an amber light and caused a number of banks here and elsewhere to review the way they were doing their business'.[38]

Countries elsewhere in Europe chose not to encourage the Eurodollar market as a major part of their international financial activities. This reflected the perceived risks to the domestic economy associated with attracting 'hot money', including increased bank liquidity and potential calls on the reserves if there were a sudden withdrawal. In mid-1960 the Swiss launched a gentlemens agreement with Swiss banks not to accept short-term foreign currency deposits in order to stop the inflow of hot money. Banks agreed not to credit interest on foreign deposits and to charge a commission of 1 per cent on deposits withdrawn from Switzerland within six months. They also agreed not to invest foreign capital in Swiss shares, property, or mortgages. France and Germany also prohibited the payment of interest to foreigners,[39] and in France and Italy private swaps from Eurodollars to local currency were prohibited.[40] In December 1963 the French banks were called in to the Banque de France and advised to reduce their Eurodollar business.[41] The Governor of the Banque de France expressed his great concern over the growth of the market at a European Central Bank Governors' meeting.[42]

Paris was the centre for the Eurosterling market which emerged parallel to the Eurodollar market in London. Evidence on the emergence of this market is patchy, mainly due to the political nature of its origins. The Bank of England believed that about half the deposits of sterling in French banks in the early 1960s were made by Eastern European countries.[43] In May 1962 about half the US$1.2 bn. in French Eurocurrency deposits was denominated in dollars, 20 per cent in sterling, 12 per cent in D-mark, 10 per cent in Swiss francs, and the rest in other currencies.[44] At this time Eurodollar deposits in London had reached US$3 bn.[45]

The major new product developed in this period was the Eurobond, an issue placed mainly in markets other than that of the country in whose currency it is denominated. The Eurobond is popularly considered to have developed in response to the USA Interest Equalization Tax (IET) of mid-1963, which made the flotation of foreign securities in New York more expensive.[46] In fact, the use of Eurodollars for loans to foreign governments began to be discussed in London as early as 1962 after the foreign bond market in London was reopened for government issues. Stamp duty kept the costs of borrowing in London relatively high, which encouraged the search for alternative means to fund loans. In mid-December 1962 the Treasury outlined the plan for a foreign currency loan, noting that 'the object of these loans is to make the facilities of the London capital market more widely available and to mop up some of the very volatile Euro-dollars at present in London'. At this point it was reported that the Belgian government had applied to raise US$30 m.[47] This first proposal fell through in February 1963[48] but a subsequent loan was completed. This was followed by a loan to IRI (Istituto per la Ricostruzione Industriale, an Italian state-owned holding) in July (just before the imposition of IET), bringing the total amount of dollars raised in international capital markets through Eurobonds to US$55.5 m. in 1963. In addition to this, a further US$13.7 m. worth of Swiss franc denominated Eurobonds were floated. Table 4.5 shows the value and denomination of Eurobond issues in the 1960s. By 1966 the volume of new Eurobond issues exceeded those of conventional foreign bonds.

Further innovations were prompted by the increasing exchange risk on medium- and long-term lending as the international payments system faltered in the 1960s. From 1964, some loans were denominated in sterling, but with

Catherine R. Schenk

Table 4.5. *Public issues on the Eurobond market ($ m.)*

	1961	1962	1963	1964	1965	1966	1967	1968	1969
Dollars			55.5	449.2	563.0	842.5	1,589.3	2,260.0	1,560.5
Units of Account	5.0	5.0	43.0	10.0		74.1	19.0	57.0	60.0
Currency Option				14.0	64.4	19.6	20.2	28.8	116.4
Deutsch Marks				91.2	67.5	50.0	15.0	700.0	1,083.5
Swiss Francs		13.7							
Dutch Guilders					48.3				
French Francs							12.2	20.2	
TOTAL	5.0	5.0	112.2	564.4	743.2	986.2	1,655.7	3,066.0	2,820.4

Source: Policy on the Bond Markets in the Countries of the EEC (Brussels: EEC, October 1970), Table E.

the option of interest and capital payable in sterling or D-mark at a fixed parity at the request of the creditor. Another method was 'parallel loans' in which the lender could choose between securities issued in dollars or in D-marks so that the subscribers determined the allocation of the loan among currencies.[49] Unit of Account loans were introduced in 1961, and were given added impetus after the imposition of IET on foreign securities in New York in mid-1963. These loans were denominated in special units of account defined in terms of a particular weight in gold. Loans could be subscribed simultaneously in various countries in various currencies, and would be repaid in any one of several currencies depending on the preference of the lender. From 1963, the value of the unit of account would change if the exchange rates of $\frac{2}{3}$ of the 17 European currencies changed in the same direction. In 1963/4 US$53 m. worth of such loans were issued. This increased to US$74 m. in 1966.

In summary, the early 1960s were a period of significant product innovation with the emergence of the Eurodollar deposit and the Eurobond. These innovations were a response to increased demand for international finance, but they were also prompted by changes in the regulatory environment that will be discussed in the next section.

2.2. *Regulatory Changes*

The direction of flows of international capital, and the roles played by various international financial centres in the global financial system were, to a large extent, determined by differences in regulatory frameworks. The British authorities deliberately pursued policies that would attract customers for international finance to London. To this end, there were no restrictions on the operation of overseas banks in London. The US authorities were more wary of the risk that the activities of US banks could generate a drain of capital from the USA. Until 1965, however, there was a passive acceptance of the multinational expansion of US banks. In France, the authorities kept a tight reign on the domestic banking system, which was extended to international transactions.

London. As noted above, the British approach to international finance was to encourage the activities of London as an international financial centre while maintaining safeguards on the balance of payments through exchange control on the use of sterling. At the end of 1958 sterling was finally made convertible with much fanfare, but it needs to be emphasized that this freedom applied only to current account transactions and only to individuals not resident in the UK or in the rest of the sterling area. Individuals not resident in the UK were free to use London as a centre for their transactions in currencies other than sterling. There were considerable restrictions on the operations of UK banks in the 1960s including controls on domestic credit and limits on the interest payable by commercial banks on their deposits. This contrasted with the relative freedom of foreign banks operating in London on account of non-residents. The regulatory framework, therefore, actively encouraged the activities of international banks in the City. As noted above, the Bank of England believed that the activities of the City enhanced the UK balance of payments by consistently attracting large deposits of dollars, and through the invisible earnings of its institutions.

New York. In contrast with the UK, the regulatory framework in the USA in the 1960s can be described as defensive. The mixture of increased controls on outflows of capital and the limits on domestic deposit rates do not conform to a competitive model of international regulation. American authorities did not aim to capture more business for New York as an international financial centre in this decade.[50] Instead, they were content to encourage US banks to perform their international transactions in European financial centres.

By mid-1963, the US authorities were concerned about the growth of the Eurodollar market. In May, a UK Treasury representative spoke with Robert Roosa, the under-secretary of the US Treasury, who claimed to have

already had some talks with one or two representatives of the banking community and reminded them that although there is no question of imposing exchange control, they should, in his [Roosa's] words, ask themselves whether they are serving the national interest by participating in this sort of activity, which adds to the volume of short term capital outflow from the US. Mr. Roosa was not too optimistic about the outcome.[51]

By December 1963, the US Treasury was reported to be less certain about the implications of the Eurodollar market. On a trip to New York and Washington,

Workman of the UK Treasury reported a general feeling that the Eurodollar market would decline after recent defaults on Eurodollar loans in Germany. He noted that 'some corporate treasurers had not quite realized the risks they had been taking in placing short term dollar funds abroad, thinking of them as deposits with a liquidity corresponding to that of deposits with the domestic banking system rather than as short term loans'. The US Treasury was divided over whether the disadvantage of short-term capital outflow which the market prompted was outweighed by the advantage of the increased incentive to hold dollars overseas. Workman reported that 'They would not claim to be able to know whether these contrary influences had been on balance favourable or adverse'.[52] This ambivalence led to a policy of benign neglect until 1969.

The famous Regulation Q, which set ceilings on the interest payable on deposits by US banks, has been widely credited for prompting the growth of the Eurodollar market in European financial centres. However, through the 1960s Regulation Q was amended with little impact on international capital flows. For example, the relaxation of the Regulation Q in 1963 for 3-month deposits from 2.5 per cent to 4 per cent was not sufficient to draw money from the London market to New York. Some concern had been expressed at the time in the Bank of England, but the increase in interest that American banks could pay on foreign dollar deposits did not prompt a withdrawal of funds from London.[53] Regulation Q was further relaxed in November 1964 when the ceilings on shorter-term deposits were raised. Despite this, the Eurodollar market accelerated.

The major regulatory change affecting longer-term capital flows in this period was the imposition in July 1963 of the already-mentioned Interest Equalization Tax on foreign securities issued in the USA by developed countries. The effect of this was to make foreign flotations in New York and other US financial centres more expensive, promoting instead recourse to the Eurobond market and direct borrowing from US banks. As a result, in 1964 the foreign credits of banks in the USA increased US$2 bn., almost twice as much as in any previous year. Japan and developing countries were the main borrowers on short-term while long-term lending was mainly to Japan and Europe.[54] In the two years 1963–4 US long-term lending to Italy amounted to US$340 m., while Japan accounted for a further US$260 m.[55] Part of the expansion in 1964 was due to the anticipated extension of IET to term loans to foreigners as well as securities. Conversely, foreign securities issued in the USA subject to IET declined dramatically from US$531 m. in 1963 to US$101 m. in 1964. In the six years 1966–71 only US$89 m. worth of such securities were issued.[56]

On 10 February 1965 President Johnson announced a Balance of Payments Programme designed to reduce the US deficit. A major part of this policy was

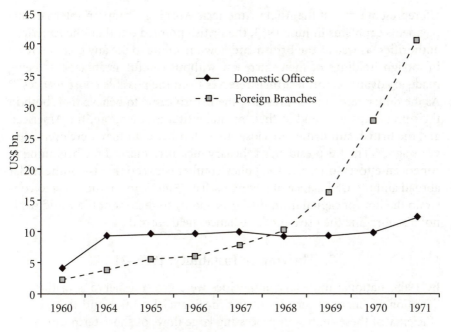

Figure 4.3. *Foreign credits of US banks*

Source: J. Kelly, *Bankers and Borders: The Case of American Banks in Britain* (Cambridge, Mass.: Ballinger, 1977), 105

the Voluntary Foreign Credit Restraint Programme, under which banks and industrial enterprises were directed to reduce their deposits abroad and their lending to foreigners. Initially proposed as a temporary measure, it continued in force until January 1974. This policy marked a turning point for the foreign operations of New York banks as their international operations increasingly went through branches in London and other international financial centres. Johnson also took this opportunity to extend IET to medium- and long-term bank loans as well as foreign securities. Initially, the tax was applied to loans by domestic and foreign branches, although foreign branches were made exempt in February 1967. Figure 4.3 shows the increase in overseas lending by foreign branches of US banks compared with the relative stability of such loans by domestic offices.[57]

In summary, by 1963 the USA was facing difficulties very familiar to British authorities. Since 1945 Britain had grappled with the conflict between the international use of their domestic currency and the threat that this posed to the capital account. Their solution had been to restrict the use of sterling to a 'trusted' group of countries in the sterling area while accepting and then promoting the use of other currencies in London. In a paper given to

US representatives of the Anglo-American Working Group on international payments problems in June 1963, the British pointed out that 'the American authorities, as well as the British, are now unwilling to see any great increase in foreign holdings of their currency, without careful arrangements being made in advance to protect their reserves from the possible consequences'.[58] As the dollar came under pressure, the British came to believe that 'both in their preoccupations and in their mental attitudes, therefore, the American and the British authorities are closer to each other than they were even a few years ago'.[59] The US president's February measures marked the beginning of American efforts to resolve the policy conflict between the use of the dollar abroad and the US balance of payments. The American solution was to constrain the flow of capital from the US economy to the rest of the world while not discouraging the use of dollar balances held abroad.

3. Thriving on Instability: 1965–71

By 1965, national monetary authorities were growing nervous of the proliferation of financial services offered in financial centres and the growing efficiency of these centres in processing large flows of short-term capital. By this time the US balance of payments was also showing the strain of persistent deficits that fed dollars into international markets, prompting regulators in the USA and West Germany to restrict capital flows through direct controls. It was widely surmised that the integration of international financial centres was threatening the economic sovereignty of national governments. This is reflected in the plethora of investigations into the economic impact of the Eurodollar market and its implications for world liquidity and inflation during this period. Conversely, the French authorities chose this period actively to promote Paris as an international financial centre by relaxing exchange controls and other restrictions on French banking.

Paris. Paris was a major international underwriting centre and French banks were among the largest in the world, but Paris did not dominate the international financial markets of Europe except in particular sectors such as the Eurosterling market. Of US$4.5 bn. of gross public issues of conventional foreign bonds in Europe in the 1960s, only US$137 m. were floated in Paris.[60] By mid-decade, however, the government had decided that France would benefit from having a major international financial centre to rival London. The commitment by President de Gaulle to promote Paris as a première international financial centre was signalled in November 1966 by the cancellation of the instruction forbidding payment of interest on non-resident franc accounts. This was followed a month later by new laws designed further to liberalize foreign financial transactions through the abolition of exchange controls. These moves formed part of a more general relaxation of the highly regulated French banking system from the beginning of 1966. Freed from restrictions, some nationalized French banks formed affiliates with other European banks in order to raise funds through the Eurobond market and to attract Eurocurrency deposits. The new affiliates were not necessarily located in Paris, however.[61] The first Eurobond denominated in French francs was issued in 1967, which raised US$12.2 m. and was followed by issues amounting to US$20.2 m. in 1968. In May 1968 efforts were made by the Banque de Paris et des Pays-Bas to establish an international gold market modelled on that of London. These developments were promoted by de Gaulle and the new finance minister Michel Debré, and they also reflected underlying internationalization of the French economy within the EEC, and the influx of US banks and corporations.[62]

Unfortunately, the initiative to establish Paris as a more diversified international financial centre was ill served by political events. The general strike and student riots of May 1968 prompted a speculative drain on the French foreign exchange reserves, which heralded the return of exchange controls. Although many controls were lifted again in August, confidence in the French franc was shaken, which inhibited both borrowing and lending internationally. The net assets in foreign currencies of French banks *vis-à-vis* non-residents fell from US$800 m. in September 1968 to US$20 m. by December. At the beginning of January 1969 French banks were told to eliminate their net foreign currency asset positions *vis-à-vis* non-residents by the end of the month or, failing that, to deposit the US$ equivalent with the Banque de France during the next three months. These restrictions led Paris to revert to its previous role as an underwriter of international bonds, with Paris banks participating in most medium- and long-term loans on the Eurobond market. In August 1969 the franc was devalued 11 per cent against the dollar.

New York. In the second half of the 1960s, New York banks were increasingly circumscribed by regulations that encouraged them to operate in European international financial centres rather than from their home base. The Voluntary Credit Restraint Programme of 1965–74 encouraged US banks in London to divert their activity away from merely repatriating most of their Eurodollars to head offices in New York, and instead to redeploy these funds within Europe, partly for export finance.[63] After 1965, assets of foreign branches of US banks exceeded foreign loans from US offices.[64] In addition, from 1966 the Federal Reserve Bank pursued a policy of tight money that restricted the attractiveness of the New York market for loans. Deposit rates in New York continued to be constrained by Regulation Q, which drained deposits into more attractive investments and encouraged US banks to replace these domestic deposits by attracting Eurodollar deposits through their branches abroad. There was a second wave of tight money in the USA in 1969 and Eurodollar deposit rates increased dramatically until the spread between the 3-month Eurodollar deposit rate and the highest rate payable at US banks peaked at 4 per cent in mid-1969, falling back to about 1 per cent a year later.[65] In February 1967 the IET was removed from loans by foreign branches of US banks.[66]

On 1 January 1968 President Johnson announced a new programme to decrease the balance of payments deficit of that year by US$3 bn. All medium- and long-term bank loans to continental Europe were to be reduced by not renewing them or re-lending the proceeds abroad after maturity. All outstanding short-term credit to continental Europe was to be reduced to 40 per cent of the level at the end of 1967, at a minimum rate of 10 per cent reduction per quarter. All net investment in foreign businesses was to be considered foreign financial assets and was to be reduced by 5 per cent or more from the level at the end of 1967. No new direct investment was to be allowed in continental Europe. The aim of these policies was to generate a reflux of funds to the USA and to encourage overseas borrowing by multinational corporations. As the Federal Research Bank acknowledged, 'It has always been clear that part of the required adjustment in international payments would have to come through increased European financing of capital investment in Europe and elsewhere.'[67] In 1968 new issues of securities in foreign markets by US corporations rose to US$2.1 bn. from US$450 m. in 1967.[68] Foreign borrowing abroad by US corporations increased from 12 per cent of total foreign direct investment in 1966 and 1967 to 39 per cent in 1968 and 34 per cent in 1969.[69] By 1971, 77 per cent of foreign credits of US banks were held by foreign branches.

The operations of banks in New York were further constrained by the Federal Reserve Bank's efforts to moderate borrowing on the Eurodollar market. In September 1969 they imposed a 10 per cent reserve requirement on net liabilities to foreign branches of US banks in excess of the average amounts outstanding in May 1969. This reduced the usefulness of foreign branches to New York banks as a channel of access for liquid funds, and after 1969 lending from branches to head offices declined. The Federal Bank estimated that 30 per cent of branch resources were used to supply parent offices in 1969 but that in 1970 this had reduced to 2.7 per cent.[70]

US balance of payments deficits that prompted capital controls in the USA also required policy responses from the surplus countries of Europe, especially Germany. The West German authorities were reluctant to lower interest rates in an environment of inflationary pressure and so used direct controls to ameliorate the balance of payments pressure. On 1 April 1964 a 25 per cent withholding tax on income from German bonds held by non-residents was announced in an effort to restrain the capital inflow.[71] Foreigners were also prohibited from buying German Treasury bonds or similar paper or fixed-interest bearing domestic stocks. This encouraged D-mark denominated Eurobonds, and by 1968 these came to rival the volume of Eurobonds denominated in dollars. In 1969 US$1,561 m. was floated in dollars and US$1,083.5 m. was floated in D-marks.

It was not until after 1973 that the Nixon administration started to restore some of the influence of New York as an international financial centre. Before this, successive administrations were content to promote US banks' branch extension overseas in the general context of support for US multinational expansion of this period.[72]

London. As noted above, the regulatory environment in New York encouraged an acceleration of foreign banking subsidiaries in London. From 1965 to 1971, 69 foreign banks opened branches in London, of which almost 40 per cent were American banks. Figure 4.4 shows the distribution of deposits among international banks in London. This clearly shows the increasing importance of US banks at the expense of other categories. Although their overall share declined, between 1965 and 1970 the British Overseas and Commonwealth Banks increased their deposits from US$1,676 m. to US$5,797 m. and their advances from US$782 m. to US$2,953 m.[73] In addition to the acceleration of the Eurodollar and Eurobond market, there were other innovations in the products offered in London. In May 1966 the London branch of the First National City Bank issued the first negotiable dollar denominated Certificate of Deposit (CD). By the end of March 1968, 11 US banks and 15 other banks had issued CDs and a secondary market had developed.[74] Until 1968, withholding tax was charged on CDs with maturity over one year, but after this was removed, the CD market flourished as part of the London Eurodollar market.

The invasion of foreign banks into London did not initially concern the Bank of England so long as they were not involved in domestic credit. As noted above, exchange control was aimed at transactions by UK residents on their own account, and constrained the use of sterling more generally. Entrepôt finance between non-residents using currency other than sterling was not restricted.[75] This separation of domestic and international business was further marked by credit controls on domestic lending by all banks operating in the UK from May 1965. Until 1965 foreign banks had not been constrained by domestic credit restrictions but they had not significantly increased this part of their business. Since sterling lending was confined to an increase of not more than 5 per cent above the level in the period May 1965 to March 1966, foreign banks that had not yet established themselves in the domestic market were effectively squeezed out.

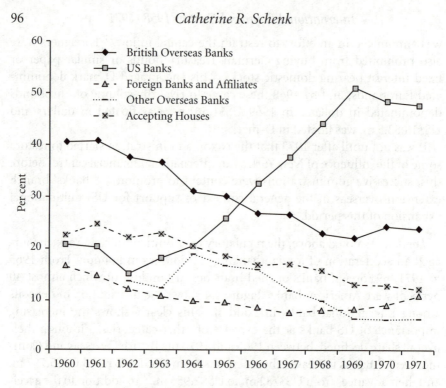

Figure 4.4. *Shares of total deposits of overseas banks in the UK*
Source: *Bank of England Quarterly Bulletin*, various issues

The continued growth in the activities of foreign banks and the relative freedom of their operations compared to domestic banks finally prompted a response from the British authorities at the end of 1971. In October the Competition and Credit Control reforms aimed to put foreign banks on a more equal competitive footing with domestic commercial banks. The interest rate cartel for clearing banks was ended and foreign banks were subjected to the same reserve requirements on sterling liabilities as domestic banks (12.5%). Eurocurrency deposits were left unregulated.

4. Conclusion

The most important factor affecting the activities of international financial centres in the 1960s was the international monetary crisis that simmered throughout the decade. The way national regulators responded to this environment, and the way service providers responded through product innovation, determined the character of international finance and the opportunities available in international financial centres. On the Continent, the

German authorities were plagued by persistent balance of payments surpluses to which they responded by restricting inward investment and ultimately revaluing the D-mark. The small public debt of West Germany precluded the use of D-mark government securities as national reserves, but encouraged the expansion of the Eurobond market. The French, with their highly regulated system, attempted to enhance the role of Paris as an international financial centre but this was unsustainable as the domestic economic and political situation deteriorated from 1968. The financial activities of Frankfurt and Paris were dwarfed, however, by the enhanced integration of New York and London.

In the 1960s financial institutions were faced with increased liquidity as a symptom of the collapse of the international monetary system, and increased demand for international financial services due to the multinational expansion of business enterprise and the integration of European economies. The response was the development of new products such as the Eurobond and the Certificate of Deposit, and new financial organizations such as branches, consortia, or banking clubs to reflect the international needs of their customers.

The international monetary crises of the 1960s brought the USA to the same problems that had plagued the UK since 1945—how to ensure convertibility at a fixed exchange rate while supporting persistent balance of payments deficits and encouraging the use of the national currency as a reserve currency. The British response was to encourage the activities of London as an international financial centre since this benefited the balance of payments by generating a persistent short-term capital inflow and invisible earnings. At the same time, however, the British were forced to restrict the use of sterling by residents of the UK and the sterling area to prevent flight from the currency. Ultimately, this policy was unsustainable and the reserve role of sterling was gradually undermined as sterling area countries sought to diversify their reserves. This culminated in the devaluation of sterling in 1967 and the organization of the Basle Agreements to encourage countries to keep sterling as their main reserve currency. By 1970 only 20 per cent of international trade was denominated in sterling compared to 50 per cent in the late 1940s.[76]

The US response was a mirror reflection of the UK approach. Regulators tried to ameliorate US balance of payments problems by discouraging the use of New York as an international financial centre. They continued to encourage the international use of the dollar, however, as this supported its value in international markets. This regulatory environment, prompted by the imbalance in the international monetary system, generated the multinational expansion of US banks and the intensification of their activities in European financial centres, in particular London. This policy, too, was ultimately unsustainable and convertibility at the fixed exchange rate was finally abandoned in 1971.

NOTES

1. H. C. Reed, *The Pre-eminence of International Financial Centres* (New York: Praeger, 1981); J. P. Abraham, N. Bervaes, A. Guinotte, Y. Lacroix, *The Competitiveness of European International Financial Centres* (Bangor: Institute of European Finance, 1993); G. Dufey and I. H. Giddy, *The International Money Market* (Englewood Cliffs, NJ: Prentice Hall, 1978); Y. S. Park and M. Essayed, *International Banking and Financial Centres* (Boston: Kluwer Academic Publishers, 1989); H. Rose, *International Banking Developments and London's Position as an International Banking Centre* (London: London Business School, 1994). For a more historical approach see C. P. Kindleberger, *The Formation of Financial Centers* (Princeton, NJ: International Finance Section, Princeton University, 1974); R. Michie, *The City of London* (London: Macmillan, 1992); G. Jones, 'International Financial Centres in Asia, the Middle East and Australia: A Historical Perspective', in Y. Cassis (ed.), *Finance and Financiers in European History, 1880–1960* (Cambridge: Cambridge University Press, 1992). See also the collection of literature in R. Roberts (ed.), *International Financial Centres* (4. vols.; Aldershot: Edward Elgar, 1994).

2. This method is used by both Reed, *Pre-eminence*, and Abraham *et al.*, *Competitiveness*.

3. Dufey and Giddy, *The International Money Market*, and Park and Essayed, *International Banking*. A. D. Smith, *Performance in International Financial Markets; The Performance of Britain and its Rivals* (Cambridge: Cambridge University Press, 1992) combines the functional approach with interviews with 'experts' to determine the most important characteristics of international financial centres.

4. S.-R. Choi, A. E. Tschoegl, and C.-M. Yu, 'Banks and the World's Major Financial Centers, 1970–1980', *Weltwirtschaftliches Archiv*, 122 (1986), 48–64, try to establish the level of interpenetration of financial centres through an analysis of bank offices.

5. The increased supply of US dollars outside the USA was due to US balance of payments deficits prompted by domestic inflation and American involvement in the Vietnam War.

6. Sterling devalued in 1967, French franc devalued in 1969.

7. *The Economist* gave an account of the competition between domestic banks and foreign branches in various European centres in 1964. *The Economist*, 21 November 1964, 845–51.

8. Quoted in Michie, *City of London*, 91. For Michie, the agglomeration of services available in London explained its competitiveness in the postwar period, see ibid. 92, 96.

9. For more detailed analysis of the sterling area see C. R. Schenk, *Britain and the Sterling Area: From Devaluation to Convertibility in the 1950s* (London: Routledge, 1994).

10. J. Kelly, *Bankers and Borders: The Case of American Banks in Britain* (Cambridge, Mass.: Ballinger, 1977), 68; S. Strange, *Sterling and British Policy* (Oxford: Royal

Institute for International Affairs, 1971), 202–3. Rose gives the sterling area some credit for sustaining international banking activities in the 1950s, see H. Rose, *London as an International Financial Centre: A Narrative History* (London: London Business School, 1994), 30–3.

11. Source: Michie, *City of London*, 26. Figures are approximate.

12. Reed, *Pre-eminence*, 34.

13. Reed attributes this to the decision to locate the International Monetary Fund and the International Bank for Reconstruction and Development in Washington rather than New York, and the decision to administer American aid programmes through London and Paris.

14. *Federal Reserve Bulletin*, 51 (1965), 362–3. The 1916 and 1919 Edge Act amendments to Section 25 of the Federal Reserve Act allowed participation by banks in special subsidiaries for foreign trade and financing.

15. *Federal Reserve Bulletin*, 51 (1965), 367–8. At the end of 1962 New York City banks accounted for over 75% of total outstanding short-term claims on foreigners, but accounted for only a little more than 0.5% of the dramatic increase in these credits in the following two years.

16. This strategy revealed its weakness after the Soviet Union defaulted on Russia's debt.

17. Italy and the Netherlands operated similar restrictions on financial transactions not linked to trade.

18. For details and analysis of the directives see A. F. P. Bakker, *The Liberalization of Capital Movements in Europe; The Monetary Committee and Financial Integration, 1958–1994* (Dordrecht: Kluwer Academic Publishers, 1996), 87–94.

19. It was easier for countries to rescind the liberalization adopted by the OECD than the EEC Council's directives.

20. *The Development of a European Capital Market: Report of a Group of Experts Appointed by the EEC Commission* (Brussels: European Economic Community, 1966).

21. This accounted for 40% of US banks' activities in London in 1969, A. F. Brimmer, and F. R. Dahl, 'Growth of American International Banking: Implications for Public Policy', *Journal of Finance*, 30 (1975), 341–63. The same was true in the early 1960s according to O. L. Altman, 'Foreign Markets for Dollars, Sterling and Other Currencies', *International Monetary Fund Staff Papers*, 8 (1961), 313–51.

22. United Nations, *Salient Features and Trends in Foreign Direct Investment* (New York: United Nations, 1983).

23. See *The Development of a European Capital Market*, 155–7, for a discussion of branching strategy by European banks.

24. R. Pringle, *Banking in Britain* (London: Methuen, 1973), 163.

25. *The Economist*, 30 June 1962, 1339. Other associations were Eurofin, Euroinvest, Negit, and Sogefina. In 1962 these five groups included 27 financial institutions from nine European countries.

26. Pringle, *Banking in Britain*, 162.

27. For a full account of the early years of the Eurodollar market in London see C. R. Schenk, 'The Origins of the Eurodollar Market in London 1955–1963', *Explorations in Economic History*, 35 (1998), 221–38. For an account of the role of the Treasury and the Bank of England see G. Burn, 'The State, the City and the Euromarkets', *Review of International Political Economy*, 6 (1999), 225–61.

28. Golberg and Saunders found that the Eurodollar market was the most important factor in increasing the overseas deposits of US banks in London from 1961–8: L. G. Goldberg and A. Saunders, 'The Causes of US Bank Expansion Overseas: The Case of Britain', *Journal of Money Credit and Banking*, 12 (1980) pt. I, 630–43. Low of the Bank of London and South America (BOLSA) told the Bank of England in October 1962 that the New York banks were more conscious of openings for business in the Eurodollar market and were more adept at developing new facilities through the market for their customers, Bank of England Archives, EID10/21, Report of a meeting between Thompson-McCausland and Low of BOLSA, 4 October 1962.

29. Bank of England Archives, EID10/22, letter from H. B. Mynors to Hambro, 29 January 1963. Hambro had expressed concern at the growth of Eurodollar deposits and had asked for the Bank of England's view.

30. Bank of England Archives, EID10/22, note by R. A. O'Brien, 16 January 1963.

31. Bank of England Archives, EID10/21, note from G. W. Lucas to R. L. Workman (HMT), 21 July 1961.

32. Bank of England Archives, EID10/21, 'UK Banks' Foreign Currency Assets and Liabilities', 29 January 1962.

33. Low of BOLSA suggested in October 1962 that more American banks' deposits were being used in Europe rather than channelled to head office. Bank of England Archives, EID10/21, report of discussion by L. P. Thompson-McCausland, 4 October 1962.

34. Bank of England Archives, EID10/15, paper for the Committee on Overseas Figures, 11 May 1962.

35. Bank of England Archives, EID10/22, draft report of BIS meeting on Eurodollar Market, 13 January 1964.

36. Bank of England Archives, EID10/22, note by R. L. Workman (HMT) of a trip to New York and Washington.

37. Bank of England Archives, EID10/22, note by Preston to Bridge, circulated to Selwyn, O'Brien, and Parsons, 4 December 1963.

38. Bank of England Archives, EID10/22, Bridge to Parsons and O'Brien, 5 December 1963.

39. Bank of England Archives, EID10/19, letter from D. E. Thompson to M. H. Locke (HMT), 23 August 1960.

40. Bank of England Archives, EID10/22, draft report of BIS meeting on Eurodollar Market, 13 January 1964.

41. Bank of England Archives, EID10/22, letter from Brunet, Governor of the Banque de France, 6 December 1963.

42. Bank of England Archives, EID10/22, note of Governor's meeting, 8 December 1963.

43. Bank of England Archives, EID10/19, note by M. J. Ive, Balance of Payment Office, Bank of England, 'Eurosterling Movements', 1 May 1962. Ive noted that regarding the Eurosterling market in Paris, 'Our factual knowledge is nil, our reasoned inferences moderate and our groundless assumption considerable.'

44. Bank of England Archives, EID10/21, note by R. G. R., 'Eurocurrency Market in Paris', 31 May 1962.

45. Bank of England Archives, EID10/15, 'Eurodollars' by Thomson-McCausland, 24 May 1962.

46. Y. S. Park and J. Zwsick, *International Banking in Theory and Practice* (New York: Addison-Wesley, 1985), 14. For the early years of the Eurobond market see also, Burn, 'The State'; K. Burk (ed.), 'Witness Seminar on the Origins and Early Development of the Eurobond Market', *Contemporary European History*, 1 (1992), 65–87; I. M. Kerr, *A History of the Eurobond Market: The First 21 Years* (London: Euromoney Publications, 1984). These sources do not discuss the Treasury and Bank of England discussion in 1962.

47. Bank of England Archives, C40/773, telegram to Commonwealth posts, 25 January 1963.

48. Bank of England Archives, C40/773, telegram to Kingston, Jamaica, from Commonwealth Relations Office, 11 February 1963.

49. The Istituto per la Ricostruzione Industriale (IRI) used this method for an issue in 1964.

50. Until 1961 New York was hampered by State constraints on the operation of foreign banks. Branches of foreign banks were prohibited from accepting local deposits and could not engage in fiduciary activities. Reed, *Pre-eminence*, 33.

51. Bank of England Archives, EID10/20, note by S. Goldman of a conversation with Roosa, 1 may 1963.

52. Bank of England Archives, EID10/22, note by R. L. Workman (HMT) of a trip to New York and Washington, 31 December 1963.

53. Bank of England Archives, EID10/22, note by G. C. Burton, Balance of Payments Office, Bank of England, 7 January 1963.

54. *Federal Reserve Bulletin*, 51 (1965), 361.

55. Ibid., 365.

56. Kelly, *Bankers and Borders*, 116.

57. Ibid., 105.

58. Public Records Office, London, T 230/641, Bank of England paper, 'Reserve Currencies', given to US representatives for US-UK Working Group, 6 June 1963.

59. Ibid.

60. Monetary Committee of the European Communities, *Policy on the Bond Markets in the Countries of the EEC* (Brussels: European Economic Community, 1970), Table E-1.

61. The Banque Nationale de Paris joined with Barclays, Banca Nazionale del Lavoro, Dresdner Bank, and Bank of America to form Société Financière Européenne.

Crédit Lyonnais and Société Générale joined with Société Générale of Belgium, Midland Bank, Deutsche Bank, AMRO Bank, and Samuel Montagu to found a medium-term credit bank located in Brussels.

62. I am grateful to Olivier Feiertag for this insight.
63. 'American Banks in Flux', *The Economist*, 20 November 1965, xxvii.
64. By 1967 foreign loans from US offices amounted to $US9.8 bn. while assets of foreign branches totalled $US15.7 bn. Park and Zwick, *International Banking*, 27.
65. Kelly, *Bankers and Borders*, 95
66. The IET on domestic banks was reduced in 1969 and finally removed in 1974.
67. *Federal Reserve Bulletin*, 54 (1968), 353.
68. Ibid., 55 (1969), 774–5.
69. Kelly, *Bankers and Borders*, 105.
70. Ibid., 101.
71. The 'Kuponsteuer' was in force from March 1965.
72. Kelly, *Bankers and Borders*, 50–2.
73. Pringle, *Banking in Britain*, 147.
74. 'Overseas and Foreign Banks in London', *Bank of England Quarterly Bulletin*, 8 (1968), 158.
75. In October 1968 exchange control authority on the use of sterling to finance trade among third countries was withdrawn.
76. Michie, *City of London*, 90.

5

Banking with Multinationals: British Clearing Banks and the Euromarkets' Challenge, 1958–1976

STEFANO BATTILOSSI

The rise of the Eurodollar system was an epitome of the awakening of international banking in the 1960s.[1] From that time, its power to contribute to the international transmission of inflation and to oil the wheels of international speculation became a source of both theoretical and political controversies.[2] Until recently, such debates have given a back-seat to the far-reaching consequences of the emergence of Eurodollar banking on strategies, organization, and business techniques of Western banks. Likewise, later developments—namely the recycling of petrodollars and the explosion of international lending to sovereign borrowers—have overshadowed the role that the demand for innovative banking services stemming from internationally-oriented companies played in the growth of the market. In fact, until the early 1970s, Eurobanking meant essentially banking with multinationals.[3]

The strong leadership of US banks in corporate Eurobanking soon emerged as a fundamental characteristic of the international financial system. Taking advantage of their firm dominant position in the Eurodollar market (by far the largest segment of Eurocurrency markets), American banks adopted an aggressive growth-oriented strategy in Europe and began to compete with their overseas counterparts by offering innovative and more efficient international banking services to European corporations. As London emerged as the hub of the Euromarkets, British commercial banks found themselves particularly exposed to such competition.

This chapter investigates their response to the American challenge. In order to exploit both growth and profit opportunities offered by Eurocurrency banking and stand up to American competition, they were forced to put their strategies, organizational patterns, and traditional banking culture under severe reconsideration. Indeed the transmutation of British clearing banks from sleeping giants, stuck to their tradition of cartelized, domestic-oriented, and retail-focused institutions, into internationally minded groups ambitiously competing in wholesale and corporate global banking has probably to be considered one of the most remarkable changes in post-war Western banking.[4] In order to account for such transformation, the main features of the competitive edge developed by American banks, along with factors accounting for their strong leadership in Eurobanking, are briefly outlined. Particular attention is devoted to the US banks' successful achievements in using Eurobranching and liability management in the international money market to strengthen their position in corporate banking overseas and launch innovative global banking and financial services. Then attention turns to the process of strategic refocusing and institutional change that clearing banks had to go through in order to develop their Eurobusiness and defend their corporate base, while at the same time circumventing restraints imposed by regulatory devices. Finally their growth and profit performance in international banking is compared to that of US banks and evaluated in the light of structural competitive disadvantages and changing market conditions in the early 1970s.

1. US Banks and the Rise of Liability Management in the Eurodollar Market

The origins of the dominant role of American banks in the Eurodollar market can be traced back to their relationships with US big business and its international expansion. Since the late 1950s major changes occurred in both financial structure and strategy of US large corporations, forced by a marked decline of gross internal funds increasingly to resort to net external-fund financing. This took the form not only of increased bank borrowing but also of innovative short-term market funding, such as direct issuing of commercial paper. At the same time, a marked change in corporate treasurers' attitude to liquidity management began to emerge. As a matter of tradition, large corporations used to keep a substantial part of their liquidity idle with commercial banks in the form of sight (thus, non-interest bearing) and time deposits: the latter were subject to Regulation Q, an inheritance of the 1930s setting low ceilings on payable interest rates. Since the mid-1950s however, responding to increased variability of domestic short-term interest rates, corporations began to rationalize their cash management by trimming bank deposits and investing substantial liquid resources in money market assets, such as Treasury bills, at a higher profit. As a consequence, banks had to meet a rising demand for credit by corporate borrowers while facing at the same time a serious threat of disintermediation, further exacerbated by increasing domestic competition from non-bank financial institutions.[5]

Innovations in liquidity management by US corporations also had an international facet. In fact, the large presence of American multinationals in the UK, the long-dated establishment of London-based branches of prime New York banks, the interdependence of New York and London as financial centres (where the largest and most efficient money markets and the most active foreign exchange markets were based) enhanced substantial transatlantic flows of short-term funds.[6] Treasurers of US companies with multinational activities proved keen to exploit profit opportunities stemming from international interest rate differentials. The emergence of the Eurodollar market in London (a market for wholesale time deposits denominated in dollars and held with banks outside the USA, including overseas branches of US banks) further contributed to expand the array of options for short-term investments at the disposal of large corporations. Eurodollars were used by US multinationals in their own liquidity management as an interest-earning liquid asset competing with other dollar-denominated money instruments. Partly such Eurodollars were switched into sterling, usually (though not by rule) covered by forward contracts against the exchange risk, and invested in UK money market assets, provided that dollar–sterling exchange rate conditions were favourable—as they indeed proved throughout most of the 1950s and early 1960s.[7] As a Report on the 1964 sterling crisis by a Committee chaired by Lord Khan emphasized in 1966:

since 1959 or 1960, when the leading American and European banks first entered the Eurodollar market, the business of moving the surplus cash of banks and industry from country to country in search of the highest short-term return had grown enormously ... A fairly detailed operational knowledge of the international money market has spread not only to a large number of bankers in the US, Canada and the Continent, who, a few years ago, hardly touched anything but routine transactions in international exchange, but also to the finance officials or treasurers of American and continental companies, whose reputation was now engaged in finding profitable outlets for their surplus cash. In the process, the knowledge and use of forward cover facilities has also spread very widely. In the autumn of 1964 there were a good number of people in places like Detroit, Dallas or Los Angeles, let alone Montreal or Paris, who were familiar with such sophistications as the latest UK local authority 7-day or 3-month deposit rates, the relevant cost of forward cover in the exchange market and the going rate offered for Eurodollar deposits.[8]

The Eurodollar market proved initially a further source of disintermediation for US banks, as British banks enjoyed the lion's share of the market. By offering competitive interest rates, they successfully competed in attracting dollar deposits from US and other international corporations. As shown in Table 5.1, merchant banks and British overseas banks resorted to Eurocurrency (mostly Eurodollar) business to revamp their fading fortunes and

Table 5.1. *UK banks' share of the London Eurocurrency market,*[a]
1958–1962 (%)

	1958[b]	1959[b]	1960[b]	1961	1962
Clearing banks	22.5	14.3	11.4	6.6	4.5
British overseas banks	33.3	25.0	18.9	20.8	23.0
Accepting houses	10.8	10.7	11.8	16.1	18.6
Other UK banks	1.0	1.3	1.5	1.1	2.6
Total UK banks	67.6	51.3	43.6	44.6	48.7
American banks	16.6	22.3	39.1	35.9	27.0
Japanese banks	—	0.9	6.0	7.3	10.8
Other foreign banks	15.8	25.5	11.3	12.2	13.5
Total (£ m.)	116	255	596	707	1,027
Growth index	100	220	514	610	885

Notes: amount outstanding, end of year.
   [a] Foreign currency deposits held by non-residents with UK banks.
   [b] Eurodollar deposits only.

Source: Bank of England Archive, EID3/335 and EID 10/21–2.

reinforce their ability to provide dollar export finance to international, often non-British corporate customers, as an alternative to traditional sterling facilities.[9]

However US banks' response was prompt. Since the early 1960s the major ones among them—such as Citibank and Chase Manhattan—began to compete aggressively for dollar liquidity by taking advantage themselves of the market funding revolution both in the USA and abroad.[10] Domestically they had strong incentives to resort to financial creativity in order to circumvent banking regulations, namely reserve requirements and Regulation Q, which handicapped them to compete for liquidity by increasing costs and setting ceilings on interest rates. The main innovation was the issue of negotiable Certificates of Deposits (CDs). Pioneered by Citibank in 1961, CDs—soon brought under Regulation Q by the Federal Bank—allowed banks to retain part of corporate liquidity that would otherwise be channelled towards competing institutions in the money market. At the international level, they successfully learnt to tap the rapidly expanding 'external' dollar money market through the extensive use of overseas (mainly London) branches to attract dollar liquid funds privately held abroad and in search of better returns than those prevailing in the USA.[11] Throughout the decade, as shown in Table 5.2, their market share rose continuously from 24.5 to 53.9 per cent, while that of British banks as a whole declined from 48.5 to 32.8 per cent.

Table 5.2. *UK banks' share of the London Eurocurrency market,*[a] *1963–1976 (%)*

	1963	1965	1967	1969	1971	1973	1976
Clearing banks[b]	4.8	3.6	2.8	1.6	1.9	4.2	13.1[c]
Other UK banks[d]	1.9	4.6	6.2	7.4	8.4	8.0	2.0[e]
British overseas[f]	24.0	18.2	18.8	16.2	18.4	17.6	
Accepting houses[g]	17.8	12.6	10.2	7.6	7.1	5.5	3.2
Total UK banks	48.5	39.0	38.0	32.8	35.8	35.3	18.3
American banks[h]	24.5	37.2	45.0	53.9	46.5	39.9	37.0
Foreign banks[i]	9.7	9.2	5.4	7.3	9.7	13.5	24.6
Other overseas[j]	17.3	14.6	11.6	6.0	6.8	8.0	13.9[k]
Consortium banks							6.2
Total (£ m.)[l]	1,798	2,930	6,329	16,902	24,512	54,373	114,833
Growth Index	100	163	352	940	1,363	3,024	6,387

Notes: amount outstanding, end of year.

[a] Foreign currency deposits held by non-residents with UK banks.

[b] London clearing banks, Scottish clearing banks, Northern Ireland banks (only parent banks).

[c] Clearing groups: parent clearing banks and their subsidiaries (including British overseas banks). Clearing parent banks' share is 5%.

[d] Among them, subsidiaries of clearing banks such as Barclays Export Finance Co.; Clydesdale Bank Finance Co.; County Bank Ltd.; Glynn Mills Finance Co.; International Commercial Bank Co.; Martins Bank (Finance) Co.; Midland Bank Finance Co.; Midland and International Bank Ltd. (MAIBL); National Provincial & Rothschild (International); William Deacon's Bank (Finance).

[e] All other banks with majority UK ownership (excluding consortium banks with foreign participations).

[f] Banks members of the British and Commonwealth Banks Association. From 1966, Eurodollar CDs included.

[g] Banks members of the Accepting Houses Association.

[h] Banks members of the American Banks in London Association. From 1966, Eurodollar CDs included.

[i] Banks members of the Foreign Banks and Affiliates Association. From 1966, Eurodollar CDs included.

[j] Banks from Japan, Africa, Near and Far East.

[k] Only Japanese banks.

[l] 1967 figure is affected by the sterling revaluation of 18 November 1967.

Sources: 1963–73, *The Bank of England Quarterly Bulletin*, various issues; 1976, *The London Clearing Banks*, Evidence by the Committee of London Clearing Bankers to the Committee to Review the Functioning of Financial Institutions (Wilson Committee), November 1977 (London: 1978), tables 26, 134.

Both CDs and Eurodollars represented key factors that allowed banks to strengthen the liability side of their balance sheet, by compensating shrinking deposits with funds borrowed at market rates. By doing so, they promoted a radically different way of banking, based on what was known as 'liability management', under which commercial banks increasingly tended to accommodate liabilities to loan demand by borrowing funds in the money markets.[12]

Along this path a critical turning point was the 1966 credit crunch enforced by the Fed, which exacerbated the liquidity strain suffered by American banks. The rise of money market rates, such as commercial paper and Treasury Bills, above the Regulation Q ceilings on bank time deposits and CDs—which the Fed for the first time refused to lift in order to signal its commitment to tight monetary policy—triggered a massive run on bank deposits.[13] During the ensuing 'controlled panic' (as Hyman Minsky put it), all major banks in search of position-making resources heavily tapped the Eurodollar market through their overseas branches: liabilities *vis-à-vis* overseas branches reached US$4 bn. at the end of the year (as shown in Fig. 5.1) and the Eurodollar inter-est rate rose to its historical peak of 7 per cent. Funds were then channelled back to head offices in the USA in order to finance domestic business.[14]

The 1966 episode was the first crucial test of liability management applied to the Eurodollar market. Indeed it has been regarded as the very moment when the new way of banking—or at least the kind of 'money-desk' or 'reserve position liability management' which banking literature refers to as 'LM-1'—actually came of age.[15] In the same period US banks promoted the issuing of Eurodollar Certificates of Deposits (certificates representing Eurodollar deposits with negotiability and potential liquidity, due to the development of a sizeable secondary market). This successful 'technology transfer' further strengthened their ability to bid for market funds and created further scope for liability management in the market. The final test came in 1968–9, when a new credit crunch, coupled with controls on US companies' foreign direct investment and US banks' overseas lending, shifted an enormous demand for credit to European subsidiaries of American banks. As shown in Fig. 5.1, time and again the Eurodollar market proved a fundamental source of liquidity for US banks: their liabilities towards foreign branches reached the highest ever level of US$14 bn., while Eurodollar rates rose to 11 per cent.[16] Beyond providing an effective alternative to domestic funds in liability management, Eurodollars also brought down banks' average reserve requirements, thus providing a new cash base for deposit creation.[17] In 1970 the gradual lifting of Regulation Q and the introduction of marginal reserve requirements (up to 20%) on Eurodollar borrowing through foreign branches, contributed to reduce incentives for US banks to resort to the Eurodollar market. In the process, however, American banks had conquered a hardly contestable leading position and the use of Eurodollar markets had become a permanent feature of their behaviour.[18]

Even more so as the Eurodollar market was soon integrated by the emergence of a medium-term Eurodollar credit market. A fast-growing business from the late 1960s (though no reliable estimate of its true size was available until 1973), the Eurocredit market successfully filled the gap

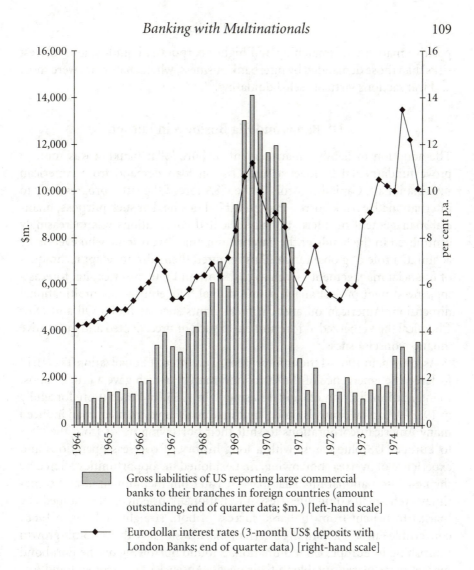

Figure 5.1. *US banks' liabilities to their foreign branches, and Eurodollar rate, 1964–74*
Sources: *FED Bulletin*, various issues; OECD Statistics, CD-Rom

between the short-term Eurodollar market and the long-term Eurobond market. It provided corporate borrowers of international standing with large-term loans (of maturity up to ten years), mainly in the form of roll-over credits at either fixed or floating rates financed by banks through short-term borrowing in the Eurodollar market.[19] This represented a further development of liability management, usually referred to as 'generalized or loan-position liability management' (LM-2), which implied substantial positive maturity mismatching and higher corporate, liquidity, and interest risks than those demanded by interbank business, where maturities were short and transactions virtually self-liquidating.[20]

2. US Banks and Big Business in Europe

The adoption of liability management in Eurodollar banking was soon to prove fundamental to meet a steep rise in loan demand from American multinationals. Capital controls in the USA forced the latter progressively to internationalize bank borrowing and capital raising. For such purpose, financial management of internationally oriented corporations was increasingly centralized in the hands of the parent companies' treasurers, who eventually acquired a role of global range. This required them also to adapt techniques of financial management—such as cash flow and return-on-capital forecasting, investment project analysis, and capital budgeting—to a multinational dimension. American oil and chemical giants such as Mobil Oil and Dow Chemical then emerged as forerunners of such unprecedented and innovative 'finance consciousness'.[21]

As known, in 1963–4 the enforcement of an Interest Equalization Tax (IET) fostered the emergence of the Eurobond market, which gave a crucial boost to internationalization of capital raising.[22] In 1965, and even more forcefully in 1968–9, capital controls on US multinationals' investment abroad induced many American corporations to shift their borrowing needs from the USA to Europe. US blue chips, with a long history of overseas operations and experience of overseas borrowing, first exploited the opportunities offered by the new international financial market. Later on, medium-sized and sometimes even small companies, less internationally oriented, also tapped the market to benefit from the large success of both straight and (since 1968) convertible Eurobonds among international investors. With economic growth flourishing in Europe, US multinationals found borrowing on the Eurobond market particularly suitable to their needs. Absence of government and foreign exchange authorities controls, tolerance for less detailed prospectuses as well as for scant disclosure of information, lower transaction costs than from raising capital piecemeal in each individual country, made Eurobonds a most convenient opportunity. From 1965 to 1972 American companies raised about $8.3 bn. in the Eurobond market—in fact, one third in 1968–9 only, when US capital controls effectively prevented them from raising capital domestically to finance foreign investment. As shown in Fig. 5.2, their issues actually accounted for some 30 per cent of the Eurobond market on average between 1965 and 1972—not to mention the 1968 peak of 60 per cent.[23] US multinationals employed the largest part of funds raised in Europe through

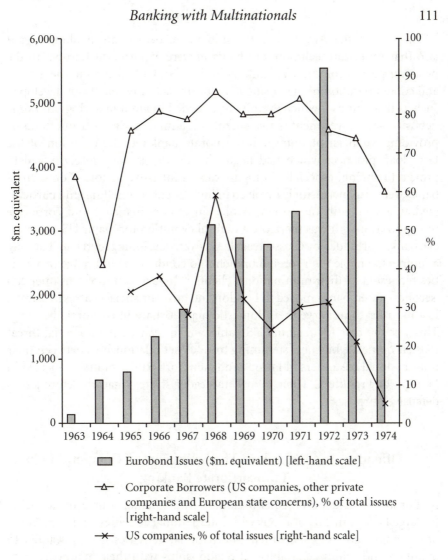

Figure 5.2. *Eurobond market's structure, 1964–74*

Source: F. G. Fisher, *Eurobonds* (London: Euromoney, 1988), 26, 58–9

Eurocredits and Eurobonds in financing overseas investments.[24] This pool of reserve funds could be quickly and easily channelled towards operating subsidiaries in different countries. Liquidity exceeding immediate financial needs was invested in the international money market in the form of short-term Eurodollar deposits with US and other international banks.

The rise of the American leadership in Eurocorporate banking meant also that American techniques of banking were exported to Europe. In the post-war period commercial banking in the USA had adapted to the growth and conglomeration of big business. Fiduciary activities had been developed such as trust funds—which eventually exceeded in amount savings and time deposits—and investment management (i.e. administering pension funds or providing financial planning). In corporate banking, the diffusion of the term loan practice, which had begun in the 1930s, was closely linked to project financing, especially in highly capital intensive sectors. Commercial banks were also increasingly involved in investment counselling, and participated, together with investment banks, in major financing and corporate reorganization.[25] It was therefore a natural evolution for major US commercial banks, forbidden by Glass-Steagall Act from developing merchant banking at home, to enable their foreign branches to conduct the full range of activities requested by their multinational clients.[26] In fact, a number of American 'second-comer' banks moved to London and other financial centres in Europe just in order to preserve their domestic market share in corporate banking. This was the case for regional US banks which realized the potential threat to their domestic business stemming from closer relationships between their multinational customers in Europe and New York banks' branches located in London or Frankfurt. Their follow-my-leader strategy had therefore also a defensive purpose.[27]

3. Offenders and Defenders: The Emergence of Competition in Eurocorporate Banking

As Eurobonds and Eurocredits became a fundamental source of financing for large European corporations with international activities, all major European banks had to expand their international activities if they wanted to maintain and reinforce established relationships with their main corporate customers.[28] In fact, far from limiting their business in Europe to local subsidiaries of American companies, US banks also began to woo major European companies.

Local bankers generally considered this attitude to be a breach of a time-honoured and widely accepted business code. Such worries were echoed in exchanges of views and information within the European Advisory Committee (EAC), a banking 'club' created in the late 1950s by Midland Bank, Deutsche Bank, Société Générale de Banque of Belgium, and AMRO Bank.[29] Complaints about US banks' aggressiveness were raised initially by Continental members of the group. Already in 1964 European branches of Citibank and the Bank of America (followed as main chief offenders by Morgan Guaranty and Chase Manhattan)[30] were reported to compete successfully with national banks on the Continent to attract international business from major national companies. Thanks to the competitive advantage stemming from their world-wide branch network, US banks were able in fact to offer innovative services (such as transfer of funds between branches in different countries) at better terms and undercut conditions. Some of them were also reported to be suc-cessfully marketing multi-currency facilities and term loans with maturity of 3–5 years, refinanced mainly through the Eurodollar market and probably backed by their head offices in the USA.[31] This 'forceful and often hardly ethical competition' (in the words of Hermann Abs of Deutsche Bank), con-ducted in the 'deliberate absence of regard for the ill-will this may cause among the national banking communities', was reputed to cause banks in West Germany, the Netherlands, and Belgium a substantial loss of business for current transactions.[32]

Alarmed by their Continental counterparts' complaints, Midland and other British clearing banks began carefully to monitor developments at home. Large British corporations with international activities (as well as American and European companies with UK-based subsidiaries) were traditionally val-ued customers of clearing banks by virtue of their large banking requirements and diversified business. Although British multinationals seemed slow to adapt their financial management to a global scale, and generally relied on local banks for their overseas banking requirements,[33] clearing banks could not afford to underestimate the appeal that the American global approach to payments and financing would exercise on them.[34] However, evidence of direct competition proved initially scant. At the end of 1964 Midland management openly emphasized that the competitive threat in the UK was not as serious as it seemed to be on the Continent. American banks' busi-ness was largely confined to London. Although from time to time they had transgressed from the accepted business code, problems could easily be rec-tified by persuasion.[35] In 1965–6 Midland's reports still regarded American banks' move to London as a mere expression of 'typical American go-getting' (i.e. offering international banking services to their customers in order to maintain and improve existing connections) and a strategy aimed at retaining dollar wholesale deposits from US companies. The outstanding growth of their current and deposit accounts throughout the first half of the decade—which had risen from £206 m. in 1959 to £1,657 m. in 1966—stemmed mainly from overseas residents (69.2% in 1966) and was due largely to dollar and other foreign currency deposits. After careful examination, the London clearers' joint subcommittees of overseas managers and chief accountants discovered that the number of accounts lost to American banks was still negligible. Moreover, American bankers officially argued that it was not their intention to compete for sterling deposits and that the bulk of their balances was provided by international and sterling-area companies and, to a lesser extent, by funds previously placed in the sterling money markets. In fact their lending business expanded rapidly, both in absolute size, from £133 m. to £1,353 m., and as a share of their own deposits, from 64.6 to 81.6 per cent. However, they focused on non-UK resident customers, who accounted for more than three-quarters of their total advances in 1966.[36] In spite of the 'aggressive attitude which characterised the American methods' and the apparent leadership reached by London-based subsidiaries of American banks among the non-clearing UK banks, American competition was perceived as confined to specialized foreign business such as foreign exchange, commercial credit, and Eurobond underwriting. As a consequence clearing banks did not spot any serious threat to their core domestic business, and considered immediate action as unnecessary.[37]

Only in the late 1960s did the unprecedented aggressiveness of American banks and the scale of their multinationalization boost clearing banks' reaction. As a number of enquiries with treasurers of various American, British, and Continental large corporations revealed, American banks in fact enjoyed a number of competitive advantages that proved hard to counteract in the short term. Among these, reports mentioned more flexible conditions in service and loan business, since special concessions made in favour of US subsidiaries abroad were easily compensated by additional business from the parent concern in the USA. Due to their large overseas branch networks, they were able to assist corporate treasurers in a variety of critical functions, such as monitoring exchange market expectations, hedging against foreign exchange risk, operating centralized international cash management, conducting arbitrage operations, and circumventing national regulation.[38] They could also offer credit facilities in all countries where they maintained branches (sometimes based on counterpart funds—a service of primary importance especially in underdeveloped, deposit-starving countries), most efficient overseas money transfers, and any kind of advising services stemming from their international know-how.[39] Moreover, advanced communication technology allowed regular monitoring of cash balances, cash flow forecasts, and quick fund transfers, speedy collection of remittances and intra-firm mobilization of cash flows in different countries in order to convert quickly working funds into capital. These services substantially reduced multinationals' borrowing costs as they enabled them to allocate liquidity efficiently within their multinational network.[40] American multinational banks acted also in the Eurodollar market as prime takers and traders in the interbank market on behalf of their corporate customers, and provided innovative credit facilities, such as Eurodollar standby lines of credit, Eurodollar revolving commitments on a standardized consortial scheme, and multicurrency lines of credit.[41]

4. Clearers in Euro-Banking: From Expansion to Consolidation

As competition from 'big internationally minded American banks' gained momentum, clearing banks were eventually urged to expand Eurodollar activities and diversify towards international and merchant banking to meet the increasingly sophisticated financial needs of large corporate borrowers and to defend their customer base from competitive attacks of American banks.[42] The 1968 merger rush—which led to the creation of National Westminster Bank and the proposed merger between Barclays and Lloyds (eventually rejected by the Monopolies Commission), which aimed at creating a global bank potentially able to tackle successfully the American challenge—gave evidence that a process of rationalization and strategic refocusing had been set in motion.[43] In fact, clearing banks were also urged towards international banking by stagnating domestic business. During the 1960s their share of total market for both sterling deposits and advances was shrinking because of keener competition from non-bank financial intermediaries and parallel money markets.[44] Moreover, domestic banking was dominated by frequent credit squeezes and the imposition of quantitative ceilings on lending, as clearing banks were considered by the Bank of England instrumental to the implementation of its monetary policy.[45] Diversification towards international banking proved, therefore, not only a response to the American challenge, but also a major opportunity of growth.

Expanding international business implied entering the Eurodollar market and adopting liability management to an unprecedented extent. In order to do that, clearing banks had to find ways to circumvent regulatory constraints which put them at a structural disadvantage. As a matter of fact, they were prevented from substantially expanding their Eurodollar business by liquidity ratios, which hampered their ability to compete in bidding for funds.[46] Not by chance, while in 1958 their share in the London Eurodollar market was still over 22 per cent, it had rapidly shrunk to 4.5 per cent in the early 1960s and further declined to 1.9 per cent in 1971 (as shown above in Tables 5.1 and 5.2).[47] As a consequence, clearing banks had to conduct the greatest part of their Eurodollar business through subsidiaries (either totally or partially controlled)–such as BOLSA and Lloyds Europe, Barclays DCO and Barclays France, Westminster Foreign Bank, Midland and International Bank Ltd. (MAIBL). These could compete outside the banking cartel and were free of reserve requirement obligations.[48] For the same circumventive purpose, specialized 'back door' subsidiaries[49] were established to compete for wholesale sterling deposits in the domestic money markets and provide innovative sterling lending such as American-style term loans (from 6 months to 5–10 years) to finance special projects of corporate customers.[50] In fact, as a result of the increasing interpenetration between the UK and the international financial system in London, Eurodollar banking turned out to be an effective training for importing the new way of banking into domestic business as well.[51]

Increasingly operating as wholesalers, clearing banks proved able rapidly to develop a wide range of international business and diversify towards corporate and merchant banking. Commercial Eurodollar lending mostly took the form of term, sometimes syndicated loans on a roll-over basis, either with fixed maturity dates or with agreed repayment schedules. Clearing banks competed in such business not only through their international banking arms but also through the establishment of multipurpose consortium banks, mainly operating on a basis of geographical specialization and specifically aimed at counteracting competition from American banks in mid-term corporate lending to US and European multinationals.[52] The move towards Eurocorporate banking was also accompanied by a gradual expansion of international merchant banking activities, such as investment banking (Euro-securities) and other advice services (legal, fiscal, and financial structuring of international operations, project manager services, evaluation and negotiation of merger, acquisitions, and joint-ventures). As a consequence, the traditional demarcation lines and division of functions between clearing banks on the one hand, and both merchant banks and British overseas banks on the other, were substantially blurred.[53]

Eurodollar banking enabled clearing banks to expand their role in more traditional international banking business, such as export finance, where the competition with merchant banks proved increasingly keen. Since the early 1960s clearing banks provided UK exporters with a series of special schemes for fixed-rate medium- and long-term credit, covered by guarantees and refinancing facilities (in order to support bank liquidity) given by the Export Credits Guarantee Department (ECGD). In order to fill the gap in the availability of export finance, in 1965 short-term credit schemes (up to two years) were introduced, again under ECGD guarantees.[54] Part of such export credit, both short and medium term, was based on the Eurodollar, but again it turned out to be difficult for British banks to counteract alternative, more flexible methods of finance proposed by American banks in such fields.[55]

Regulation restrained the growth of clearers' Eurobusiness through the early 1970s. In 1971, however, deregulation brought about by Competition and Credit Control lifted all major constraints on parent banks and paved the way to organizational refocusing and profit consolidation. Clearers' corporate restructuring of international banking activities was subject to a variety of organizational patterns, although banks, assisted by external consultants (such as McKinsey in the case of National Westminster), generally opted for a divisional approach. Barclays, probably the British bank with the larger global branch network and service diversification, introduced a full divisional organization in 1972 by separating its operations into three main divisions. While domestic operations were put under the responsibility of Barclays Banks UK Management Ltd., overseas activities, traditionally carried out by Barclays DCO, were integrated into an International Banking Division and finally concentrated into Barclays Bank International, a separate bank responsible for all international operations (both UK and foreign located). Other diversified activities were co-ordinated and controlled by a Financial Services Division, subdivided into a series of individual operating companies. In Lloyds' case, a step towards a divisional organization was taken in 1971 through the merger of its international subsidiary, Lloyds Bank (Europe), with the Bank of London and South America (BOLSA), thus forming Lloyds and BOLSA International Bank (LBI). The latter was subsequently acquired by Lloyds in 1973 and transformed into the international arm of the Lloyds' group, largely focused on Latin America. However neither were overseas departments of Lloyds and LBI amalgamated, leaving to the parent bank direct control of expansion in the USA and New Zealand, nor were separate corporate banking departments created. Similarly, National Westminster implemented a multidivisional organization where each 'product' or 'geographical' division operated as a separate centre of profit. While NatWest's clearing bank operations were carried out by a Domestic Banking Division (responsible for the branch network on a rather decentralized decision-making structure), an International Banking Division was created and given responsibility for the growing international branch network and the group's interest in other multinational banking ventures—including its association with Chase Manhattan and other international banks in the Orion consortium venture.[56] NatWest's rapid growth, however, led to frequent restructuring, including the establishment of a Corporate Financial Services Unit to market the group's international services, especially to multinational corporations. Finally a Related Banking Service Division was held responsible for new financial services, conducted as a series of separate profit centres traded as a distinct subsidiary (County Bank for merchant banking, and the like). By doing so, Barclays, Lloyds, and NatWest clearly moved towards a universal-banking pattern.[57] On the other hand, Midland was slower to adjust its group-pattern and continued to operate more as a holding company. Major financial service subsidiaries continued to operate independently, and the bulk of the Eurodollar business remained concentrated in the parent bank's overseas branches,

while geographical specialization was attained through multiplying participation in specialized consortium banks and other international cooperative
ventures. Only in 1974 were the group's international operations eventually
brought under the control of an International Division and direct representation in major international banking centres was officially recognized as a basic
goal in order to promote Midland as a major international banking group.[58]

5. Catching Up: Clearers' Growth Performance

Was the clearing banks' response up to the American challenge? Were they
able to exploit all the growth potential of international banking business?
Did they meet successfully the American competition? Parent clearing banks
had traditionally performed a marginal role in the London Eurocurrency
market throughout the 1960s. However their position gradually recovered
after the 1971 reform. As shown in Fig. 5.3, since then the growth rate of their

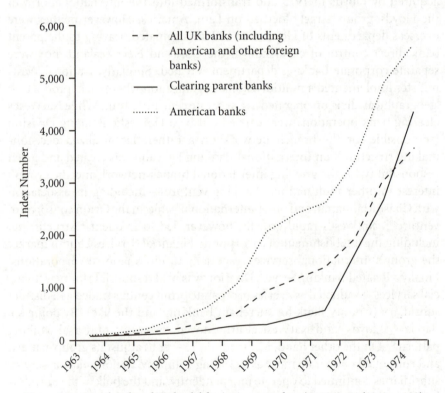

Figure 5.3. *Growth index of UK banks' foreign currency deposits, 1963–74 (1963 = 100)*
Source: *Bank of England Quarterly Bulletin*, various issues

international banking business eventually outpaced that of the UK banking system as a whole and caught up with US banks' performance.

In spite of such remarkable growth, clearing banks' market share as parent banks reached just 5 per cent by the mid-1970s (from less than 2% in 1971). This figure, however, represents a rather inaccurate benchmark of their actual standing. Table 5.2 above gives evidence that the role of clearers as banking groups—encompassing all international, wholesale, and merchant subsidiaries of clearing banks and included in 'other UK banks' and 'British overseas banks'[59]—was far more influential. As reported by the Committee of London Clearing Bankers in 1978, throughout the first half of the 1970s the foreign currency deposits of the London clearing bank groups rose in fact from 20 to 32 per cent of their total deposits. At the same time, their market share out of the total foreign currency deposits of all British banks reached 14.2 per cent, though afterwards it slightly declined to 13.1 per cent in 1976. This figure provides a far more realistic assessment of the extent to which clearing groups came rapidly to establish themselves as leaders among all British owned institutions in the Eurocurrency market.[60]

The quality of clearing banks' Eurocurrency market—on the basis of their Euro-liabilities' structure—also improved rapidly after 1971. As shown in Table 5.3, they proved able to reduce substantially their dependence on the interbank market (UK banks accounted just for 23.3% of the parent banks' total Eurocurrency liabilities in 1974, against 48.3% in 1969), thanks also to sizeable issues of Euro-CDs. Even more remarkably, such a result was attained in spite of the outstanding growth of their total liabilities as bank groups, which in 1976 were over £15,000 m. and almost equalled those of all other non-clearing UK banks (American and other overseas and foreign banks excluded). Likewise they proved quite successful in attracting funds from overseas residents (central and foreign banks, international financial institutions, industrial and commercial corporations). These accounted for nearly 60 per cent of the clearing parent banks' currency liabilities in 1974, compared with 26.4 per cent five years earlier—thus substantially reducing the gap with American and foreign banks. They were able also to retain the bulk of funds channelled towards the market by non-bank UK residents (British corporations and wealthy individuals). These played a marginal role because of binding UK exchange control restrictions, but continued to place their Eurodeposits with clearing banks rather than with other British or foreign banks.

As a matter of fact, however, British clearing banks proved unable to catch up with the process of internationalization of the British banking system as a whole. Currency advances of all UK banks grew up at a faster pace than domestic advances, to such an extent that they accounted for 52.3 per cent of

Table 5.3. *UK banks' gross deposits in foreign currency,*[a] *1969 and 1974*

	Currency deposits as % of total deposits		Total gross currency deposits (£ m.), of which vis-à-vis:		UK Banks		Other UK residents		Overseas residents		US$ CDs	
	1969	1974	1969	1974	1969	1974	1969	1974	1969	1974	1969	1974
Clearing banks	2.2	12.9	265	3,726	48.3	23.3	25.3	11.4	26.4	59.8	—	5.5
Other UK banks	48.3	40.2	1,212	4,584	43.6	46.1	2.3	1.4	54.1	48.2	—	4.3
Accepting houses	52.8	55.0	1,291	2,649	24.7	31.5	5.8	9.9	69.5	55.1	—	3.5
British overseas	66.1	76.9	2,763	11,081	24.1	23.7	2.3	4.7	73.6	62.2	—	9.4
American banks	92.9	85.9	9,059	24,671	24.3	18.2	2.3	3.6	73.4	67.0	—	11.2
Other foreign	80.4	92.8	2,215	18,698	18.2	23.2	1.0	1.2	80.8	71.3	—	4.3

Note:
[a] Including currencies of overseas sterling countries; end of year figures.

Source: Bank of England Quarterly Bulletin.

total advances in 1976 (only 24.4% in 1968). Likewise, advances to non-UK residents reached a peak in 1971 (44.6% of total advance from just 28.4% in 1968), although slightly declined afterwards to 39 per cent. In spite of the remarkable expansion of their international business in terms of both currency lending and advances to non-UK residents, clearing banks proved unable to keep up with such a trend. As shown in Table 5.4, when considered as banking groups (including both parent banks and their subsidiaries), at the mid-1970s, currency advances, though expanding, accounted for just 24.2 per cent of clearer groups' total advances. Advances to non-UK residents, though expanding, reached just 20.7 per cent. Moreover, the clearing banks' weight in the international business remained a long way behind their overall role in the UK banking system. While in 1976 their total advances (both in sterling and currency) accounted for 40.4 per cent of all UK banks' total advances—although after a period of continuous decline (they were at 62% in 1967)—their share of the currency lending market was 18.7 per cent, and 21.3 per cent was their share of total lending of the banking system to non-UK residents.

Therefore, in spite of a decade of outstanding expansion of their international business, at the mid-1970s clearing banks were still mainly nationally oriented institutions—a fact that sharply contrasted with the widespread ambitions of their managers to establish their banks' name as real international banking groups. This should be hardly surprising, however. Due to the nature of clearing banks, it was natural that the bulk of their business continued to be provided by UK residents and sterling lending, while international business was bound to prove essentially instrumental in defending their core customer base.

The bulk of the clearing bank Eurocurrency lending (over 50% of total) was in fact represented by interbank business. More than half the remainder was channelled towards UK residents, mainly corporate and financial institutions, in order to finance overseas capital and portfolio investments, working capital or acquisitions. A substantial portion was also lent to the public sector for domestic purpose (included participation in international syndicated loans to the Treasury). Lending to non-UK customers focused instead on advances to foreign corporations for normal commercial purposes, and on participation in syndicated loans to overseas borrowers, both corporate and (to an increasing extent after the crisis of 1973–4) sovereign. Eurocurrency banking was also instrumental in developing project finance business, a relevant part of which was related to financing North Sea oil and gas development by UK and American corporations, often on a syndicated basis together with American and other British or foreign banks. In 1977 London clearing bank groups and Scottish clearing banks were reported to account for more than 40 per cent

Table 5.4. *Foreign currency and non-resident advances of London clearing banks,*
1967–1976

	1967[a]	1970[a]	1973[b]	1976[b]
Clearers' total advances[c] to UK and non-UK residents (£ m.)	5,040	6,161	15,668	23,283
Clearers' market share of total advances to both UK and non-UK residents[d]	62.0	43.5	44.7	40.4
Clearers' market share of currency advances to both UK and non-UK residents[e]	n.a.	0.2	15.8	18.7
Clearers' market share of total advances to non-UK residents only[f]	25.5	16.1	21.5	21.3
Incidence of currency advances on clearers' total advances[c] to UK and non-UK residents	n.a.	0.2	14.4	24.2
Incidence of currency advances on clearers' total advances[c] to UK residents	—	0.1	7.2	15.9
Incidence of currency advances on clearers' total advances[c] to non-UK residents	n.a.	0.9	48.3	55.8
Incidence of non-UK residents on clearers' total advances[c]	7.9	15.5	17.5	20.7

Notes:
  [a] Only London clearing parent banks.
  [b] London clearing groups (parent banks and their subsidiaries).
  [c] Both in £ and foreign currency.
  [d] Clearers' advances (both in £ and foreign currency) as % of all UK banks' total advances.
  [e] Clearers' currency advances as % of all UK banks' total currency advances.
  [f] Clearers' advances (both in £ and foreign currency) to non-UK residents as % of all UK banks' total advances to non-UK residents.
  Source: *The London Clearing Banks* (see Table 5.2), 87–8.

of total facilities extended by banks to the North Sea project, with American banks accounting for 36 per cent.[61]

Competition and Credit Control also removed constraints on clearing banks' direct participation in the sterling wholesale deposit market to finance the outstandingly rapid expansion of their advances.[62] Subsequently, the proportion of wholesale deposits on total sterling deposits of clearing banks rose to 45 per cent in 1974–5. Clearing banks became able to bid successfully for new sources of funds, and sterling wholesale deposits largely replaced, and performed more effectively, the liquidity buffer function once fulfilled by call money placed by banks with the discount market. Likewise clearing banks, either directly or through their subsidiaries, began successfully to issue sterling CDs in October 1968. Such activity reached its peak during the lending boom of 1971–3, but a large part of sterling CDs issued (around 60% at mid-1970s) was held by other banks, to such an extent that the market in sterling CDs could be considered a mere extension of the interbank deposit market.[63]

In spite of such remarkable achievements, however, the ill-considered opinion that the competitive advantages enjoyed by American banks could be confined within the boundaries of US subsidiaries and international business proved eventually short-lived. From the early 1970s onwards, after the removal of restrictive credit ceilings, American banks became increasingly involved in the domestic lending market. Their lending techniques—based on the so-called 'going-concern approach' (focused on the borrower's ability to generate cash flow as the source of repayment), as opposed to a more traditional 'liquidation approach', focused on asset-based security—was considered a fundamental lever of their success with British companies.[64] Indeed, as early as 1966 they were reported to offer sterling mid-term loans at better conditions than British counterparts, sometimes by using Eurosterling transactions handled by their Paris-based branches.[65] As a matter of fact, dominance in Eurobusiness proved to American banks an effective launching-pad for the rapid conquest of substantial shares in domestic business in Britain. Throughout the 1960s the traditional dominance of the clearers cartelized oligopoly within the British banking system—under which lending and borrowing rates were collectively agreed and set in conventional relationship to Bank rate, and competition was carried out essentially on a non-price basis—began to fade. Exploiting the opportunities stemming from the absence of regulatory constraints on foreign uncartelized banks, Americans were able to parallel international banking with successful domestic business development, by expanding a sterling wholesale interbank market and lending business in short-term loans at market-determined rates.[66] In the long run therefore American banks succeeded in biting remarkably into the clearing banks' traditional domestic business, especially in large-volume lending, to such an extent that they were reported to account for some 20 per cent of all bank lending to UK manufacturing industry at the mid-1970s.[67]

6. International Profits: Clearing Laggards?

Were clearing banks able to compete with the Americans in terms of profit-making out of their international business? Here we are entering fairly hostile territory. Still at the end of the 1970s only the largest American banks were considered to have adopted highly sophisticated and profit-oriented information systems in order to evaluate performance indicators (such as the incremental return on capital or assets of loan transactions) and calculate the appropriate level of leverage, dividend pay-out, allocation of capital, loss reserves.[68] Whereas the American banks' senior international managers proved keen on publicly emphasizing dynamism, competition, and long-term profitability for stockholders as ultimate goals of their aggressive growth-oriented behaviour,

UK bankers (as much as their Continental counterparts) still preferred to emphasize the priority given to meet the requirements of their existing customer base.[69] Moreover, British banks were permitted to conceal their true profits in published accounts (thanks to a special dispensation under the Companies Act), and disclosure to the public arrived only in the late 1970s. However estimates available for major clearing banks as to the profitability of their international activities—broadly defined as the income stemming from a wide range of services offered through both their UK-based overseas branches and specialized subsidiaries and their foreign branches, subsidiaries, and affiliates—showed that their performance plodded way behind that of top multinational American banks. A study carried out in 1974 by the Stanford Research Institute on behalf of Midland Bank estimated international earnings of the four major parent clearing banks to average 23.5 per cent of total earnings after tax, against 36.8 per cent of six top US international banks.[70] Such figures are roughly consistent with those provided by the Committee of London Clearing Bankers, which in 1977 estimated international banking to have contributed 30 per cent of clearers' total profits in the first half of the decade, while 60 per cent had been derived from the mainstream domestic banking activities.[71] Profits earned by clearers from their international business therefore clearly failed to compete with the American performance.

Some authors incline to ascribe such results mainly to organizational and strategic uncertainties.[72] However these factors account for only a partial explanation. In fact the Stanford Report—whose findings are summarized in Table 5.5—gave evidence that, once compared to American banks with similar characteristics as to size, geographic coverage, and service diversification, clearing banks' profit performance did not look too shabby at all.

A more comprehensive explanation can be worked out in terms of structural features of Eurobanking, competitive advantages of American banks, and changing market conditions in the early 1970s. Eurobanking was a highly competitive business, with high product standardization and narrow spreads. As profits originating from interest differentials were narrow, they were extremely sensitive to marginal variations in spreads and influenced by slight differences in economies of scale (the global volume of funds intermediated) and operating, transaction, and organizational costs.[73] Profit performance therefore depended very much on fee-generating business.[74] Under all such respects, top-notch, technologically advanced American banks enjoyed a number of structural advantages. As primary Eurodollar takers and price makers, they could afford to bid for funds at lower rates than the rest of the participants in the market. This was reflected in the multi-tier structure of the market itself, which assigned different risk premiums to different kind of banks—with the biggest American banks as top-rankers, while British banks

Table 5.5. *Profits from international banking, 1973*

	Total assets (average) $ bn.	Net total profits[a]/ total assets (%)	International net profits[a] (% of total net profits)
Global banks[b]	39	0.47	37.8
Mid-size international banks[c]	20	0.63	21.0
Small-size international banks[d]	14	0.41	14.4
First National City Bank	44	0.57	60.0
Bank of America	49	0.45	32.0
Chase Manhattan	37	0.44	41.0
Manufacturers Hanover	20	0.49	33.0
Chemical Bank	19	0.35	35.0
Continental Illinois	17	0.50	20.0
Barclays (BBI)	31	0.73	26.0
National Westminster	28	0.83	17.0
Midland	19	0.77	21.0
Lloyds	18	0.85	30.0

Notes:

[a] Earnings after tax.

[b] Banks with total assets over $30 m., extensive overseas networks, global geographic coverage, and full-range service diversification,* First National City Bank, Bank of America, Chase Manhattan Bank, Barclays Banks International, Banque Nationale de Paris.

[c] Banks with total assets over $15 m., middle-size overseas networks, regional geographic coverage, and partial service diversification. National Westminster, Lloyds Bank, Midland Bank, Manufacturers Hanover, Chemical Bank, Continental Illinois.

[d] Banks with total assets under $15 m. (Fuji excluded), limited overseas networks, narrow geographic coverage, and low service diversification. Securities Pacific Bank, First National Bank of Boston, Fuji Bank, Commerzbank, Skandinavinska Enskilda Bank.

* Service diversification includes: banking services (international banking, foreign domestic banking); specialized banking services (factoring, finance, instalment credit, leasing, merchant, mortgage, real estate, ship, trust, other); non-banking services (travel, insurance, consulting, international credit card franchise).

Source: Stanford Research Institute, 'Managing the International Development of Banks. A Survey', November 1974 (unpublished), in Midland Bank Archives. Figures on international earnings officially reported by FNCB, Bank of America, Chase Manhattan, Manufacturers Hanover, and Barclays (BBI). For other banks, estimates by banks or Stanford Research Institute.

were ranked below together with other foreign banks and regional American banks.[75] As lenders, US banks' large customer base and global branch network generated an outstanding volume of business.[76] Their London-based branches also enjoyed a substantial advantage in syndicated Eurocurrency loans, as the strength of their balance sheets and the guarantee of credit lines from their US headquarters enabled them to take directly a large portion of their loans. They also invested large resources in developing securities functions and Eurobond primary placing and secondary trading power—a major competitive factor in

Eurobond business. They increasingly integrated Eurobond and Eurolending business, a fact that further strengthened their appeal on large corporate borrowers and enabled them to compete with Continental universal banks.

By contrast, British clearing banks, as Eurodeposit takers, were not only subject to narrower spreads on the average but also much more exposed to the potential risks of profit squeeze and liquidity gap.[77] They also had to espouse a prudential attitude not only as to liquidity and exchange risk, but also as to capital adequacy, refraining from expanding their business beyond unsound capital ratios.[78] Issuing Eurobonds and Euronotes to raise loan capital helped them overcome this problem only partially.[79] Moreover, British clearers proved pretty reluctant to embark on Eurobond underwriting. In fact, at the beginning of the 1970s only Lloyds (through its international banking arm) and Samuel Montagu (participated in by Midland) were ranked among the main managers and co-managers in the market. In fact, their placement power was severely harmed by UK exchange controls, which deterred potential UK-resident investors from participating in the Eurobond market by requiring them to use 'investment dollars', usually at a premium against sterling. Similarly, the potential corporate customer base of their Eurobond and Eurocredit business was to some extent reduced by regulatory constraints related to the chronic weakness of sterling. As British multinationals were forbidden to use sterling finance raised domestically in order to fund their investments abroad, foreign currency borrowing—generally through Euromarkets—represented the main source of financing for their overseas expansion: the expansion of UK multinationals in the USA was financed largely this way. On the other hand, however, British companies were reluctant to resort to Eurodollar borrowing, especially after 1971, because of the risk of seeing the benefits of lower international interest rates offset by adverse movements in the pound exchange rate to the dollar. At the mid-1970s British companies were in fact estimated to have lost £3 bn. because of foreign currency borrowing. This might partially explain why, even in giant companies such as Courtaulds, General Electric, ICI, and Unilever, long-term foreign currency borrowing was reported to account for no more than 10–20 per cent of their total long-term finance.[80] Moreover, UK corporations wishing to float Eurobond issues had to be authorized by the Bank of England. The latter used to apply no particular restrictions to funds raised to domestic investments. However, when the proceeds were to be used for overseas investments, the Bank required that the indebtedness was funded by foreign currency remittances to the UK; moreover, no repayments of principal were allowed during the first five years of the loan.[81]

On an overall basis, therefore, American banks enjoyed a dominant position based on strong market leadership, substantial cost advantages, and general dominance through their size. Changes of market conditions in the early 1970s made such advantages even more important. Since 1968, due to both increasing competition and evolving interest rate structure of the Euromarkets (higher and more volatile interest rates, increased maturity mismatching, keener competition), opportunities for banks to obtain significant returns without an equivalent degree of risk substantially decreased. A number of studies demonstrated that attempts to derive profits from mismatching based on mechanical rules, generally adopted in the early phase of the Euromarkets, ceased to produce any neutral or positive result from 1969 onwards. Rising interest rates or a loss of confidence in the viability of a bank's portfolio (leading to a premium to be paid over the normal rate in order to borrow funds) could then more easily force a bank to face a profit trimming. As a rule, therefore, the potential for mismatching to achieve profits required increasing expertise as banks moved into the 1970s. To cope with this change, banks had to develop a much more flexible and sophisticated approach to liability management. Quick access to inter-bank borrowing (or to other market-based deposits) and securitization or marketization of assets were to prove fundamental in order to reduce liquidity risk.[82] This suggests that structural factors and market conditions substantially reduced scope for profits in international banking not only for British clearing banks, but also for any banks with similar characteristics.

7. Conclusions

The 1973–4 financial turmoil[83] triggered the first serious crisis of confidence suffered by Euromarkets since their emergence. At that time British clearing banks' Eurobusiness was still in transition. In the early 1960s clearers had regarded Eurocurrency banking as a useful way to ease transitional liquidity restraints, and an additional tool for strengthening their traditional international business. In the second half of the decade they had seen it turned into a twofold phenomenon: a promising opportunity of growth and business development, paralleled by a totally unprecedented competitive threat. They had reacted to such challenge first by developing specialized arms in order to circumvent domestic regulation and enter the new business, subsequently— after deregulation brought about by Competition and Credit Control in 1971—by consolidating their expansion into more coherent organizational patterns. Commercial business was increasingly supplemented by diversification towards corporate banking and merchant services. The growth of their currency deposit base was remarkable since the early 1970s, to such an extent that clearing groups turned out to be the only British actors with a say in thriving Euromarkets. Their profit record was not a match with true global US banks, but it was in step with comparable competitors. In fact, British clearers seemed to have exploited extensively the scope for profits left to mid-size, non-US international banks, in the given structural and market conditions of the early 1970s.

The 1973–4 upheaval found clearing banks still halfway in their consolidation of international banking and forced them to reconsider their strategies and performances. The result was the decision to upgrade the challenge and devote their efforts to establish themselves as real global banking groups.[84] Their ambitions were soon reinforced by relaxation of international financial strains at the mid-1970s, which increasingly enabled them to shift business from the stagnating domestic field to international lending. However, in the mid-1970s Eurobanking was already moving along a path quite different from that of the past decade. New business opportunities were coupled with unprecedented foreign exchange risk. At the same time the corporate crisis of the mid-1970s and the enormously increased financial needs of governments and public institutions began to induce a rapid shift of international banking from corporate to country and sovereign lending, with widening maturity gaps and higher credit and political risks. Such ever-changing challenge, with its riskier and crisis-prone evolution, was to drag clearing groups far from the core strategy which originally motivated their expansion into Eurocurrency banking and bring a new, even harder challenge to their global ambitions.

NOTES

I am grateful to the Bank of England Archive and the HSBC Group Archive for granting access to their records, and particularly to Sarah Millard and Edwin Green for their help and assistance. I am also indebted to the participants in the Conference on European Banking and the American Challenge (organized by the Business History Unit at the LSE in March 1999), and in particular to Marcello De Cecco, Geoffrey Jones, and Dick Roberts for their valuable comments. Financial support for research from the Consiglio Nazionale delle Ricerche (CNR) and the British Council under a joint scheme is gratefully acknowledged.

1. The concept of 'international banking' includes a wide range of activities that might be classified according to different criteria (currency of denomination, residence of customer, location of bank). This chapter focuses essentially on wholesale transactions in time deposits denominated in dollars and booked by banks located outside the USA, and more specifically in Europe (Eurobanking). For a methodological discussion see R. Pecchioli, *The Internationalization of Banking* (Paris: OECD, 1983), 127–31; and R. Bryant, *International Financial Intermediation* (Washington, DC: The Brookings Institution, 1987), 6–18.

2. R. C. Bryant, 'Eurocurrency Banking: Alarmist Concerns and Genuine Issues', *OECD Economic Studies*, 1, (1983).

3. M. De Cecco, 'Inflation and Structural Change in the Euro-Dollar Market', in M. De Cecco and J. P. Fitoussi (eds.), *Monetary Theory and Economic Institutions* (London: Macmillan, 1987), 203.

4. G. Jones, *British Multinational Banking 1830–1990* (Oxford: Clarendon Press, 1993).

5. A seminal contribution is A. Woynilower, 'The Central Role of Credit Crunches in Recent Financial History', *Brookings Papers on Economic Activity*, 10 (1980), 2, 277–339. See also T. M. Podolski, *Financial Innovation and the Money Supply* (Oxford: Basil Blackwell, 1986), 129–30.

6. At the end of the 1950s the Bank of England began to pay systematic attention to the inflow of short-term funds and the rapid increase of non-official holding of foreign currencies as a potential source of expected variations of the sterling parity exchange. See Bank of England Archives, EID 3/335, draft by the Balance of Payments Office, 31 March 1959.

7. Bank of England Archives, EID 3/122, note from the Balance of Payments Office, 11 August 1960; and EID 10/19, note, 23 May 1961.

8. Bank of England Archives, C43/127, Kahn Report, 1 June 1966.

9. See P. Einzig, 'Dollar Deposits in London', *The Banker*, 110 (1960), 23–7 and O. L. Altman, 'Foreign Markets for Dollars, Sterling, and Other Currencies', *IMF Staff Papers*, 12 (1961), 4, 313–52. On BOLSA see R. Fry, 'Introduction', *A Banker's World: The Revival of the City 1957–1970. Speeches and Writings of Sir George Bolton* (London: Hutchinson, 1970), 32–7.

10. A. J. Meigs 'Recent Innovations in the Functions of Banks', *American Economic Review*, 56 (1966), 2, 167–77; G. W. Woodworth, *The Management of Cyclical Liquidity of Commercial Banks* (Boston: The Bankers Publishing Co., 1967); and F. Tamagna, 'Commercial Banking in Transition: From the Sixties to the Seventies', in International Banking Summer School, *Banking in a Changing World* (Rome: Associazione Bancaria Italiana, 1971), 39–58.

11. D. Hester, 'Innovations and Monetary Control', *Brookings Papers on Economic Activity*, 11 (1981), 1, 141–89.

12. For a general survey see J. Young, 'International Banking: The Background to Asset and Liability Management', in J. S. G. Wilson (ed.), *Managing Bank Assets and Liabilities* (London: Euromoney, 1988), 71–83.

13. The critical relevance of the 1966 credit crunch is stressed by Wojnilower, 'The Central Role'.

14. V. Argy and Z. Hodjera, 'Financial Integration and Interest Rate Linkage in Industrial Countries', *IMF Staff Papers*, 20 (1973), 1, 1–77 and R. C. Marston, 'American Monetary Policy and the Structure of the Euro-Dollar Market', *Princeton Studies in International Finance*, 34 (1974).

15. E. J. Kane, 'The Three Faces of Commercial Bank Liability Management', in M. P. Dooley, H. M. Kaufman, and R. E. Lombra (eds.), *The Political Economy of*

Policy-Making: Essays in Honor of Will E. Mason (Beverly Hills and London: Sage, 1979), 150–65.

16. A detailed outline of the 1966–70 events is provided by the Bank for International Settlements, *Annual Report*, 37 (1966–7), 138–46, and 40 (1969–70), 145–63.

17. Midland Bank Archives (located at Hong Kong Shanghai Banking Corporation Group Archives), Acc 206/2.6, Chemical Bank of New York, Economic Research Department, US Banking Developments, 'Euro-Dollar Float', 11 August 1969.

18. L. L. Kreicher, 'Eurodollar Arbitrage', Federal Reserve Bank of New York, *Quarterly Review*, 7 (1982), 2, 10–23.

19. A floating rate was determined as a fixed spread over the costs of funds in the market and adjusted every three or six months to prevailing short-term Eurodollar interbank rate (LIBOR). See P. Howard, 'Medium Term Lending: Lead Managers and Medium-Term Loans', *Euromoney*, 4 (1972), 1.

20. S. I. Davis, *The Euro-Bank: Its Origins, Management and Outlook* (London: Macmillan, 1981), 72–6, stressed that positive maturity mismatching was a natural consequence of long-term loan maturity. Therefore risk was higher for banks heavily depending on the interbank market as their main source of funds. On the same point, H. D. Gibson, *The Euro-Currency Markets, Domestic Financial Policy and International Instability* (London: Macmillan, 1989), 125–9, 142–59.

21. Insights in L. C. Nehrt, *International Finance for Multinational Business* (Scranton, Pa.: International Textbook, 1972), which included a number of contributions by American corporate treasurers.

22. See Richard Sylla's and Catherine Schenk's Chapters in the present volume.

23. A history of the market in I. Kerr, *A History of the Eurobond Market: The First 21 Years* (London: Euromoney, 1984); a concise outline in F. G. Fisher, *Eurobonds* (London: Euromoney, 1988), 5–15.

24. While US 'giants' regarded Eurobond financing as strictly related to their activity abroad, smaller companies tended to use a more substantial portion of their Eurobond borrowing in order to refund existing debts or finance working capital, often channelling part of the proceeds back to the USA.

25. W. Curran, *Banking and the Global System* (Cambridge, Mass.: Woodhead-Faulkner, 1979), 31–48. Curran was chairman of the First Chicago Investment Banking Group.

26. A broad picture of the American banks' activities in London is offered by J. Kelly, *Bankers and Borders: The Case of American Banks in Britain* (Cambridge, Mass.: Ballinger, 1977), 22–37.

27. This aspect has been emphasized by De Cecco, 'Inflation and Structural Change', 188.

28. See *The Economist*, International Banking Supplement, 15 November 1969.

29. A. R. Holmes and E. Green, *Midland: 150 Years of Banking Business* (London: Batsford, 1986), 252–3.

30. On Citibank, H. van B. Cleveland and T. F. Huertas, *Citibank 1812–1970* (Cambridge, Mass.: Harvard University Press, 1985), 258–71. On Chase

Manhattan, J. D. Wilson, *The Chase: The Chase Manhattan Bank, N.A. 1945–1985* (Boston: Harvard Business School Press, 1986), 172–84.

31. Midland Bank Archives, 200/291, Deutsche Bank Memorandum 'Aggressiveness of US Banks in Europe', 4 December 1964, MA 200/291. See ibid., 200/160, the discussions held at the EAC Meetings in Brussels, 28 September 1964, and London, 14 December 1964.

32. Midland Bank Archives, 200/190, EAC Meeting, Brussels, 14 March 1966 and 26 September 1966.

33. Jones, *British Multinational Banking*, 324. He quotes from the Monopolies Commission Report that rejected the Barclays-Lloyds merger in 1968: 'As a general rule companies operating overseas go to the bank which provides the cheapest and most efficient local service, including often a local branch network. In many countries these banks are indigenous banks, but even where they are British banks the companies are influenced by local conditions and not by their relationships with the parent banks in this country.'

34. Midland Bank Archives, 200/190, EBIC Foreign Managers' Meeting, Brussels, 10 July 1967.

35. Midland Bank Archives, 200/160, EAC Meeting, London, 14 December 1964.

36. This was considered also a natural result of the relatively small organization of their European branches, which made them unable to evaluate credit risks of medium and small companies.

37. Midland Bank Archives, 200/160, Midland Bank Memorandum 'US Banks in London', June 1965; and ibid., 200/215, Midland Bank Memorandum 'American Banks', March 1966. See also ibid., 200/291, The Committee of London Clearing Bankers, Minutes of the Meeting of Overseas Managers, 27 January 1966. During the sterling crisis of 1965, the Bank of England obliged all UK banks to limit their advances up to March 1966 to about 105% of the March 1965 figure.

38. R. M. Rodriguez, *Foreign Exchange Management in US Multinationals* (Lexington: Lexington Books, 1980), 16–32.

39. Midland Bank Archives, 200/190, EBIC Foreign Managers' Report, 'EBIC's International Policies with Special Reference to the Competition of American Banks', November 1967. Also ibid., 200/634, EAC Meeting, 11 March 1969.

40. H. Strasser, *Finance for Industry and Commerce* (London: Institute of Bankers, International Banking Summer School, 1973), 64–6. C. P. Lunn, *British Banks and International Trade* (London: Institute of Bankers, 1972) argued that US banks had developed extremely sophisticated technological systems of fund transfer, far more advanced than any other established by either British or Continental banks at that time. Lunn was deputy general manager at Barclays Bank International.

41. Committee to Review the Functioning of Financial Institutions (Wilson Committee), *Evidence on the Financing of Industry and Trade*, 8; 'Written Evidence by the American Banks Association in London' (London: HMSO, 1980), 49–51.

42. R. J. Clark, 'The Banking System: Changes in the Traditional Structure', in The Institute of Bankers, *British Banking: Changes and Challenges* (London: Institute of Bankers, 1968), 1–16. Clark was economic adviser at the Westminster Bank. See

also *The London Clearing Banks*, Evidence by the Committee of London Clearing Bankers to the Committee to Review the Functioning of Financial Institutions (Wilson Committee), November 1977 (London: Blades, East & Blades, 1978), 123.

43. Notably, together with rationalization of branch networks, the pooling of costly investments in computerization programmes was a major incentive to mergers. See Channon, *British Banking*, 42–4.

44. P. Einzig, *Parallel Money Markets* (London: Macmillan, 1971).

45. J. H. B. Tew, 'Monetary Policy-Part I', in F. T. Blackaby (ed.), *British Economic Policy 1960–1974. Demand Management* (Cambridge: Cambridge University Press, 1979), 237–57; M. Collins, *Money and Banking in the UK: A History* (London: Croom Helm, 1988), 456–87.

46. Clearing banks were obliged to hold additional sterling liquid assets of 28% of their currency deposits: *The London Clearing Banks*, 134.

47. Fresh evidence has been provided recently that Midland Bank had engaged in such business since 1955. See C. Schenk, 'The Origins of the Eurodollar Market in London: 1955–1963', *Explorations in Economic History*, 35 (1998), 224–9.

48. Jones, *British Multinational Banking* 262–72 and 322–7; Holmes and Green, *Midland*, 253–7.

49. An example of these was Midland Bank Finance Corporation, established in 1967: Holmes and Green, *Midland*, 240–1.

50. G. W. Taylor, 'New Techniques in British Banking: An Examination of the Sterling Money Market and the Principles of Term Lending', *Kings' College Gilbart Lectures* (London: 1973).

51. J. H. Forsyth, 'Financial Innovation in Britain', in M. De Cecco (ed.), *Changing Money: Financial Innovation in Developed Countries* (London: Basil Blackwell, 1987), 144–7, emphasizes the spill-over of new techniques and processes from international into domestic banking.

52. A new view in D. M. Ross, 'European Banking Clubs in the 1960s: A Flawed Strategy', *Business and Economic History*, 27 (1998), 353–66.

53. Channon, *British Banking*, 52–3; *The London Clearing Banks*, 27–8 and 187–8.

54. *The London Clearing Banks*, 129–33. Also W. J. Benson, 'The Role of the Banks in Exporting', in Institute of Bankers, *Banks and the British Exporter* (London: Institute of Bankers, 1977), 37–56.

55. Midland Bank Archives, 200/190, Minutes of the Seminar of the Committee on Foreign Trade Promotion and Development, London, 24 February 1966.

56. A history of the Orion venture in R. Roberts (with C. Arnander), *Take Your Partners: Orion, the Consortium Banks and the Transformation of the Euromarkets* (New York: Palgrave, 2000).

57. Advantages and disadvantages of universal and specialized banks are extensively debated; for a review, J. Canals, *Universal Banking: International Comparisons and Theoretical Perspective* (Oxford: Clarendon Press, 1997), 83–126.

58. On Midland, see Holmes and Green, *Midland*, 255–60, 286–98.

59. According to the Wilson Report, at the end of the 1970s the wholesale and merchant banking subsidiaries of London clearers accounted for about two-thirds

of the sterling and four-fifths of the foreign currency deposits of the 'other British banks' category. See Committee to Review the Functioning of Financial Institutions, 2/Appendices (London: HMSO, 1980), 414–15.

60. Indirect participation through consortium banks is not taken into account. All consortia accounted for a market share of 6% at the mid-1970s.

61. *The London Clearing Banks*, 134–8, 234–8.

62. C. J. Montgomery, *The Clearing Banks 1952–77: An Age of Progress* (London: Institute of Bankers, 1977).

63. Clark, 'The UK Financial', 145–6; Channon, *British Banking*, 52–3; *The London Clearing Banks*, 49–50, 273.

64. Committee to Review the Functioning of Financial Institutions (Wilson Committee), *Evidence on the Financing of Industry and Trade*, 8, 'Written Evidence', 26: 'The going-concern approach . . . recognises the medium term nature of much borrowing, aims to match this with appropriate lending terms, monitors progress, examines forecasts and identifies major deviations. This approach requires a close involvement with the borrower, and in order to predict cash flows (future events) the analyst must reconcile forecasts with historical patterns.' See also ibid., 53–4, the hearing of American bankers' representatives.

65. Midland Bank Archives, 200/291, Williamson to Graham, 3 February 1966. Later on in 1968 Citibank was reported to compete actively for deposits of UK residents.

66. J. S. Fforde, 'Competition, Innovation and Regulation in British Banking', *Bank of England Quarterly Bulletin*, 23 (1983), 363–5.

67. *The London Clearing Banks*, 77–8, 188, 213. The Report emphasized that competition in domestic lending business by American banks played a relevant role in the loss of market share in sterling advances suffered by clearing banks since the mid-1960s.

68. S. I. Davis, *The Management Function in International Banking* (London: Macmillan, 1979) enumerates a variety of means of measuring profit performance.

69. Davis, *The Management Function*, 40–5.

70. Midland Bank Archives, 200/756, Stanford Research Institute, 'Managing the International Development of Banks: A Survey', Draft Report, November 1974.

71. *The London Clearing Banks*, 166. This was in spite of the fact that international profits were reported to have grown regularly, while domestic ones had been subject to wide fluctuations.

72. Channon, *British Banking*, 60, who referred to clearing banks at the mid-1970s as 'over-bureaucratised' institutions far behind their rivals in corporate banking as to 'innovation and speed of decision making', and to their managers as 'narrow, conservative, and short of marketing skills'.

73. J. A. Frenkel and R. M. Levich (1975), 'Covered Interest Arbitrage: Unexploited Profits?', *Journal of Political Economy*, 83 (1975), 325–38, estimated that total transaction costs (including the bid–ask spread, the brokerage fee in the interbank market, and the cost of foreign exchange transactions) accounted for 0.15% or less for each transaction.

74. In the case of syndicated Eurocurrency loans, a management fee to the managing banks, plus participation and commitment fees to participating banks to cover the cost of undrawn funds could be charged on borrowers.
75. C. R. Weston, *Domestic and Multinational Banking* (London: Croom-Helm, 1980), 308.
76. Special concessions were usually made in favour of US subsidiaries or branches abroad that were expected to be compensated by additional business from the parent company in the USA.
77. On techniques to minimize liquidity risk, Davis, *The Management Function*, 84–5.
78. Moreover, since their equity was sterling-denominated, the declining value of the British currency in the early 1970s advised them to keep under tight control the expansion of foreign currency deposits.
79. *The London Clearing Banks*, 138.
80. J. M. Samuels, R. E. V. Groves, and C. S. Goddard, *Company Finance in Europe* (London: Institute of Chartered Accountants, 1975), 238–50; W. A. Thomas, *The Finance of British Industry 1918–1976* (London: Methuen, 1978), 321–3; K. Midgley and R. G. Burns, *Business Finance and the Capital Market* (London, 1979), 106–9.
81. In order to avoid such regulation, together with UK taxes and stamp duties and stricter prospectus rules, a number of UK companies established foreign wholly-owned subsidiaries for the purpose of making the Eurobond issue on the security of the parent company's guarantee. As a response, the Bank of England imposed conditions on such borrowing to the effect that, if the UK company was called upon to make payment under this guarantee during the first 5 years after the issue of the loan, the guarantor would be required to fund his obligation with investment currency or by other foreign borrowings or with the proceeds of the sale of other foreign investments.
82. Weston, *Domestic and Multinational Banking*, 318.
83. Beyond the collapse of the fixed exchange system and the oil shock, international banking suffered a strong setback after the failures of Franklyn National Bank in the USA and Herstatt Bank in West Germany and the emergence of the UK secondary banking crisis.
84. Jones, *British Multinational Banking*, 333–5.

6

Clubs and Consortia: European Banking Groups as Strategic Alliances

DUNCAN M. ROSS

European cooperation in the international banking market can be dated to the confluence of two crucial factors in the 1960s. The first of these is the challenge that American banks began to set their European counterparts from the early part of that decade. By following US-based multinational companies to Europe, and by competing aggressively with the European banks only not for American business, but also for the business of European multinationals, they were seen as predators in what had hitherto been a relatively peaceful and protected set of domestic markets. The European banks considered the incursions—or, more specifically, the tactics—of the Americans to be hardly ethical and they set about trying to find a way of combating this. Ongoing European integration represented the second explanatory factor for the development of international cooperation. Harmonization of regulations and the creation of a single European market for the provision of banking services were seen as important elements of the process of political and monetary convergence. Large banks in each of the main European countries, therefore, began to think about how they could best supplement the services and products that they offered, partly in order to combat the growing American presence, partly to take advantage of the opportunities afforded by, and to play a role in shaping, what they saw as an emerging *Europe bancaire*. In an earlier paper,[1] I suggested that there was a third main explanation for the choice of a cooperative strategy; that, greatly constrained by their own resources of time and expertise, as well as by the regulatory barriers to entry that existed in the various domestic European markets in the 1960s, it was the only option available. This chapter makes use of the concept of strategic alliance to explore these cooperative relationships, and suggests that the subsequent history of the institutions established can be explained by reference to the managerial commitment and focus with which they were provided at the outset.

From the late 1960s until the mid-1970s, the growth of cooperation by European banks took two distinct but related forms. Consortium banks and banking clubs were both means by which groups of institutions sought to develop their international presence in consort with other banks. The more common of the two approaches was consortia. Defined as 'a joint venture bank separately incorporated and owned by two or more shareholders who are banks themselves and usually of different nationalities', by 1971 35 of the world's 50 largest banks had participated in establishing a consortium, and by 1974 there were 29 based in London, with well over 100 shareholders.[2] Other European banks were established and based in Brussels, Luxembourg, Zurich, and Paris, while the emerging Pacific economy—notably Australia—hosted an important group.[3] The main business of the consortia was the provision of medium- and long-term funding in specific regional locations or industrial sectors; Euromarket flotation became their chief arena of expertise. Banking clubs, by contrast, were less numerous and more broadly focused. They represented coalitions of large commercial banks, which were designed to extend the services of their members throughout Western Europe without the need for direct representation. They can be seen as early attempts to integrate banking across borders, and some of their members certainly perceived the process as being the creation of fully integrated European banking institutions. The first of these was formed in 1959, and was made public in 1963. The four groups that existed a decade later—Associated Banks of Europe Corporation (ABECOR), Europartners, European Banks International Company, and Inter-Alpha—each included some of the largest commercial banks in Europe.[4]

1. Strategic Alliances

One recent application of strategic alliance literature to bank behaviour suggests that they can in general be understood as a class of joint venture.[5] Jacobsen and Tschoegl cite Kogut's analysis of the motivations for engaging in joint ventures, which stresses three possibilities: reduction of transaction costs, strategic and competitive positioning, and the opportunity to engage in organizational learning.[6] Similarly, Doz and Hamel identify three 'fundamental imperatives' in the construction of strategic alliances. These are the gaining of competitive capabilities through co-option from partners, the leveraging of co-specialized resources, and the gaining of competence through internalized learning.[7] The similarities are clear. Both approaches indicate that firms seek to take advantage of opportunities or develop resources in a way that would be difficult or expensive operating individually. Doz and Hamel argue, however, that alliances differ from traditional joint ventures in a number of ways.[8] Together, these differences reflect the greater fluidity and uncertainty of alliances—the notion that they are evolving or transitional organizational forms, and that their success should be measured not necessarily in longevity of the institutional arrangement, but in how the initial partners transform their competitive position. The process of competitive collaboration is one in which a range of partners engage with a view to achieving particular strategic or competitive goals. These strategic goals are optimally shared by all the partners, but beyond the current scope of any of them individually. Such goals might be the achievement of competence in a particular technology, access to a range of markets or a customer base, the enhancement of learning capabilities, or gaining economies of scale or scope without full merger or acquisition.[9]

Alliances can take both defensive and offensive forms. Among explanations for the latter, the literature stresses positive strategic goals such as gaining access to markets, setting industry standards in a new market, competitive or technical environment, or anticipation of political changes.[10] Defensive alliances are often characterized by avoidance of investment and reduction of risk—that is, the capabilities could be produced internally, but only with significant costs, either of money or time. These capabilities may relate to the acquisition of a new and expensive technology or to the achievement of economies of scale or scope by gaining access to the production processes or capabilities of partners.[11] These forms (representing a co-option strategy in Doz and Hamel's terminology) may be particularly prevalent where alliances are constructed on a bilateral model derived from joint ventures. This tactical element, however, allows us to understand that alliances may be seen as a temporary solution to a pressing competitive difficulty, but should not disguise the fact that the eventual outcome will be determined by the abilities of the partners—individually or in concert—to exploit the synergies represented by the alliance itself.[12] The role of uncertainty is the crucial element in understanding the move towards the construction of cooperation. Urban and Vendemini note that 'co-operation is the new way of adapting to the uncertainties of the market economy', and describe three constant features: cooperation gives firms more time to adjust to instability, it reduces the risks involved in managing new processes or introducing new products, and it accelerates the acquisition of skills, technology, or expertise.[13] By stressing these issues, of course, there is the realization that, largely because of the increased pace of innovation, individual firms are no longer able quickly to internalize and extract first-mover advantages from many specific functions.[14]

Organizational learning has been identified as one of the key incentives to engage in alliances. Mody has stressed that an alliance may have higher short-term transaction costs than a full merger or hierarchy based mainly on the *ad hoc* nature of the organizational architecture and the need to guard against opportunism on the part of one or all of the partners.[15] These managerial challenges, however, should force participants to improve their communicating and bargaining procedures: they need to learn to work together and to trust each other if the strategic goals are to be realized, 'learning is thus at the heart of successful alliances'.[16] Since the architecture of the alliance must reflect this commitment to learning, those that seek to build networks of trust and that place great importance on flexibility and the evolution of the relationship are those that are most likely to have successful outcomes. Flexibility and learning fit together because alliances allow a measure of strategic experimentation.

There is, then, a series of benchmarks against which it may be possible to measure the clubs and consortia as strategic alliances. Jacobsen and Tschoegl suggest that their Nordic banking consortia are best understood in terms of a strategic motivations approach and they note the conclusion of Marois and Abdessemed that 'learning cannot be seen as a motivation for international alliances in the banking sector'.[17] They also, however, note the approach of Johanson and Vahlne, in which learning can be achieved in incremental steps, and in which the evolution of the alliance may ultimately lead to its demise.[18] This last observation is of course more in the spirit of alliances as fluid, flexible, and disposable organizational innovations. Again, longevity is not necessarily an indication of a successful alliance. Development or transformation of the competitive capabilities of one or all of the partners is usually seen as the appropriate indicator.

2. The Origins of Consortia and Clubs

The first consortium bank of the period was formed by Midland Bank and its partners the Toronto Dominion, the Commercial Bank of Australia, and the Standard Bank of New York. Created in 1964, the consortium was universally known as MAIBL (Midland and International Banks Ltd.). The reasons for its founding are well known. The Midland had for some time been dissatisfied with its own ability to react to the requests for international financing that it had been receiving, and was seeking some way of responding to this new business.[19] Geoffrey Jones has used the term 'administrative heritage' to identify the managerial and competitive inertia that suffused the large British banks in this period.[20] Hampered by market segmentation and the strict demarcation of domestic and international banking activities, they tended to rely on their long-established networks of correspondent relationships to undertake international business. In doing so, suggested Pringle, 'British banks' international performance lagged sadly behind their potential. The period, which can be dated roughly from 1955 to 1965, when British banks might perhaps have scooped the pool, i.e. after the U.S. corporations had begun to move overseas but before their banks followed them, was allowed to slip by'.[21]

The Commonwealth-based cooperation of MAIBL was one of two strategic moves in what the Midland directors referred to as their 'Grand Design' for developing an international presence.[22] The other important move was to join the first of the European banking clubs. Founded in 1959, the original members of the *club des celibataires* (Banque de la Société Générale de Belgique SA, Deutsche Bank, and Amsterdamsche Bank NV) had sought to establish institutional links so that they could monitor and be prepared to respond to the ongoing process of 'economic and perhaps also political integration of Europe'.[23] The Midland, conscious of banking developments in Europe such as the merchant bank dominated Eurosyndicat, and explicitly linked to the UK's application to join the Common Market in 1961, decided to include a European dimension in their 'Grand Design'.[24] It was agreed to open negotiations with the Deutsche Bank and in 1963 the Midland joined the *club des celibataires*, or the European Advisory Committee, as it was henceforth to be known.

The differences between the clubs and the consortia are well illustrated in the differences that the Midland recognized in its two-pronged approach to international banking. The MAIBL consortium was explicitly conceived as a joint venture in which the rights and responsibilities of each participant would be reflected in their shareholding. The 'separateness' of the new bank was established and recognized by each of the shareholder-partners, and this was to be a general feature of consortia. This individual and legal identity that the consortia had, therefore, allowed them to develop their own strategies and management focus in a more independent format than was possible, or even envisioned, for the clubs:

it is important to draw the distinction between the loose nature of the relationships in this European club which calls for no investment of capital and at the outset would be little more than image forming, and the more concrete form of association which is being contemplated between the English speaking banks, the latter involving as it would not only the willingness to take part in approved joint ventures but also the investment of sizeable funds.[25]

It was, of course, the clubs that represented attempts to exploit much grander and more extensive organizational synergies. The *Banker* distinguished them by describing the consortia as 'a rather loose relationship between banks formalized only to the extent necessary to conduct a specific type of business transaction, usually by the establishment of a joint venture which is then granted a considerable degree of operational autonomy'.[26]

It is clear, however, that joining with other European banks—in a club or a consortium—represented a safety-first approach to the development of an international banking presence.

There are three main explanations for the emergence of the clubs, however, at least one of which should be interpreted as a positive or offensive move. It was noted above that the original founders of the *club des celibataires* sought to participate in the emerging European project. The joining of Midland was publicly announced in 1963, and the club was justified on the grounds that 'impending European integration was seen as a fact'.[27] The Europartners Group explicitly saw the creation of a European bank as its goal. It described itself as a 'quasi merger' between the Banco di Roma, the Commerzbank, and the Crédit Lyonnais. This was generally understood to be the most tightly organized of the banking groups, and it sought to take the lead in developing an integrated European institution. The members even went so far as to sign their alliance in Rome, symbolically to invoke the Treaty of Rome itself.[28]

In participating in the European project in this way, the banking clubs sought to establish a position from which they could provide an integrated suite of banking services to multinational corporations operating on the Continent. By doing so, they had to face the challenge of American competition. A number of factors contributed: larger and more sophisticated demands on international financing in the 1950s and 1960s often exceeded the capacity and skills of individual banks, and the European institutions had to respond quickly in order to compete with the American banks that had developed many of the required skills in their domestic markets. One of the directors of the EAC group noted that, faced with the onslaught of American competition in this market, 'time is running out for European banks'.[29] An alliance was, therefore, a sensible response; 'by co-operating together, a group of European banks, each with extensive networks in their own countries, would be able to offer a *superior* European service to their customers'.[30] (emphasis in original).

3. Clubs and Consortia as Strategic Alliances

Both these forms of alliance recognized that there were synergies to be gained from cooperating with counterpart banks in other countries and that, by doing so, the participants would be able to take steps towards establishing an international position without the enormous investment that such a strategy would have required were it to be independently pursued. This is precisely the kind of situation in which a strategic alliance is a sensible managerial choice. Ohmae stresses the role of fixed costs in forcing companies to seek partners when developing new markets,[31] while Dunning, by extending his eclectic approach to the organization of multinational activity to include strategic alliances, brings transaction costs to the forefront of discussion.[32] Cost and, therefore, risk reduction is a powerful incentive to explore the possibilities offered by strategic alliances. Hamel, Doz, and Prahalad point out, however, that, if used as a means of avoiding investment, rather than appraising opportunities, alliances are unlikely to be successful.[33] Both consortia and clubs, therefore, can be understood as defensive responses to a changing competitive environment. They sought to minimize the expense and exposure to risk involved in developing an international presence in a variety of banking markets. But positive elements can also be discerned. MAIBL and the other consortia were formed essentially to take advantage of the medium- and long-term financing opportunities in the developing Euromarkets. Park and Zwick note that participation in consortia was the only way that many of the smaller banks could gain entry to the growing Eurocurrency business of the late 1960s, and that 'banks of all types combined their resources to form consortia to exploit international lending opportunities for their domestic or foreign clientele'.[34] New market penetration, it has been noted above, is an offensive strategy, and the uncertainty of international lending in this period, as well as the greatly enhanced demands for liquidity of multinational business made alliances a sensible—and in some cases, the only—choice. Consortia were also able to bring together a wide range of expertise and experience from different financial and regulatory settings. Weismuller describes the 'catalytic effect of a subsidiary able to develop its own expertise in certain specialized fields that were not open to the direct action of the parent'.[35] The appendix to his paper is revealing in that, of the 28 consortia listed, some have as many as 10 shareholders, with the average number being in excess of five. Organizational learning was clearly an important aspect of the incentives for what was in many cases a highly disparate group to join together. Lorange and Roos, in offering a definition of a consortium strategic alliance, note that the business of the consortium tends to be core to each of the partners, and that the resources generated will flow back to them, thus improving individual competitive performance.[36] On the other hand, but not necessarily in contradiction to this, it has been noted that alliances themselves will be more successful if the precise activities undertaken do not duplicate those of any of the individual partners. In such a situation, the potential for conflict is too great. Charles Ganoe predicted the failure of many of the consortia, based on these 'built-in weaknesses'.[37]

Despite affording considerable opportunities for organizational lending, the disparate nature of the partners in many cases would be considered an obstacle to successful interaction and communication in the subsidiary company. The degree of proximity among the partners is seen as a crucial determinant of the outcome of the process, with heterogeneity a source of tension.[38] The key issue, however, is not necessarily the range of activities undertaken by the individual partners, but the strategic focus of the subsidiary and the extent to which their complementarities contribute to its achievement. In this, by having a relatively clear idea of what they were designed to achieve, the proximity of the partners, and the synergies which they were able to exploit, were thought to be sources of considerable strength for the consortia.[39]

There were, then, offensive and defensive elements in the creation of both the clubs and the consortia. In both cases, the strategy of alliance-forming was seen as a way of anticipating or adapting to changing political and market circumstances. Alliances offered the opportunity of responding to these changed circumstances in a way that limited their exposure to fixed and transactions costs and which offered the opportunity to learn new skills while exploiting the synergistic benefits of working with a wide range of institutions. The consortia became established as individual and separate institutions, but the clubs were more nebulous. As a defensive response to market penetration from their competitors, and with a much broader but less clearly defined strategic goal, the clubs could be expected to achieve less success than the consortia; 'a successful co-operative effort presupposes, in the first place, that the aims of the operation to be undertaken have been clearly defined and unambiguously formulated'.[40]

4. The Construction of Cooperation: The Case of Barclays

It is clear that the advent of European integration and the new market for medium- and long-term lending brought a fundamental shift to the European banking market. There were a number of elements in this shift, which in turn dictated the banks' responses:

- Their domestic markets were cartelized, protected, and static. International competition offered an opportunity to revitalize their income streams without breaking their domestic cartel agreements.
- There emerged a new pan-European customer, which wanted a new pan-European service, the multinational corporation. The logic of transaction costs implies that this customer preferred to deal with one bank rather than many across the entire Continent.
- The variety of regulatory structures across Europe meant that banks domiciled in particular countries were unable to undertake particular activities. By engaging in cross-border alliances, a superstructure of

universal banking provision could be created, without violating the domestic regulatory strictures.

- The changing regulatory and market structure in Europe offered opportunities but brought considerable uncertainty. Construction of alliances was the best way of attenuating the risks attached to such uncertainty.

It is clear that each of these played a part in the emergence of the cooperative spirit in European banking in this period. The differences between the consortia and the clubs need to be addressed in this light, therefore. In particular, we need to focus on the relationships between what the banks saw as the competitive opportunities and the particular form of strategic response. Assessment of the extent to which these can be considered 'successful' can then be undertaken.

Barclays' overseas representation was long-established and successful. Trading as an independent bank, Barclays Bank Dominion, Colonial, and Overseas (DCO) operated primarily in the Caribbean, Latin America, and Africa. This was a British overseas bank of the classic type; it conducted no business in Britain or Europe, and concentrated on commercial banking in its established regions. In 1959 Barclays decided to appoint an advisory committee to consider the implications and possibilities of European and overseas business. As a result of their deliberations, a European representative of the bank was installed in Zurich in 1961, 'to enable the bank to be kept well informed on business developments in Europe'.[41] In contrast to the Midland Bank, Barclays had no Grand Design for its international strategy, preferring instead to rely on cautious pragmatism and a refusal to rule out any good opportunities for potential profit. A number of issues quickly arose which, taken together, reveal Barclays' attitude towards the construction of alliances, to the position of Europe as a strategic opportunity for the extension of its international business, and to competition from American banks.

Emerging Europeanization was first signalled to Barclays in 1962, when the Banque de Bruxelles launched a take-over of the Banque de Commerce of Antwerp, in which Barclays held close to a 50 per cent stake. In preparing the ground for this take-over, the directors of the Banque de Bruxelles indicated to Barclays that they wished to be involved in a European venture, and would greatly value the latter's participation, 'whether Britain joined the common market or not'.[42] The *Financial Times* heralded this move as a 'useful expansion in the European business of Barclays Bank . . . the chief reason for the deal is the need by Barclays for larger facilities to handle the increased business now being done with Europe'.[43] This relationship came under serious strain a few years later, however, when Chase Manhattan Bank acquired 'a substantial interest' in the Banque de Commerce. In February 1966, it was clear that the Banque de Commerce 'was to become little more than a branch of the Chase Manhattan

Bank' and that, in this circumstance, Barclays would be unable to maintain its relationship; 'Barclays Bank Ltd would in future regard itself as having a close association in Belgium with Banque de Bruxelles but not with Banque de Commerce'.[44] The fragility of the old correspondent and relationship banking arrangements were coming under serious threat from American competition, but Barclays' attitude towards Europe remained ambivalent.

A second development revealed a similar story. Towards the end of 1962 Barclays were sought out by the merchant banking firm of Samuel Montagu, who were keen to explore the possibilities offered by the British application to join the Common Market. It was the view of Montagu that 'institutions in the City would have to prepare themselves to offer the financial services and facilities which would be needed, and that a number of associations would be bound to arise'.[45] Their proposal was to establish a consortium involving a merchant bank, an insurance company, and a major commercial bank, which, together, 'could offer practically every kind of service' to both British and European companies. This proposal fits well with the typology of incentives outlined above; it was designed to help the British commercial bank develop a series of activities more in line with European banking practice of undertaking investment, new issue, and broking business, while at the same time offering an opportunity to the insurance company, which sought to 'extend its business to Europe, for which it is prepared to put up a fair amount of long term money'. It lacked, however, the necessary introductions and contacts.[46]

Barclays took a sceptical view of the opportunities outlined by Montagu, and eventually refused to participate. Essentially, their international strategy had not yet evolved as far as that of Montagu, or beyond their traditional activities. The role of DCO remained powerful within the Barclays Group, and they could not decide whether to maintain correspondent relationships with other major banks in Europe (in which case they saw no harm in developing a servicing company) or whether they should develop 'best friends or even sole friends' in some European countries. In the latter case, they saw no room for the consortium proposal. The view of the bank was that they needed complete freedom of action 'while things [in Europe] develop'.[47] Two years later, things in Europe still had not developed sufficiently to interest the bank. Their response to the announcement of Midland's participation in the European Advisory Committee was not to take any initiatives, but to 'maintain such relationships with its European correspondents as would make them feel free to suggest to the Bank the setting up of such an association'.[48] In June 1966, the Bank's foreign committee noted the increased business in Europe since the appointment of the bank's representative in Zurich, and considered a number of possible additional locations. Beirut was considered to have the best claim.[49]

Barclays' international strategy was, therefore, rooted in its traditional approach of representatives and correspondents. It had been made aware of the American challenge, but was not sufficiently committed to the idea of European expansion to feel a strong need to do anything about it. A third development—their involvement in a consortium based in Switzerland— was to force the bank to change these attitudes. The bank became aware in February 1965 that there was a company based in Switzerland with approximately £100 m. available for investment.[50] Barclays' initial reaction was to attempt to secure some of these funds on deposit with their subsidiary in South Africa and they entered into negotiations with Mr Saager, of the Union Bank of Switzerland, who was managing the transaction, with this goal. Saager had approached a number of European banks—including the Banca Commerciale Italiana, the Banque de Bruxelles, Crédit Lyonnais, and the Dresdner—to determine their interest in creating a European financing company, whose primary purpose would be the 'granting of first rate middle- and long-term credits . . . for the most part in Western Europe'. The goal of creating a 'truly European financial policy' was explicit.[51] For this reason, the participation of any American banks—the idea of involving the Chase Manhattan had been raised—was ruled out,[52] but Barclays continued to negotiate on two fronts; one regarding their own involvement in the consortium, and one in which they tried to persuade the group to place a large deposit with DCO in Johannesburg. Their functional, as well as administrative, inheritance appears to have played a significant part in shaping their responses to the idea of European cooperation.

By the end of 1965, Barclays' thinking in this matter had evolved somewhat. It had become clear that there was to be no deposit for or participation by their South African subsidiary, and they had begun to stress the positive aspects of engaging with European partners. Two elements, in particular, carried weight; it was clear that participation would allow Barclays to extend their services to their customers and offer direct access to the European capital market. Secondly, they took the view that 'Britain and Europe are bound to come closer together some time or other', and it was prudent, therefore, to begin to develop the 'best friends' strategy noted above.[53] The position of UBS had also clarified; they were creating a separate and independent 'European *banque d'affaires* dealing in medium and long term finance', with a number of shareholders, all of whom were banks. In doing so, they 'could have travelled alone but they subordinate selfish views to the conception of a European cooperation'.[54]

These ultimately fruitless negotiations displayed many of the classic features of consortium activity. They also played an important role in focusing the attention of Barclays' management on Europe and the possibility of cooperation as a way of developing new markets and new business. By the time they engaged in a successful consortium, these issues were much less difficult for the bank to face. The Société Financière Européenne (SFE) was incorporated in April 1967 as a consortium of six major banks: Algemene Bank Nederland, Banca Nazionale del Lavoro, Bank of America, Banque Nationale de Paris, Barclays Bank Ltd., and the Dresdner Bank. It existed to finance investments by multinational companies in Europe, as 'the process of European integration is under way and is irreversible'.[55] The bank dealt mainly in the Euromarkets and in its first year lent 136m. francs. Barclays introduced eight propositions to the bank in this period, all of which were taken up.[56] The SFE was a typical consortium bank; it had a range of bank shareholders (including an American bank), it had legal autonomy and it undertook a fairly well-specified range of tasks, mostly long- and medium-term financing in the Euromarkets, which were of course a rapidly expanding source of business in the early 1970s.

The evolution of Barclays' cooperative endeavours underlines three important points. First, it is clear that they were reluctant to participate in the new European banking market until there was no viable alternative. In this sense, their history and traditions as a great British overseas bank hampered their ability to detect important shifts in the market. Second, their participation in strategic alliances, although reluctant, reflected some of the standard incentives. They sought to engage in the new market by co-opting some of the skills and capabilities of their partners, and they were aware that in European customer service terms, the sum of the various contributions to the SFE were very much greater than the parts. Third, the SFE, as a consortium bank, benefited from the operational independence granted by its shareholders.

5. Successful Alliances: The Consortia

The Bank of England began to report on the activity of the consortia in March 1972, and the heyday of their Eurocurrency operations was in the mid-1970s.[57] In September 1973—the high point—consortia accounted for 8.2 per cent of all non-sterling claims held by banks in London. Weismuller points out that this is an underestimate, since it excludes in-house funding— loans subscribed by the consortium and then either partly or wholly passed on to its shareholders.[58] It also, of course, excludes activities of consortia outside London. Nevertheless, a comparison with the American banks, who held 39.2 per cent of claims at the same time, provides some context. Analysis of

Table 6.1. *Percentage share of various maturity categories held by consortia, 1971–1979*

	<8 days	8 days –1 month	1–3 months	3–6 months	6–12 months	12–36 months	>36 months
Oct. 1971	3.61	3.48	1.98	3.58	5.36	15.20	18.54
Oct. 1972	4.10	3.98	3.59	3.07	5.45	17.16	18.18
Sept. 1973	7.85	6.88	6.33	6.05	7.31	20.24	20.35
Nov. 1974	5.86	4.38	4.38	4.38	7.68	16.48	14.29
Nov. 1975	4.57	4.91	4.16	3.17	5.61	11.51	10.53
Nov. 1976	4.56	4.69	4.69	4.57	5.99	11.14	10.88
Nov. 1977	4.25	4.87	4.58	3.89	7.07	12.27	10.08
Nov. 1978	4.33	4.38	4.82	4.22	5.71	13.44	9.36
Nov. 1979	4.34	4.41	3.50	3.86	5.58	13.69	9.92

Source: Bank of England Quarterly Bulletin, various issues.

maturity holdings reveals the specialism of the consortia clearly to have been in medium- and longer-term funding. Table 6.1 shows the percentage share of each maturity category accounted for by consortium banks. It shows that the consortia managed to achieve considerable penetration in their target market, at the longer end of the maturity spectrum, where they were able to gain as much as 20 per cent of the total business in 1973. This was the high point of their activity, however, and their role in medium- and long-term funding began to fall off in the rest of the decade. There are a number of explanations for this decline. The crisis of 1974 raised the spectre of insufficient capitalization and inadequately protected loan portfolios. Many consortia suffered losses in the crisis, and had to issue 'comfort letters' to the Bank of England, in which their shareholders promised to provide financial support in the event of failure.[59] This clearly undermined their independence to some extent, and many shareholders began to reappraise their consortium involvement. This was particularly so as financial innovation in the Euromarkets involved many of the shareholding banks directly.

It was noted above that one of the key elements of a successful alliance is that there is non-duplication of activity between the alliance and any of the partners. While this had been the case in the initial phase of consortia, it had become less true from the mid-1970s onwards. As their spreads came under pressure, the shareholders became more demanding of them and in many cases began to take over the consortia themselves. Here we see the playing out of the alliance as a learning tool that allowed the participants to gain access to the market, develop the particular skills, and then establish their own competitive position: 'the consortium bank served as a vehicle for its shareholders to enter and adjust to this type of market . . . the shareholding banks themselves learned Eurocurrency banking quickly and many of the consortia no longer served a useful purpose for them'.[60] In this sense—the development of competitive capabilities by the participants—these strategic alliances achieved considerable successes.

6. Unsuccessful Alliances: The Clubs

The banking clubs had a less well-defined strategic goal. They did not involve the creation of separate and formally constituted subsidiaries, but represented attempts to bring together a whole range of banking activities. They had a much grander and more integrationist agenda, but one which was, there-fore, more reliant on exogenous factors and more difficult to achieve. It was noted above that the concept of cooperation was the banks' response to the opportunity, on the one hand, of European integration and the problem, on the other, of American competition—particularly in the market for multi-national financing. Regulatory and competitive (defensive) imperatives forced the pace of the clubs in their early form, but it is clear that they also played a significant role in determining their fate.

The Treaty of Rome envisaged the creation of a single European market in which a single set of regulations would apply to banking business throughout the Common Market. This would therefore allow the development of single, integrated banking groups delivering services and products without reference to national borders or jurisdiction. The banking clubs sought to ride this integrationist wave and create cross-border banking groups in preparation. The European ideal of an integrated market, coupled with the beginnings of deregulation (for example in France in 1967) offered the opportunity for Continental banks to rediscover the link between retail and commercial bank-ing, at the same time as the British banks began to reassess their attitude towards corporate lending.[61] There was clearly much that, in principle, the largest European commercial banks could learn from each other.

In the first instance, the European Advisory Committee members signed up to an information-sharing commitment. The original agreement—which was to remain in place for five years—envisaged that:

- Each bank would endeavour to provide a special service to the customers of the other EAC banks.
- Each bank would endeavour to pass its European business through the EAC banks.
- Each bank would use the facilities and branch networks of their partners, and would therefore refrain from opening branches.[62]

There are contained within these general aims some of the elements of an interim strategic alliance; each bank sought to gain access to and use the expertise of its partners, while offering its own in return. Exclusive relationships were part of this arrangement, although it is not clear that these were in fact adhered to.[63] The worrying aspect of this agreement from such a perspective, however, is that there is no clear and unequivocal strategic goal in sight; rather, a set of vaguely expressed aspirations. While this allows for growth within the relationship, the potential for conflict is clear. In particular, asymmetric commitment to the ideals of integration can be discerned in a series of papers prepared for a meeting to consider the future aims and objectives of EAC in 1969.[64] The Deutsche Bank referred to the need to create 'by means of maximum co-ordination . . . a banking group corresponding in both geographical coverage and in size, to the European market'. Société Générale de Banque stressed their past willingness to adapt to the expansion and integration of the Common Market, and their hope for an acceleration of integration and joint operations in the future. Amsterdamsche-Rotterdamsche Bank suggested that, although a full merger of the banks was not at the time desirable, 'closer co-operation is an absolute necessity'. The Midland, by contrast, took the view that 'a loose association is all that is needed' and that the membership needed to be expanded to include banks from all the Common Market countries. Such divergence of attitudes towards the club and its operation can be explained not only by the differences in the structural and competitive approaches of the banks as they entered the alliance, but also by their divergent estimates of what they hoped to gain from it. This contrasts with the position of the consortia, in which the partners' expectations were similar and reasonably consistent. This is one of the key elements in determining the success of an alliance.[65]

The members of the European Advisory Committee sought to share information with each other and trade expertise. They did this by establishing a series of study groups, designed to improve the flows of communication between the participants. There were originally four of these: the foreign managers group, the economic research group, the investment research group, and the foreign trade promotion group. These performed the function of cementing the relationship and of developing a sense of unity and tangibility to the alliance. There were differences and difficulties in the approach of the various banks—the Midland could not engage in providing investment advice for example, and it alienated its partners by sending junior, rather than senior management personnel to some meetings, but on the whole these were considered fairly successful.[66] Their proliferation provides some evidence of the information-sharing achievements of the club. Groups on such issues as security, public relations, advertising, legal issues, stock markets, and staff training were all established. The verdict of the training group is typical; 'by mixing in this way the EBIC men not only learned more about the member banks, but also about each other and about the national characteristics in evidence'.[67]

The ongoing business of the club was, therefore, a fairly limited exercise in communication, valuable but constrained by the partners' own levels of commitment. The lack of progress in achieving full integration was recognized by the strategic review in 1969, and the conflict of interest of duplicated services is revealed by the report of the Economics Research Group (ERG); 'in considering the appropriate content of confidential internal studies, the ERG is often torn between relevance to EBIC and relevance to the member banks individually'.[68] The *Banker* took the view that 'as long as international co-operation does not result in a real merging of activities, the natural instinct of any bank will always be to keep the most interesting business deals on its own books'.[69] Similarly, the requirement not to compete with partner institutions in their own domestic markets was a consistent source of friction among members. The Deutsche Bank developed a favoured strategy of opening its own full service branch in London, and both Société Générale de Banque and Société Générale (France) actively developed London-based merchant banks in the early 1970s. The implications here are clear. Frustrated by the difficulties involved in maintaining exclusive relationships and attracted by the incentives offered by the fast-developing London money and capital markets, the banks were lured towards competition on their own account.[70] When the Midland eventually decided to pursue an alternative strategy for its inter-national ambitions, it had learned little from its partners about cross-border banking, and it still lacked an international staff development programme. Its competitive capabilities (at least in this sphere) had changed little in the decade of the club's existence.

7. Why Did the Clubs Fail?

That the clubs were less successful than the consortia is, in some ways, sur-prising. Ganoe, for example, expected the consortia to experience difficulties related to the weakness of decision making, but the clubs to survive thanks to their flexibility and less prescriptive goals.[71] The absence of a clear sense of independent purpose, however, meant that they were unable to resolve the conflict of interests that existed within the alliance. The alliance itself duplicated the activities of each of the partners and there was no large or new competitive opportunity that offered a focus for their activities. The Clubs' failure can be explained by reference both to the strategic alliance approach and to the exogenous factors that precipitated their formation in the first place. It is clear that European integration did not proceed as had been hoped; exchange controls remained within the EEC into the late 1970s, economic and monetary union receded along with the difficulties of that decade and yawning gulfs remained between the discrete tax and legal structures in each country. Given that European integration could not be relied upon, and that the competitive and market environments changed less than had been anticipated, The *Banker* took the view that 'any attempt to merge managements or control systems, is probably ruled out for the time being. And yet it is a unified administration and command structure that . . . is one of the keys to really big economies of scale in banking'.[72] It was only towards the end of 1968—three years after its foundation—that EAC agreed to appoint a co-ordinator, 'to convey a somewhat more institutionalized character' to the activities of the group. In a similar vein, the institutional opacity of the committee structure used to run the group was identified by at least one of EAC's subgroups as a serious problem.[73]

This criticism is explicitly related to many of the issues that dictate a successful alliance. The importance of unified and well-informed management structures, a clear strategic goal, and a good fit between the partners are often stressed in determining the outcome of an alliance.[74] Alternative explanations of why the clubs failed to develop deep and committed relationships lie, according to this view, in the differences in their approach. Table 6.2 describes some of the features of financial structure in Germany, France, Italy, and the UK in 1963. It reveals that, at the outset of the relationship at least, the corporate finance market in these countries was significantly different. Banks emanating from these markets would no doubt reflect these differences. By the end of this period, in the mid-1970s, some convergence had taken place in the field of corporate and financial structure, but the differences

Table 6.2. *Financial structure of enterprises in West Germany, France, Italy, and the UK, 1963*

	Ratio of owners equity to fixed assets	Ratio of long-term capital to fixed assets	Ratio of net working capital to stock	Ratio of medium- and long-term credit to cash flow	Ratio of medium- and long-term credit to owners equity
West Germany	0.90	1.27	0.72	2.44	0.41
France	0.94	1.31	0.68	2.64	0.39
Italy	0.67	1.07	0.25	4.31	0.59
UK	0.26	1.49	1.04	—	0.18

Source: *The Development of a European Capital Market: Report of a Group of Experts Appointed by the EEC Commission* (Brussels: European Economic Community, 1966), table 11.

between countries remained more marked than the similarities.[75] The anti-cipated possibilities for the leveraging of co-specialisms and exploitation of learning opportunities did not, therefore, develop to the extent foreseen.

If European integration did not provide the spur for committed cooperation, and the various banking sectors and markets remained distinct from each other, then the value and business to be gained from financing European multinationals in a pan-European context should have provided the incentive to construct clearly focused alliances competing with the American banks establishing branches throughout Europe. There are two issues to be addressed here. First, there is the question of whether European multi-nationals, or even multinational business in Europe, developed to the extent expected. Second, there is the issue of whether that was indeed the sector in which these alliances were most able or best suited to provide banking ser-vices. It is clear that the banks themselves considered multinational financing to be a key competitive opportunity that they would be able to exploit; the discussions of the EAC repeatedly stressed this point.[76] Table 6.3 measures the outflow of foreign direct investments from the United States, Japan, and some European countries in this period. It reveals clearly that, not only was the European share a fairly small proportion of the total, but that its growth was less than spectacular, despite the decline of the position of the USA. In the second half of the 1970s, of course, European foreign direct investments began to grow more strongly, but by this time, initial enthusiasm for the clubs had waned, the difficulties of co-ordinating and developing an integrated group marketing programme among the loosely organized clubs had become clear, and the individual banks had revised their competitive strategies towards separate representation.[77]

Neither continued European integration nor a large-scale demand for fund-ing from European multinationals materialized to the extent necessary to

Table 6.3. *Outward flow of direct investment of selected countries, 1965–1974 (% of total)*

Country	1964	1965	1966	1967	1968	1969	1970	1971	1972	1973	1974
USA	69.8	72.9	66.1	63.3	60.6	62.9	59.3	53.2	50.2	42.1	56.9
France	3.7	3.1	4.5	4.1	0.8	3.1	3.1	4.0	4.0	3.6	4.1
West Germany	4.3	4.8	4.6	5.0	7.2	7.2	8.2	10.6	7.3	8.9	8.0
Netherlands	2.1	3.5	4.1	4.1	5.1	4.3	3.5	4.5	3.7	7.3	5.3
UK	12.0	10.4	10.6	11.8	13.4	10.9	12.8	12.7	17.6	17.1	9.7
Japan	1.1	1.4	1.7	2.6	2.1	3.0	2.8	4.9	8.4	9.3	7.0

Source: United Nations Centre on Tansnational Corporation, *Salient Features and Trends in Foreign Direct Investment* (New York: UN, 1983), table 8.

encourage much more tightly organized or committed banking clubs. Their decline was signalled in the mid-1970s when groups such as EAC and the Europartners began to allow associate and partial membership. This obviously represented the end of the hopes for tightly integrated groups, and it also intimated the beginnings of fragmentation. The strategic alliance approach allows us to explain the failure of the banking clubs in terms of, first, the asymmetric expectations of the various partners to the alliances, and, second, their consequent varying levels of commitment. The lack of authoritative managerial direction or independence was exacerbated by the lack of a clear strategic focus. Fundamentally, the incentives for the banks to make deep and lasting commitments to each other were not, in the early phase, obvious enough, nor, in the later phase, strong enough.

It is ironic that the area in which the banking clubs did achieve some significant successes was in the construction of consortia to undertake and facilitate financing activities in the Euromarkets and those of developing countries. Banque Européenne de Credit a Moyen Terme was the first of the subsidiaries established by the EAC banks in 1967, and this was followed a years later by the establishment of European-American Banks. Midland had to be persuaded by Deutsche to merge its own New York branch with this consortium and 'given the wider business catchment potential, multicurrency support and the valuable licences' they eventually agreed to participate.[78] This was agreed to be one of the most successful of the joint activities of the EAC members, and its success indeed contributed to the agreement in 1969 to establish a subsidiary holding company and to extend the partners' international banking ambitions in the consortia and financing-related fields. In the following few years, group presence was established in Australia, the West Coast of the USA, Japan, and the Middle and Far East.

The clubs' main success, therefore, was to be found in those areas in which they had not developed individual strategies, that offered the greatest opportunities for profitable and competitive development, and in which they established specific institutional subsidiaries and specific strategic goals. The strategic alliance approach adopted in this chapter suggests that the relative success of the consortia is explicable in terms of the nature of their cooperation. This is true also for the consortia created by the clubs, since it was in these areas that the benefits of cooperation, in terms of reduced costs and shared risks, were greatest. The clubs themselves suffered from asymmetric expectations, from a failure to establish either a clear strategic goal or effective managerial systems, from duplication of activities with many of their partners, and from a reliance on exogenous factors to set their agenda. As strategic alliances, they had little chance of success.

8. Appendix

Table A.1. *European Banking Clubs, 1974*

Club	Headquarters
Associated Banks of Europe	
Banque Nationale de Paris	Paris
Barclays Bank	London
Banca Nazionale del Lavoro	Rome
Dresdner Bank	Frankfurt
Algemene Bank Nederland	Amsterdam
Bayerische Hypotheken und Wechsel Bank	Munich
Banque du Bruxelles	Brussels
Banque Internationale à Luxembourg[a]	Luxembourg
Osterreichische Landerbank[a]	Vienna
Europartners	
Crédit Lyonnais	Paris
Commerzbank	Düsseldorf
Banco di Roma	Rome
Banco Hispano Americano	Madrid
European Banks International Company	
Deutsche Bank	Frankfurt
Société Générale	Paris
Midland Bank	London
Banca commerciale italiana	Milan
Amsterdam Rotterdam Bank	Amsterdam
Société Générale de Banque	Brussels
Creditanstalt Bankverein	Vienna
Inter-Alpha	
Kredietbank	Brussels
Crédit Commerical de France	Paris
Berliner Handels-Gesselschaft-Frankfurter Bank	Frankfurt/Berlin
Nederlandsche Middenstandbank	Amsterdam
Williams and Glyn's	London
Banco Ambrosiano	Milan
Privatbanken	Copenhagen

Note:
[a] Associate members.

Source: Banker, International Banking Annual Review, August 1974.

Table A.2. *Clearing Banks' Investments in Consortium Banks, 1977*

	Location	Percentage shareholding	Specialization
Barclays			
Anglo-Romanian Bank	London	30	East Europe
Banque de la Société Financière			
Européenne	Paris	12	West Europe
Euro-Latinamerican Bank	London	5	Latin America
International Energy Bank	London	15	Energy
Iran Overseas Investment Bank	London	6	Iran
Midland			
Banque Européenne de Crédit	Brussels	14	
Banque Européenne pour l'Amerique			
Latine	Brussels	16	Latin America
European-American Bancorp	New York	20	United States
European Arab Holding and			
subsidiaries:	Luxembourg	5	Middle East
European Arab Bank	London		Middle East
European Arab Bank (Brussels)	Brussels		Middle East
Europaische-Arabische Bank	Frankfurt		Middle East
European Asian Bank (branches in			
Asian centres)	Hamburg	14	Asia
European Asian Finance (Hong Kong)	Hong Kong	10	
European Banking Company	London	14	Merchant banking
Euro-Pacific Finance Corporation	Melbourne	15	Australia
Iran Overseas Investment Bank	London	6	Iran
Midland and International Banks	London	45	
Ship Mortgage International Bank	Amsterdam	25	Shipping
UBF Bank	London	25	Middle East
National Westminster			
Libra Bank	London	5	Latin America
Orion Bank and its subsidiaries,	London	20	
including:			
Orion Pacific (75%)	Hong Kong		Far East
Roy West Banking Corpopration	Nassau	40	
Saudi International Bank	London	5	Merchant banking
Williams and Glyn's			
Development and Investment			
Bank of Iran	Teheran	4	Iran
Inter-Alpha Asia	Hong Kong	14	Far East
United International Bank	London	10	

Source: *London Clearing Banks*, evidence by the committee of London Clearing Bankers to the Committee to Review the Functioning of Financial Institutions (London, 1979), table 48.

NOTES

My thanks to HSBC Group, Barclays Bank, and their respective archivists, Edwin Green and Jessie Campbell, for access to and advice on this material. This paper has also benefited from discussions with Brian A'Hearn, Catherine Schenk, and the participants in the LSE conference on 'European Banking and the American Challenge, 1950s–1970s'. Particular gratitude is due to Stefano Battilossi and Steven I. Davis. Adrian Tschoegl provided help at a crucial stage.

1. D. M. Ross, 'European Banking Clubs in the 1960s: A Flawed Strategy', *Business and Economic History*, 27 (1998), 353–66.

2. Y. Park, and J. Zwick, *International Banking in Theory and Practice* (Reading, Mass.: Addison-Wesley, 1985), 54.

3. M. von Clemm, 'The Rise of Consortium Banking', *Harvard Business Review*, 49 (May–June 1971), 125–41.

4. There is a listing of the members of these groups, as well as of the British clearing banks' participation in consortia, in the Appendix.

5. S. F. Jacobsen and A. E. Tschoegl, 'The Norwegian Banks in the Nordic Consortia: A Case of International Strategic Alliances in Banking', *Industrial and Corporate Change*, 8 (1999),137–65.

6. B. Kogut, 'Joint Ventures: Theoretical and Empirical Perspectives', *Strategic Management Journal*, 9 (1988), 319–32.

7. Y. Doz and G. Hamel, *Alliance Advantage: The Art of Creating Value Through Partnering* (Boston, Mass.: Harvard Business School Press, 1998), 36–7.

8. Ibid., 6–7.

9. G. Hamel, Y. Doz, and C. Prahalad, 'Collaborate With Your Competitors—And Win', *Harvard Business Review*, 67 (Jan.–Feb. 1989), 133–9.

10. C. Bronder and C. Pritzl, 'Developing Strategic Alliances: A Conceptual Framework for Successful Co-operation', *European Management Journal*, 10 (1992), 412–21. A review and extensive discussion of the literature on strategic alliances can be found in R. Spekman, T. Forbes, L. Isabella, and T. MacAvoy, 'Alliance Management: A View from the Past and a Look to the Future', *Journal of Management Studies*, 35 (1998), 747–72.

11. K. Ohmae, 'The Global Logic of Strategic Alliances', *Harvard Business Review*, 67 (Mar.–Apr. 1989), 143–54; P. Lorange, and J. Roos, *Strategic Alliances: Formation, Implementation and Evolution* (Oxford: Blackwell Business, 1993).

12. Hamel, Doz, and Prahalad, 'Collaborate', 133–9.

13. S. Urban and S. Vendemini, *European Strategic Alliances: Co-operative Corporate Strategies in the New Europe* (Oxford: Blackwell Business, 1992), 121. In a similar vein, Segil uses a pyramid approach to alliances, in which take-overs/mergers have the highest risk and cost, while joint marketing and distribution ventures have the lowest risk, cost, and use of human resources: L. Segil, *Intelligent Business Alliances: How to Use Today's Most Important Strategic Tool* (London: Century, 1996), 16.

14. This is the intuition behind such work as R. Miles and C. Snow, 'Organizations: New Concepts for New Forms', *California Management Review*, 28 (1986), repr. in P. Buckley and J. Michie (eds.), *Firms, Organizations, and Contracts* (Oxford: Oxford University Press, 1996), 429–41.

15. A. Mody, 'Learning Through Alliances', *Journal of Economic Behaviour and Organization*, 20 (1993), 151–70.

16. Doz and Hamel, *Alliance Advantage*, 170. See also Y. Doz, 'The Evolution of Cooperation in Strategic Alliances: Initial Conditions or Learning Processes', *Strategic Management Journal*, 17 (1996), 55–84, and G. Hamel, 'Competition for Competence and Inter-partner Learning Within International Strategic Alliances', *Strategic Management Journal*, 12 (1991), 83–103.

17. Jacobsen and Tschoegl, 'The Norwegian Banks'; B. Marois and T. Abdessemed, 'Cross-Border Alliances in the French Banking Sector', *International Studies of Management and Organization*, 26 (1996), 38–58.

18. J. Johansen, and J. E. Vahlne, 'The Internationalization Process of the Firm—A Model of Knowledge Development and Increasing Foreign Market Commitments', *Journal of International Business Studies*, 9 (1977), 23–43.

19. A. Holmes and E. Green, *Midland: 150 Years of Banking Business* (London: Batsford, 1986), 252.

20. G. Jones, *British Multinational Banking, 1830–1990* (Oxford: Oxford University Press, 1993), ch. 10.

21. R. Pringle 'The British Big Four Stake their Claim', *Banker*, 127 (Aug. 1977), 113.

22. Midland Bank Archives (located at Hong Kong Shanghai Banking Corporation Group Archives), Management Committee Files, 200/289, 'Grand Design: record of a meeting of participants', 5 December 1963; note of Mr Thackstone's talk to the Royal Commonwealth Society, 20 February 1964.

23. Midland Bank Archives, Management Committee Files, 271, paper prepared by Amsterdam-Rotterdam Bank for the 23rd meeting of the European Advisory Committee.

24. Midland Bank Archives, Management Committee Files, 200/52, 'Common Market Developments', note by Hellmuth, August 1961.

25. Midland Bank Archives, Management Committee Files, 200/289, appendix to Mr Hellmuth's memo on MAIBL, October 1963.

26. 'Co-operation is Good: Control is Better', *Banker*, 127 (Aug. 1977), 85.

27. L. Gall, G. Feldman, H. James, C. -L. Hotfrerich, and L. Buschgen, *The Deutsche Bank, 1870–1995* (London: Weidenfeld & Nicolson, 1995), 752.

28. M. Green, 'New Model Multinational Bank', *Banker*, 121 (May 1971), 483.

29. Midland Bank Archives, Management Committee Papers, 190, 11th meeting of the European Advisory Committee, Brussels, 26 September 1966.

30. Midland Bank Archives, Management Committee Files, 200/749, 'The Strategy of Midland Bank Group and International Banking', memo prepared by R. L. Wyatt, November 1974.

31. Ohmae, 'Global Logic', 143–54.

32. J. H. Dunning, *Explaining International Production* (London, Harper-Collins, 1988). For a review of the extension of international production literature to include strategic alliances, see J. Hammill, 'Changing Patterns of International Business: Crossborder Mergers, Acquisitions and Strategic Alliances', Strathclyde International Business Unit, Working Paper Series, 91/4.
33. Hamel, Doz, and Prahalad, 'Collaborate', 133–9.
34. Park and Zwick, *International Banking*, 55.
35. A. Weissmuller, 'London Consortium Banks', *Journal of the Institute of Bankers*, 95 (1974), 205.
36. Lorange and Roos, *Strategic Alliances*, 46.
37. C. Ganoe, 'Banking Consortia: Are They Here To Stay?', *Columbia Journal of World Business*, 7 (August 1972), 51–7.
38. Lorange and Roos, *Strategic Alliances*, 13; Spekman *et al.*, 'Alliance Management'; B. Borys and D. B. Jemison, 'Hybrid Arrangements as Strategic Alliances: Theoretical Issues and Organizational Combinations', *Academy of Management Review*, 14 (1989), 234–49.
39. The Segré Report recognized in 1966 the possible synergies among quite different institutions: 'the establishment of European bank consortia might provide a useful source of refinance ... the consortium would have the advantage of knowing the needs and capacity of a diversified clientele embracing several markets', *The Development of a European Capital Market: Report of a Group of Experts Appointed by the EEC Commission* (Brussels: European Economic Community, 1966), 160–1.
40. Urban and Vendemini, *European Strategic Aliances*, 189.
41. Barclays Bank Archives, board minute books, 719, 21 July 1960; see also ibid., 484, 12 February 1959, and ibid., 970, 27 June 1963, for the appointment of the committee and an assistant to the European manager respectively.
42. Barclays Bank Archives, 2219/3, Banque de Commerce and Banque de Bruxelles, chairman's note, 7 August 1962.
43. *Financial Times*, 16 October 1962.
44. Barclays Bank Archives, board minute books, 631, 11 February 1965 and 10 February 1966.
45. Barclays Bank Archives, 2219/4, Montagu Proposition, note by Thornton, 25 October 1962.
46. Barclays Bank Archives, 2219/4, note by Thornton, 10 December 1962.
47. Barclays Bank Archives, 2219/4, notes by Thornton, 14 February 1963 and 8 April 1963.
48. Barclays Bank Archives, 80/93, Barclays Bank Foreign Committee minutes, 7 January 1965.
49. Barclays Bank Archives, 80/93, Barclays Bank Foreign Committee minutes, 13 June 1966.
50. Barclays Bank Archives, 38/441, Interhandel, letter from Aitken, chairman of Barclays DCO to Lambert, European representative, 3 February 1965; replies

8 February 1965 and 19 February 1965. For a detailed description of this company and how the money came to be available for investment, see D. O'Reilly, 'IG Farbenindustrie A.G., Interhandel and General Aniline and Film Corporation. A Problem in International Political and Economic Relations Between Germany, Switzerland and the United States, 1929–1965', Ph.D. thesis (Cambridge, 1998).

51. Barclays Bank Archives, 38/441, Interhandel, letter from Lambert to Aitken, 2 July 1965; letter from Schaeffer (UBS) to Thornton (Barclays), 13 July 1965.

52. Barclays Bank Archives, 38/441, Interhandel, letter from Charleston to Thornton, 28 July 1965; letter from Lambert to Thornton, 25 October 1965.

53. Barclays Bank Archives, 38/441, Interhandel, meeting between Schaeffer and Thornton, 22 November 1965. They did, however, add the caveat that 'we must not overlook the effect that this might have on other correspondents in Europe': note by Thornton, 21 December 1965.

54. Barclays Bank Archives, 38/441, Interhandel, note by Thornton, 21 December 1965.

55. Barclays Bank Archives, 3/4617, Société Financière Européenne, long- and medium-term credit bank.

56. Barclays Bank Archives, board minute papers, 300/465, ref. board minute 547, 25 April 1968.

57. 'The Eurocurrency Business of Banks in London: Maturity Analysis as at End of October 1971', *Bank of England Quarterly Bulletin*, 12 (Mar. 1972), 56–63; D. Channon, *British Banking Strategy and the International Challenge* (London: Macmillan, 1977), 183–7.

58. Weissmuller, 'London Consortium Banks', 203–17.

59. Park and Zwick, *International Banking*, 56–7.

60. Ibid., 58. See also C. Parker, 'Consortium Banks Find the Going Tough', Eurofile supplement to *Banker*, 128 (April 1978), pp. vi–ix.

61. Midland Bank Archives, Management Committee files, 200/749, 'The Strategy of Midland Bank Group and International Banking', memo prepared by R. L. Wyatt, November 1974; also Management Committee Papers, 271, 23rd meeting of European Advisory Committee, 4 September 1969, paper prepared by Amsterdam-Rotterdam Bank. See also D. Vittas, P. Frazer, and T. Metaxas-Vittas, *The Retail Banking Revolution: An International Perspective* (Dublin: Lafferty, 1988).

62. Midland Bank Archives, Management Committee files, 200/749, 'The Strategy of Midland Bank Group and International Banking', memo prepared by R. L. Wyatt, November 1974.

63. *The Economist* (Nov. 1964), 851, reported that some correspondents had been the recipients of extra business from the participants 'to reassure them that they will not be neglected'.

64. Midland Bank Archives, Management Committee papers, 271, 23rd meeting of European Advisory Committee, 4 September 1969.

65. Ohmae, 'Global Logic', 143–54, see also C. Freidheim, *The Trillion Dollar Enterprise: How the Alliance Revolution Will Transform Global Business* (Reading, Mass.: Perseus, 1998), ch. 5.

66. Midland Bank Archives, Management Committee files, Greenwell papers, 200/215, notes for meetings of 19 February and 15 May 1964.

67. Midland Bank Archives, Management Committee files, 200/749, 'The Strategy of Midland Bank Group and International Banking', memo prepared by R. L. Wyatt, November 1974, appendix report on EBIC training group (EBIC stands for the European Banks Investment Company, the name adopted for the holding company formed after the strategy discussions in 1969).

68. Midland Bank Archives, Management Committee files, 200/749, 'The Strategy of Midland Bank Group and International Banking', memo prepared by R. L. Wyatt, November 1974, appendix report on Economics research group.

69. 'Co-operation is Good', *Banker*, 127: 87.

70. U. Steuber, 'International Cooperation and Competition among Banks in Europe', in J. Wadsworth, J. Wilson, and H. Fournier (eds.), *The Development of Financial Institutions in Europe, 1956–76* (Leiden: Sijthoff, 1977), 175–9.

71. Ganoe, 'Banking Consortia', 51–7.

72. 'Banking Clubs Still in Fashion', *Banker*, International Banking Annual Review, 124 (August 1974), 947.

73. Midland Bank Archives, Management Committee files, 335, minutes of a meeting on 9 September 1968; see also ibid., 200/749, 'The Strategy of Midland Bank Group and International Banking', memo prepared by R. L. Wyatt, November 1974, appendix report on Economics research group.

74. Urban and Vendemini, *European Strategic Alliances*; Borys and Jemison, 'Hybrid Arrangements'; Doz and Hamel, *Alliance Advantage.*

75. See e.g. the various descriptions contained within J. Samuels, R. Groves, and C. Goddard, *Company Finance in Europe* (London: Institute of Chartered Accountants in England and Wales, 1975).

76. See, e.g. Midland Bank Archives, Management Committee papers, 271, 23rd meeting of European Advisory Committee, 4 September 1969.

77. Midland Bank Archives, Management Committee files, 200/749, 'The Strategy of Midland Bank Group and International Banking', memo prepared by R. L. Wyatt, November 1974.

78. Ibid.

7

European Aspirations and Market Reality: Paribas, the Crédit Lyonnais, and their European Strategies in the 1960s and 1970s

ERIC BUSSIÈRE

The aim of this chapter is to analyse the way in which French banks envisaged their development strategies in the context of the construction of Europe in the 1960s and 1970s. The main feature of the period for the six-member Community was the recent establishment of the Common Market which, from the customs point of view, had become a reality. At the time those involved saw it as leading to the introduction of European-scale firms, a development which, as we have seen, has taken place much more slowly than expected. Europe was then still very heterogeneous, largely because of the lack of a homogeneous monetary and banking framework. The hope that one could be put in place persisted throughout the 1960s and led to the first attempt to create economic and monetary union between 1969 and 1973. Such is the institutional framework for the present study. In addition to the European factor, however, that of American competition must also be taken into account. For over a decade, Continental bankers felt that their American competitors were in a better position to benefit not only from integration but also from the growth of international capital markets providing finance in Europe than they were themselves. Here, we shall examine the reactions to such developments, basing our analysis on the examples of the chief French credit bank of the time, the Crédit Lyonnais, and the major merchant bank, the Banque de Paris et des Pays Bas.

What can be learnt from their particular experience, however, is valid for each and every Continental bank, as their German, Italian, Belgian, and Dutch counterparts were all involved in the type of strategy we shall be discussing. As will be seen, British banks too were associated with the creation of banking clubs. Each and every European bank had to reconsider its Continental strategies in the late 1970s. It is clear that the way things have recently been going for the establishments in question is not connected with the experiences described here, which comprise only part of their international activities.

1. Factors Determining French Banks' European Strategies

The dynamics of the Common Market is of fundamental importance to any understanding of the steps taken by French banks at several key points in their strategies of alliances and locating in Europe from the late 1950s. Time and again, French banks were so carried along by the mystique of the new Europe being built that each major new advance led to intentional and would-be anticipatory steps. These were in conformity with the choices expressed by a considerable section of French and, at the wider level, Continental employers, particularly through organizations such as the European League for Economic Co-operation, which was linked to the European movement and very representative of the banking world. A leading supporter of a free-market policy, the League had quickly come out in favour of faster integration and monetary union amongst the six Common Market member states.[1] The positions taken up by the banks, and to an even greater extent the modifications in their strategies, constantly reflected such options.

It was for reasons of this kind that in 1948 Paribas had put forward the idea of a European banking committee and an international financial company to encourage cross-border investments in Western Europe. Even more revealing was the idea, proposed in 1949, of closer cooperation between its Belgian and Dutch branches, since they were both going to be 'economically in one country' as a result of the creation of Benelux. The signing of the Treaty of Rome in 1957 led to new moves by Paribas, with the creation of two bodies to form part of the movement towards closer cooperation between firms which, it was thought, would go hand in hand with the introduction of the Common Market. These were the SEDI (Société Européenne de Développement Industriel)—the name alone summarizes its programme, which had been drawn up with the Deutsche Bank—and the SFIDI (Société Franco-Italienne de Développement Industriel) with Banca commerciale italiana.[2]

As is shown by a note dated 1975 from the archives of the Crédit Lyonnais setting out the circumstances in which its policy of European alliances had been defined five years earlier, the same kind of move was made again in the late 1960s and early 1970s, when the Common Market and the Werner Plan for economic and monetary union had been achieved. It talked of the part played by the 'mystique' of Europe, the supranational option adopted and the deep disappointment some years later when 'Europe stopped short'.[3] In the very early 1990s, the prospect on the one hand of the launch of the new extended market that followed the signing of both the Single Act and on the other of a further attempt to create a monetary and economic union led to the adoption of new positions in favour of European union. Thus André Levy-Lang, the chairman of the board of directors of Paribas, declared that 'in every country in Europe there are great financial establishments, but no great European financial establishments. That is why I am in favour of European union'. And in 1991, the same André Levy-Lang was still deploring the inordinately long time it was taking to put economic and monetary union into effect.[4]

The American challenge was always one of the European banks' reasons for supporting integration, as was clearly expressed at the time of the first attempt to set up EMU in the early 1970s. Their position was based on both defensive and offensive considerations. The former were a reflection of their anxiety at the increasingly strong presence of American banks in Europe during the 1960s and 1970s, which the leading figures in the Crédit Lyonnais saw as threatening to create heightened competition both within and outside Europe. The response to the challenge was seen to be for European banks to form associations amongst themselves in order to avoid harmful penetration of the European banking network by the big American banks. This explains the views of the Crédit Lyonnais in 1973: 'Should we keep our network European or seek American support? We have chosen Europe in order to be sure of preserving our identity as a result of the balance of our respective forces and in order to try to produce a vigorous response to the action of American banks in Europe'.[5] The positive aspect of analyses of the American challenge has to do with the size of the market for, as André Lévy-Lang said in 1994, its growth as a result of monetary union was the essential opportunity for rationalizing structures and modelling them on those made possible by the American example of a major market. It should be noted that references to challenge and the major American market had been one of the permanent features of arguments in favour of European integration since the 1920s, and by no means only in relation to the banking world. Indeed, for over 70 years it has been just as important a characteristic of the case made by the proponents of a pan-European economy.[6]

The consequences of these options in terms of the banks' choice of strategy are as follows. Each of the institutional modifications mentioned above was analysed by the banks in terms of the market structures prevailing in its own particular context and expressed in a series of strategic initiatives intended to accompany (and more particularly to anticipate) changes in the market in order to capture the new flows they would lead to. In 1957, Paribas was chiefly interested in the industrial dimension of the Common Market and its effect on the structure of firms. In 1967–8, what led both Paribas and the Crédit Lyonnais to think about their strategy of locating in other European countries was the imminent prospect of monetary union. In 1970, as was later to be also the case in 1990, that prospect gave rise to analyses of the opening up of the money market at both the merchant banking and market activities levels. Strategies were thus differentiated in terms of actual banking activities, and even though those of the Crédit Lyonnais and Paribas tended to become more similar from the 1960s onwards, the former remained largely a merchant bank moving into close and permanent contact with its customers as a result of its physical presence and new locations, and its rationale was, in fact, a highly territorial network within Europe. On the other hand, the European strategy adopted by Paribas was based rather on a rationale of alliances and partnerships at the level of the major states, with the new international locations established during the 1960s being chiefly concerned with the main financial markets such as London, Geneva, Luxembourg, and New York, where business was less directly linked to the economy of the host country. For a long time, therefore, it was the first of these two approaches that was more closely linked to the process of European integration, and the second did not follow suit until later. At the end of the 1980s, however, as a result of a combination of linked causes (a degree of specialization, globalization, and the prospect of monetary union), the two strategies tended to merge.

This meant that firms had two possible ways of establishing a European presence, namely a strategy of either alliances or direct physical location. What decisions were taken depended on a whole range of factors. Traditionally, the major establishments had organized their foreign business through a network of correspondents, and this strongly influenced choices until the end of the 1960s. Many of the French banks' European partners told them that the tradition of keeping to one's own backyard had to be maintained, and location on their national market was deemed to be hostile.[7] A preference for alliance-based strategies also had the advantages of costing less and offering the possibility of benefiting more quickly from the network effect. It also seemed more defensive, since margins were preserved. Direct location was slower and more expensive. It could be achieved by creating networks, necessarily a gradual and slower process, but also by taking over establishments. This tactic was adopted later, but here too there were many obstacles, and in many cases it was difficult to penetrate national markets.

2. From Anticipating the Future to Differing Strategies: Initiatives around 1960

In the late 1950s and early 1960s, during the early years of the Common Market, both Paribas and the Crédit Lyonnais attempted to fit their strategies into the new institutional framework, but in very different ways. Paribas wanted to be proactive and forward-looking, the Crédit Lyonnais more defensive, even if quite ambitious in scope. Part of the interest in the comparison is the fact that in both cases the target was the Deutsche Bank.

At the end of the 1950s, Paribas's sphere of influence in Europe centred around its old branches in Brussels, Amsterdam, and Geneva. The hold on their respective domestic markets, however, was very variable and had in fact strengthened, particularly since the end of the war, in ways appropriate to each of them, a trend which continued during the 1960s.[8] The signing of the Treaty of Rome quite naturally led to a desire to establish a presence in the two major EEC markets: Italy and, first and foremost, Germany. The policy Paribas was tentatively developing for Germany in the late 1950s was profoundly in phase with the idea of a Franco-German, industrially based Europe and was instigated by a group of officials coming mainly from the bank's industrial department along a path unbroken since the 1950s. In 1957 it led to the creation of the Société Européenne de Développement Industriel (SEDI) in partnership with the Deutsche Bank. The latter wanted to encourage every possible type of cooperation between the industrial firms of both countries and, in particular, a policy of furthering links in accordance with the industrial orientation Paribas had been affirming since 1945, and of anticipating the integrative effects of the Common Market. The form the new cooperation took was thus at once limited in its means, as the capital at its disposal was more like that of a study group than that of a holding company, but it was essential in terms of its potential political impact. Paribas wanted the announcement to come as something of a surprise, which rather turned the Paris market against the new institution. Paribas was quick to realize that the SEDI was a failure: business proposals tended to emanate largely from its top echelons and to come to nothing. Working meetings of the SEDI, which had originally attracted such personalities as Jean Reyre and Hermann Abs, became less frequent and dynamic. The failure marked the limits of an approach organized from above on the basis of a contractual agreement between two major institutions. It had not taken Paribas long to realize that the Deutsche Bank and its president, Hermann Abs, believed in keeping to one's own territory and that such a way of seeing things could not give rise to a policy of major industrial *rapprochements* conducted by the two partners.[9]

The first move by the Crédit Lyonnais to develop connections involving more than merely correspondent relationships with the major banks in the Common Market dates from April 1962, and was a result of the trip to Frankfurt by the director of the 'major bank' and foreign agency department to discuss the situation regarding competition in Europe. The developing European market looked as if it might make it possible for European multinationals to benefit more from better conditions abroad for the support they needed for their national currencies than by applying to their usual banker in their country of origin. Thus we find, in an internal Crédit Lyonnais memorandum, that 'Italian companies use Switzerland for the financing of their lire requirements, their German counterparts use France for theirs in marks, and so on'.[10] If it were to become widespread, such a situation might cast doubt on the way in which the operation was being carried out if it involved by-passing national regulations and agreements on rates, which themselves might well be challenged. The move by the Crédit Lyonnais was thus defensive and aimed at preserving operating margins. As the bank's worries seemed to coincide with those of the Deutsche Bank, it launched the idea of a club bringing together the main banks in the Common Market for joint discussion of problems of competition and ensuring that certain rules were adhered to. In the view of the Crédit Lyonnais, membership involved two commitments: promising not to engage in any new direct or indirect location in other Common Market countries, and respecting 'the dominant position of bankers in a particular country in the business of firms in that country, i.e. to limit direct steps and indirect relations likely to divert business normally entrusted to local banks'. More positively, members of the club could, in terms of future institutional and regulatory developments at the European level, look forward to more formal cooperation agreements and indeed joint projects.

The club envisaged was to bring together leading establishments in the main Community markets—the Crédit Lyonnais, the Deutsche Bank, and the Banca commerciale italiana—and later a major Belgian bank and a major Dutch bank (the Banque de Bruxelles or Banque de la Société Générale and the Amsterdamsche Bank), and even a British and a Swiss establishment. There were to be meetings at several levels, with those involving presidents and managing directors serving to establish general directives and principles that each bank would try to ensure would be accepted and applied by establishments in its own country of origin. Even a system of sanctions for infringements was envisaged. The initial meetings of April 1962 led to no practical agreement, and the club of which the Crédit Lyonnais had wanted to form the linchpin never came into being.

Over the next few years the Crédit Lyonnais and the Deutsche Bank developed correspondent relationships with each other, and the German bank played a modest part in developing its French partners' new establishments in sub-Saharan Africa. Both banks also cooperated in the international issues field. It was not until November 1966, however, that talks aimed at creating a more structured relationship along the lines envisaged four years earlier were resumed, once again at the initiative of the Crédit Lyonnais. One of the reasons given at the time by G. Cazès for the Crédit Lyonnais was the increasing competition from American banks in Europe. The two banks agreed, as had been envisaged in 1962, to regular and frequent exchanges of views on various fields of activities likely to lead to important areas of bilateral cooperation. They decided not to seek any formal agreement, but the Crédit Lyonnais did persuade its partner to commit itself to prior consultation if it envisaged 'engaging in negotiations relating to a major project with French establishments other than the Crédit Lyonnais'. If it did, the latter would be offered the opportunity of 'formulating proposals' if it felt itself to be in a position to do so.[11]

The documents consulted do not clarify the motivation of the two partners in this step. For the Deutsche Bank, participation in the *club des celibataires* founded in 1959 and renamed the European Advisory Committee (EAC) in 1963 had enabled it to enter into sustained, if informal, relations with the Banque de la Société Générale de Belgique, the Amsterdamsche Bank, and the Midland Bank.[12] With no French institution playing a central part in the club, the German bank's desire to establish a similar kind of relationship with the main French bank was understandable. For the Crédit Lyonnais, the logical step was to establish an indirect foothold in the club to ensure that it would be associated with any activities it might engage in. Once again, the French bank was in the position of a suitor in the new *rapprochement*. G. Cazès therefore informed his German contact, Pirkham, that he hoped it would be possible to 'start exploratory talks . . . that might lead to much wider prospect'.[13] The way relations between the two banks developed was a great disappointment for the Crédit Lyonnais. The working parties set up during the first meeting in November 1966 never got beyond discussing technical matters and did not lead to any structured cooperation. In the words of the head of the Crédit Lyonnais's general German delegation, the working meetings involving representatives of the two banks 'produced merely friendly gestures and no practical result', and did not seem likely to do so.[14] The announcement of the creation of the European Banks International Company (EBIC) in July 1967 by the members of the EAC was a major disappointment for the directors of the Crédit Lyonnais, who were to all intents and purposes faced with a *fait accompli*, as Thursday 13 and Friday 14 July were public holidays in France. In the opinion of the bank's representative in Germany, the attitude of the Deutsche Bank, which was simultaneously fuelling intermediate-level discussions with the Crédit Lyonnais and preparing a formal association with other banks, left much to be desired.[15] It did, however, sanction the choice of the Deutsche Bank as the axis of its European strategy. The Crédit Lyonnais had not in fact remained idle in the face of the first European medium-term financing institutions. In early 1967, when a group of European banks, including the

Dresdner Bank and the Banque Nationale de Paris (BNP), were getting ready
to set up the Société Financière Européenne, the Crédit Lyonnais had submitted a similar project to both its German partner and a Swiss concern. It
had not been taken further, as at the time the Deutsche Bank was no doubt
preparing to make other arrangements.[16]

It is hard to understand the Deutsche Bank's attitude towards its French
partner. The main reason for it, which was unofficially mentioned during
private conversations between representatives of the two banks in 1967, was
the status of the Crédit Lyonnais, which was a nationalized bank, a fact that
had been stressed by the Deutsche Bank's partners and probably also among
a section of its top echelons.[17] In 1970 the matter was also raised again in
an internal memorandum in the Crédit Lyonnais.[18] More purely political
reasons—in particular, the general attitude of the French authorities and
banks to European banking regulations—may also have played a part. In
1969 one of the officials of the Deutsche Bank alluded to General de Gaulle's
attitude towards British entry into the Common Market, an attitude which
might have explained the persistent refusal of the British partner in the EBIC:
'We do not want a de Gaulle in our association'.[19] The events of 1967 left
a sense of unease between the two concerns despite attempts on all sides to
wipe out all traces of it. Thus the Crédit Lyonnais, followed by other bodies, eventually rejoined the EBIC, and the bilateral working-party meetings
began again in autumn 1967. In fact the members of the EBIC group followed their strategy of alliances through the creation of a series of specialized
or regional consortial establishments without the knowledge of the Crédit
Lyonnais. Total confidence was a thing of the past. By July 1967 the Crédit
Lyonnais's representative in Germany was advising a change in direction and
a move towards another establishment, the Commerzbank, whose president,
Lichtenberg, had approached him.[20] That shift in direction, a new stage in the
Crédit Lyonnais's strategy, became more marked during 1970.

3. The Strategies of the 1970s

The initiatives of the early 1970s shaped the approach of Paribas and the Crédit
Lyonnais to the European market for over 10 years. Here again, however, the
two banks differed in their tactics. The Crédit Lyonnais involved itself more
deeply in the clubs option, while Paribas explored the path of direct location.

For the Crédit Lyonnais, 1970 was a year of overall stocktaking with regard
to its strategy of establishing a physical presence in Europe. A preparatory
summary for the meeting of the international affairs co-ordinating committee produced in April 1970 by Feuilhade de Chauvin, the assistant managing
director responsible for international financial affairs, provides a clear idea of

what were seen as imperatives at the time. There were two possible strategies for cooperation. The first, conceived with an economy of means in view, was aimed at tackling the problem on a case-by-case basis and hence succeeding in establishing a network of alliances varying in its geometry in terms of geographical sectors and specialized services. Most members of the international affairs committee were in favour of this approach was more realistic and more effective if the right partners were targeted. It would also mean that the Crédit Lyonnais could keep a firm hand on the operation by avoiding a largely exclusive (and probably more constricting and less effective) association with one or more 'stars'. Their experience with the Deutsche Bank had left its mark.

The second option, which involved a series of special alliances that might lead to a greater integration of establishments and was based on the perceived threat of new and much sharper international competition, was clearly that favoured by Feuilhade de Chauvin. It was a matter of 'defending essential positions in the face of ever more threatening competition' and of 'uniting in order to resist'. Two spheres of action in particular were involved. The first was the business of merchant banks, for which the danger seemed clearly to be 'seeing our European competitors opening agencies in France' in order to drain off resources and jobs arising from intra-Community trade and companies operating in several countries. The second concerned the activities of investment banks for which, given the prospect of Britain's entry into the Common Market, the competition from British merchant banks and with them 'the intervention of American interests' could well pose a threat. In the latter special field, the need to acquire both the necessary skills and direct access to Anglo-Saxon markets and powerful assets made it particularly important to implement a strategy of effective alliances. Such a step seemed all the more necessary as the Crédit Lyonnais, which had just created the Crédit Lyonnais Corporation in New York, felt the need to join in with partners to ensure its development. If that were to be to be the case, the note concluded that there would be a need for 'a clear and resolute policy to move, even if gradually, towards wider integration'.[21]

The argument for a limited series of special alliances was supported by the analysis of competitors' attitudes it would then be possible to make. An examination of the creation of the BEC and the subsequent developments in the EBIC seemed to indicate the need for further integration of the banks involved: 'they have allowed the BEC to carry out operations they would not perform themselves, and have very quickly taken the route of outside cooperation by combining to create a bank in New York. No doubt it will only be a matter of time before they combine their networks, or at very least follow a joint policy at the European level'.[22] If such a forecast were to prove correct, an all-out strategy of case-by-case alliances might well be harmful and isolate the

Crédit Lyonnais. In an address in January 1973, Feuilhade de Chauvin spoke publicly of a vague but 'deeply felt' sense of isolation amongst the bank's senior executives. However that may have been, given the prospect of the integrationist option that seemed to be emerging in spring 1970, the selection of partners depended on a political choice that would be 'more fundamental the longer the commitment lasted and would consequently make a return to the *status quo* more unpredictable'.[23]

The April 1970 survey of the state of the Crédit Lyonnais's relations with its partners looked first at Germany. Only contacts with the Commerzbank and the chairman of its board of directors, Lichtenberg, seemed to provide any hope of movement towards a special alliance. Lichtenberg agreed in principle to support the French bank in its move to set up the Crédit Lyonnais Corporation, and thus a combination of cooperation in international-scale investment banking in European merchant banking looked possible. The highly confidential negotiations started in spring 1970 led to the two banks signing an agreement in December of that year. The circumstances that led them to make a reality of their discussions were as follows. An article by Paul Lichtenberg, the managing director of the Commerzbank, which appeared in an in-house publication of the Crédit Lyonnais gives an idea of the state of mind in which the agreement was signed and implemented during its first year of existence.[24] Lichtenberg's analyses show that both sides saw things in largely the same way and that there was a certain continuity. Two factors were stressed: American competition and European integration. The American challenge primarily meant competition from major American banks with branches in Europe and the whole range of services they could offer to European multinationals at Common Market level, thus possibly depriving European banks of the benefits of integration. The scrutiny of the American challenge was still cautious, however, and did not imply anti-Americanism:

Our idea of European organization has sometimes been wrongly seen as a direct riposte to the activities of American banks in Europe. We have never sought a direct confrontation of that kind. It is simply that we are convinced that the Europe of the Common Market will soon play such an important part in the world economy that it will have to be reflected in huge banking institutions.

The process of European integration was put forward as the chief factor in the action taken as a direct result of the realities of commercial integration and as a medium-term prospect in the framework of EMU. In Lichtenberg's view, 'banks have benefited from the achievement of the customs union and the consequent regularly increasing levels of trade. They have analysed the perhaps hesitant progress of the EEC towards economic union and confidently look forward to seeing monetary union in the early 1980s'. We should bear in mind the work of the Werner committee, which began in early 1970, its report, published on 17 October of the same year, the difficult compromise reached on it in February/March 1971, and the agreement of 21 March 1972 leading to the European monetary snake, by which European governments agreed upon joint flotation of their currencies against the dollar. It certainly seems that a perception of a real and necessary solidarity decided the move. Lichtenberg's assessment was corroborated by Feuilhade de Chauvin's in January 1973, when he highlighted the combined effect of the American factor and integration to justify the December 1970 agreement and the choice of a European-scale grouping.

The movement towards creating a structured entity was cautious. Right from the start the two partners, joined by the Banco di Roma in 1971, declared their determination to finish up with a structured rather than an excessively flexible club. In Lichtenberg's phrase, it was to be a marriage of permanent partners. The notion of a structured club, however, did not go as far as providing for the merger of the entities involved. Preserving identity, as Feuilhade de Chauvin suggested, also implied that, as distinct from American banks, European ones do have their own identity, but that there is also a national identity that the method used must make it possible to safeguard. The way of organizing cooperation embarked on in January 1971 included setting up a pyramid of committees: a general management committee bringing together managing directors and taking decisions, coordinating committees in every bank to coordinate and stimulate cooperation, and specialized working parties. At the client-services level, the objectives were to make use of complementary networks by offering, in Common Market countries, individuals, and more particularly firms, maximally integrated merchant bank services, and to set up through specialized subsidiaries and joint locations, particularly outside the Common Market, services for major clients and advice in the financial field. Such a strategy clearly turned on the complementarity of partners and even envisaged merging several departments, but not purely and simply merging the three concerns. In the formula of Schlogel, the vice-president of the Crédit Lyonnais, 'everything short of a merger, which is ruled out'. We need to examine the reasons for stopping short of a merger, a policy adopted by the partners from the outset. In a way, the banks' project as outlined was less ambitious than the project for EMU, which envisaged a common currency by 1980. The reasons for the reservations were essentially institutional. On the one hand, there were differences in status amongst the banks involved (some were nationalized, some semi-public, and others private), and on the other there was a variety of regulations governing the instruments of monetary policy and the banking activities involved. It can also be suggested that if as a nationalized bank the Crédit Lyonnais was in a position to act as an essential brake on the French side, its weight, in comparison with that of its original partners, might account for their reluctance to envisage the possibility of a merger. In the same spirit, a memorandum to the higher management of the Crédit Lyonnais in March 1971 stresses 'the major (but not necessarily dominant) part that it is incumbent on the Crédit Lyonnais to play in such co-operation'.[25] And it should be added that the overall idea of the association was also part of the concept of a gradual contractually founded construction based on a 'Europe of banks' and subject to the limits the French authorities wished to impose on the march towards supranationality.

The assessment by the leading figures of the Crédit Lyonnais of the first four years of cooperation within an association that in the meantime had acquired the name of Europartners was fairly negative, as is shown by a note of January 1975: 'Given the breadth of perspective and the initial mystique surrounding the venture, it is hard now not to feel really disappointed'.[26] The idea behind the project was that of a supranational Europe, and the agreements were supposed to lead to a gradual integration of the establishments involved, based on the principle of exclusive preference in their actions. The January 1975 assessment was harsh ('that idea is now dead') even if it had in fact led to one or two embryonic joint actions and achievements, such as emergency finance, joint representation, shared subsidiaries, the Luxemburg joint holding company project, and a shared secretariat. The failure of the venture was linked in the first place to institutional factors ('Europe has stopped short') and changes in the banking sector which could not 'happen before political developments'. In addition, the rules introduced by Brussels encouraged the freedom to set up establishments rather than the cooperative strategy imagined in 1970. Another observation pointed out that 'the woof and warp of banking houses is inimical to relinquishing autonomy and cries out for freedom to develop'. The note went on to say that managing joint institutions was found to be difficult, particularly when parity reigns within them, and joint representations to be a failure, because they are merely juxtapositions and do not lower costs. The solution the assessment proposed was that there should be an end to the idea of sharing markets and giving up operations on other institutions' territory, and that joint operations and collegial management should be discontinued. What was really being suggested was thus a return to the idea of a club for exchanging ideas and experiences and forming a framework for implementing occasional initiatives for cooperation. With regard to joint creations, it was suggested that they should be set up on a non-parity basis, with one man having the decisive vote and exercising the reality of management. Otherwise, it would be a case of 'total freedom of action and creation for all'. The note did not therefore come to the conclusion that Europartners should be dissolved, but that it should develop into a loose form of cooperation and not be seen as leading towards merging the entities involved. There is no doubt that the uneasiness the upper echelons of the Crédit Lyonnais felt after a few years of cooperation was also felt by those of the Commerzbank. Although Europartners was not dissolved at once, later attempts to revive it fully confirmed the assessment made in 1975 and led the Crédit Lyonnais to shift the general direction of its European strategy towards a direct presence on the main markets of the Community.

The experience of Paribas in this area began before that of the Crédit Lyonnais, but shows the difficulties inherent in the alternative strategy, as witnessed in its establishment of a presence in West Germany. The advent of the full Common Market in 1968 brought the question of the presence of Paribas in West Germany and the ways of achieving it to the forefront once more. The arguments in favour of the move, which were set out in a note in 1970, were based on the vitality of the Common Market, the importance of flows between Germany and its European neighbours (with France in the first rank), and the chance of Paribas beginning to play a part in financing such flows.[27] The strategy proposed therefore corresponded not only to the role of the merchant bank (with the short-term aim of accompanying Paribas clients to Germany) but also to that of the industrial bank (with the chance of participating in interesting long-term joint ventures). For a long time, however, just how such a presence could be achieved was unclear. Apart from the reluctance of German banks to contemplate the possibility of French banks moving into their home market, Paribas hesitated for a long while between a policy of acquiring existing establishments and directly setting up new ones. In 1961 and again in 1962 Paribas was obliged to give up two attempts to acquire institutions, and a further series of attempts with two German banks at the end of the decade also had no tangible result. The decision to initiate direct location was taken in 1970. Caution was the order of the day, and at first the bank settled for an agency in Frankfurt, which became a branch in 1973. The Paribas German network then began to grow (Düsseldorf, 1973, Stuttgart, 1979, and Hamburg, 1984) but slowly and cautiously.

An assessment of Paribas's direct presence in West Germany is fairly disappointing. Industrial banking activities did not grow as had been hoped, and it was therefore fairly soon necessary to broaden activities to include credit to large firms which, although they did not give rise to any significant setbacks, brought in little profit. After all, the German domestic market, and the clientele provided by medium- and large-scale firms in particular, had proved to be difficult to penetrate, as it was largely controlled by German banks. The lively competition amongst foreign banks for control of the available sections of the market reduced margins and made operations less viable. What little success Paribas had in West Germany was limited to market slots using the expertise available from head office rather than the effects of a direct presence.[28] From the 1970s, there were better results from locations in Italy and Spain, but here too switching between direct location, acquisition, and cooperation was the rule. In Italy, Paribas acted through both its subsidiary and the International Lombardy Bank jointly owned with Banca commerciale italiana, with whom a cooperation agreement had also been signed.[29] The overall picture we can form of the results of Paribas's European strategy and of the 1980s is rather mixed. The general impression is a fairly heterogeneous one, with a juxtaposition of, on the one hand, a series of national locations unevenly integrated into the corresponding domestic economies, and on the other a range of international locations. Presence in Europe was therefore not synonymous with the Europe-wide integration of the bank's network, particularly as the various component parts of the European network enjoyed very varying degrees of autonomy with regard to head office.

4. Conclusions

The construction of Europe very clearly played an important part in the French banks' internationalization strategy from the 1960s. In this context, the American challenge was taken into account in their assessments but was not of crucial importance. All the banks wanted to 'go European' in terms of the priorities linked to their role. For Paribas, which was primarily a market bank, an international presence took precedence over a strategy of 'occupying' the territory of Europe. For the Crédit Lyonnais, where merchant bank operations were the prime consideration, expanding in Europe was the continuation of expanding in France. The two establishments took different paths towards Europe. The preference for cooperative strategies in the form of clubs that was so marked until the 1970s was part of both the traditional practices of European banks (with their implicit code of international good behaviour that outlawed competition with their correspondents in their own domestic markets) and a contractual conception of building Europe that was dominant until the 1970s. Their moves were gradual, however, and the chief players aimed at anticipating the institutional integration of the money markets once the possibility of monetary union emerged. But all that was envisaged was friendly, gradual, and negotiated progress. In their entirety the strategies were unsuccessful.

The major factor in the failure was without doubt the institutional dimension. The lack of convergence in the institutional framework in the fields of monetary policy and the regulation of banking reduced interest in the *rapprochements* that had been envisaged by preserving the heterogenous nature of the European market and the specific nature of each national market in the relations the great banks had with their customers. In addition, the fact that most of the major French banks were nationalized was no doubt a serious handicap which stopped them formulating offers or seizing opportunities that private institutions with greater freedom of movement could have more easily grasped. Explanatory factors of a political nature should also be considered alongside the institutional dimension of the problem. For a long time French banks came up against the handicap of their size compared with that of their European partners, for whom merger operations were perhaps not possible or acceptable. From that point of view, the attitude of the German banks, and particularly of the Deutsche Bank, can be seen as a successful management of the time factor, which would subsequently re-establish a balance that is now in their favour.

NOTES

1. On the Ligue Européenne de Coopération Economique, see M. Dumoulin and A. M. Dutrieue, *La Ligue Européenne de Coopération Economique* (Brussels: Peter Lang, 1993).
2. Archives Paribas, Département étranger, Dossier SFIDI, 1959–65; and Dossier SEDI, 1956–9.
3. Archives Crédit Lyonnais, 143 AH 2, handwritten note following a meeting held on 10 January 1957 in the president's office, 14 January 1975.
4. A. Lévy-Lang, 'Défense ou guerre economique?', *Défense* (September 1994) 24–6.
5. Archives Crédit Lyonnais, 143 AH2, address of M. Feuilhade de Chauvin, Hotel Bristol, 17 January 1973.
6. E. Bussière and M. Dumoulin, 'L'Emergence de l'idée economique Européenne d'un après-guerre . . . l'autre', in R. Girault (ed.), *Identité et conscience Européennes au XXe siècle* (Paris: Hachette, 1994), 67–105.
7. Archives Paribas, interview with F. Durand, 23 July 1991.
8. On these aspects of the question see E. Bussière, *Paribas, Europe and the World* (Antwerp: Fonds Mercator, 1993), 156–9.
9. Archives Paribas, Département étranger, Dossier SEDI, 1956–9.
10. Archives Crédit Lyonnais, DHB 4952, senior magement of the bank to O. G. Pirkham of Deutsche Bank, 21 April 1962.
11. Archives Crédit Lyonnais, DHB 4952, meeting with the representatives of the Deutsche Bank, 16 November 1966.
12. Supplement to the Lettre de l'EFMA, n. 26, March 1963.
13. Archives Crédit Lyonnais, DHB 4952, G. Cazès to O. G. Pirkham, 20 November 1966.
14. Archives Crédit Lyonnais, DHB 4952, note from permanent representative in Germany, 'Our Relations with the Deutsche Bank', 17 August 1967.

15. Archives Crédit Lyonnais, DHB 4952, note from representative in Germany, 17 July 1967.
16. Archives Crédit Lyonnais, DHB 4952, meeting of working party, no. 2, 20 April 1967.
17. Archives Crédit Lyonnais, DHB 4952, note from representative in Germany, 17 July 1967.
18. Archives Crédit Lyonnais, 143 AH2, 'Problem des alliances internationaux du Crédit Lyonnais', reflections by Feuilhade de Chauvin, 23 April 1970, and minutes of meeting of 30 April 1970.
19. Archives Crédit Lyonnais, DHB 4952, account of a discussion at the Deutsche Bank, 11 March 1969.
20. Archives Crédit Lyonnais, DHB 4952, note from representative in Germany, 17 July 1967.
21. Archives Crédit Lyonnais, 143 AH2, 'Problème des alliances', and minutes of 30 April 1970.
22. Archives Crédit Lyonnais, 143 AH2, 'Problème des alliances'.
23. Archives Crédit Lyonnais, 143 AH2, address of M. Feuilhade de Chauvin, 17 January 1973.
24. Archives Crédit Lyonnais, 143 AH2, notes and opinions, 12 April 1972.
25. Archives Crédit Lyonnais, 143 AH1, communication by M. Smolarski at the meeting of the senior management of the Crédit Lyonnais, 19 March 1971.
26. Archives Crédit Lyonnais, 143 AH2, handwritten note following a meeting held on 10 January 1957 in the president's office, 14 January 1975.
27. Archives Paribas, Paribas delegation to Germany, note of July 1970.
28. Archives Paribas, A History of Paribas in Germany, 1992. Départment étranger, dossiers 'Projected establishment of a financing company in Germany' and 'Bayrische Vereinsbank'.
29. Archives Paribas, Paribas in Italy, 5 November 1991.

8

German Banks and the American Challenge

ULRICH RAMM

Despite all the difficulties and setbacks, the German economy recovered fairly quickly from the aftermath of the Second World War. It largely benefited from the Marshall Plan and was put back on a track of fast and stable growth from the early 1950s. Gradual liberalization of exchange and capital control were consequences and additional factors of the 'German miracle'. In the second half of the 1950s, the restrictions on the West German capital market were gradually eased—with tax disadvantages in particular being dismantled—and the market was opened up internationally. One important aspect was the introduction of free convertibility for the D-mark in December 1958. Two years earlier, in May 1956, German residents had been permitted to buy foreign securities, which had an especially positive impact on the Frankfurt stock exchange. In September of that year, unofficial trading began in six foreign shares, all of them US industrial stocks. In the two following years, the first foreign-currency and foreign D-mark bonds were introduced on the German market. But it was not until the end of the 1960s that business involving non-German securities became more significant.

Very soon, Frankfurt am Main became the most important domestic financial centre. The ground for this development was prepared back in 1948, when the US military government managed to get Frankfurt accepted as the seat of Bank Deutscher Länder and also of Kreditanstalt für Wiederaufbau. This advantage was explicitly reconfirmed when Bank Deutscher Länder was transformed into the Deutsche Bundesbank in 1957. Together with other factors, such as the proximity of a large airport and the increasing economic importance of southern West Germany, Frankfurt became a magnet, prompting the German Big Three—Deutsche, Dresdner, and Commerzbank—to move their head offices to the city on the Main. Numerous other German institutions, such as Berliner Handels- und Frankfurter Bank (BHF), DG Bank, Deutsche Bau- und Bodenbank AG, and Hessische Landesbank, also had their legal seats in Frankfurt. Foreign banks also recognized the attractiveness of this financial centre. In the mid-1980s, 40 of the world's 50 largest banks had a presence in Frankfurt, and 80 per cent of the foreign banks represented in West Germany had established themselves in Frankfurt.[1]

The rapid expansion of the leading German banks' international activities, which began during the 1960s and gathered momentum in the 1970s, was more a reflection of the revival of West German business and its international expansion than an autonomous response to any 'American challenge', either actual or alleged.

Although the presence of US banks in West Germany rose substantially in the 1960s and 1970s and was sometimes perceived as unduly aggressive (see section 1), by no means should the international expansion of German banks be regarded as a mere reaction to the American competition. Major German commercial banks—the Big Three—went abroad to assist German multinational concerns in their international operations, as well as to compensate for slow domestic growth, hampered by regulation and increased market shares conquered by public sector banks and cooperative credit institutions, and eventually to pursue autonomous global strategies (section 2). The increasing role of the D-mark as an international currency, promoted by West Germany's leading position as a trading country, critically enhanced their international thrust (section 3). Since the late 1960s this was largely influenced by the establishment of the European Economic Community as well as by recurring debates on European monetary union. All major German banks participated in cooperative arrangements with traditional European partners in the form of clubs and consortia—a strategy bound to produce controversial results and gradually abandoned since the 1980s (section 4). In their penetration into the US market, on the contrary, German banks opted for a direct presence, by opening branches, acquiring participations, and establishing joint subsidiaries as part of cooperation agreements. This choice proved by far more successful and allowed them not only to further develop their international activities, but also to gain a footing in the American market and build up a significant base of domestic customers (section 5). Perhaps paradoxically, a much more effective American challenge was brought home to German banks on intellectual and political grounds at the mid-1970s. Then the failure of Bankhaus Herstatt triggered a large public debate on the advantages of the US-style dual banking system—a controversy eventually resolved in favour of the preservation of universal banking (section 6).

1. US Banks in West Germany

In the foreign business of American banks, operative units outside the United States were of little significance until the end of the 1950s. The extensive, traditional network of correspondent banks was quite adequate for handling international transactions. First National City Bank was the only institution to maintain a sizeable branch network in other countries, comprising 100 international outlets in 1964. Due to the increasing foreign direct investment of US industrial firms and their need for finance, American commercial banks stepped up their activities outside the USA during the second half of the 1960s. In part, this was also a reaction to US government policy, as capital-market restrictions were introduced to contain the country's balance-of-payments deficits. The Interest Equalization Tax (IET) levied from 1963 onwards on foreign bonds in the United States excluded many non-residents from the New York capital market and London became the beneficiary. The Voluntary Foreign Credit Restraint Programme of 1965, which required US banks to limit loans to non-residents, had a similar impact. At the same time, direct foreign investment out of the United States was subject to controls. Consequently, American multinationals wishing to invest abroad increasingly raised capital, either themselves or via subsidiaries, in the expanding London Euromarket. In order to avoid being at a competitive disadvantage, US banks found themselves obliged to establish units of their own in London or in continental Europe. Another reason for the international expansion of banking business was probably the above-mentioned restriction on setting up outlets in the United States itself, which encouraged banks to look for new markets further afield.[2] Moreover, since restrictions set by the Glass-Steagall Act of 1933, which installed the dual banking system, did not apply to operations abroad, this meant that US banks in Europe were able to conduct commercial and investment activities under one roof.

The strong international expansion of the banks primarily took the form of foreign branches. At the same time, though, they founded a series of subsidiaries, acquired participations and, to a lesser extent, set up joint ventures with other institutions. Between 1965 and 1972, the number of foreign outlets of American banks rose worldwide from 211 to 627. The total assets of these branches increased over the same period from US$9.1 bn. to US$77.4 bn. Purely in terms of the number of outlets, the regional breakdown shows a predominance of the Latin American countries. Yet if the total assets of the units are compared on a regional basis, the United Kingdom clearly tops the list at 57 per cent, followed by continental Europe with 18 per cent (1970).[3]

A number of factors—namely West Germany's significance as a major trading and industrial nation, the D-mark's increasingly prominent role in the Euromarkets and its emerging function as a reserve currency, together with liberal market setting (regulation on lending and borrowing interest rates ceased to be effective early in 1967)—all helped to raise the number of operative units and representative offices maintained by foreign banks in West

Germany, above all during the 1970s. Whereas 22 foreign banks with an aggregate business volume of DM6.8 bn. had been active in the Federal Republic in 1968, there were 42 institutions from abroad by 1973 with a business volume of DM28.2 bn., and five years later their total had risen to 53, with a combined business volume of DM38.2 bn. The US banks represented the largest group, with 13 banks maintaining some 30 outlets as of the mid-1970s. Altogether, their share amounted to two-thirds of the business volume of all foreign banks in West Germany. At the same time, the largest institutions also came from the USA, namely Citibank AG and Chase Bank AG, both in Frankfurt am Main, with total assets of DM2.6 and DM2.3 bn. respectively (figures relate to 1978).[4] The American units defended their top position for a long time and it was not until the 1980s that they were relegated to second place by Japanese institutions.[5]

The first offshoots of foreign banks in West Germany after 1945 were those of Chase Manhattan Bank and First National Citibank in Frankfurt am Main and that of Bank of America in Düsseldorf; they opened for business between 1947 and 1953. However, their sole purpose was to provide the US Army with financial services; they were prohibited from accepting deposits from German customers or from conducting securities transactions with them.[6] In 1965, First National Bank opened two more branches in West Germany and Morgan Guaranty Trust Company of New York transformed its Frankfurt representative office into an operative unit. Further branches followed, such as those of American Express Bank GmbH and First National Bank of Chicago (1966), Bank of America and Chemical Bank New York (1969), as well as of National Bank of Detroit (1972). In 1973, Chase Manhattan Bank (National Association) was established with its seat in Frankfurt am Main. In addition, a round-up from the 1970s shows there were a number of American participations in German institutions. Bankers Trust, for instance, held a 75 per cent majority interest in Deutsche Union Bank, Citibank acquired majority shareholdings in Trinkaus & Burkhardt (51%) and KKB Kundenkreditbank (75%), while Bank of America bought a stake in Centrale Credit AG. There was also an interest of over 25 per cent held by Wells Fargo in Allgemeine Deutsche Creditanstalt and a stake of more than 40 per cent acquired by First National Bank of Wisconsin in Bankhaus Koch, Lauteren & Co. Chase Manhattan Bank pursued another approach, when it established Familienbank AG in 1973 as a wholly owned subsidiary for retail business.

In the 1980s and 1990s, the trend for American banks to set up shop in Germany continued; among others, J. P. Morgan (1984), Morgan Stanley (1986), First Commercial Bank (1991), Bankers Trust (1994), and Merrill Lynch (1996) deserve to be mentioned here.[7] Credit institutions that are majority-held by foreign banks have the same rights and obligations as their German counterparts. The banking supervision authorities and the Bundesbank treat them as legally independent institutions whose liable funds have to be secured by means of adequate capital backing. In accordance with a bilateral agreement between Germany and the US, which is largely based on the fourth amendment to the German Banking Act of 1993, the offshoots of American banks no longer need to be endowed with capital. The equal treatment accorded to foreign and domestic credit institutions and also the unrestricted possibility for banks to invest in trading and industrial enterprises make Germany an extremely attractive location for foreign banks.[8]

In 1968 and 1969, when US international monetary policy was especially restrictive, the foreign offshoots of American banks raised funds for their parent banks in the Euromarket more reasonably than they could have done at home. Once the situation in the US money market became less tense, lending to non-banks increased substantially. American banks' foreign units served US companies operating on the spot, but increasingly they were attracting major local companies as well. In West Germany, they were keen to do business with export-oriented firms in the chemical, steel, mechanical engineering, electronics, and car industries in particular, whereas only Citibank made concerted efforts to acquire retail customers.[9] By the end of the 1970s, foreign banks in the Federal Republic accounted altogether for 2.9 per cent of the overall business volume of all groups of banks; on both asset and liability sides of foreign banks' balance sheets, however, interbank business predominated.[10] Overall, the focus on interbank transactions, the provision of services for large companies and, most recently, involvement in off-balance-sheet business represented a typical pattern for all foreign banks in Germany. By contrast, foreign banks play virtually no role whatsoever for retail German customers, if Citibank is left out of consideration, which sees itself as a provider of financial services that is active worldwide in all segments of business.[11] For a variety of reasons, the attempts during the 1990s by institutions such as Crédit Lyonnais, Barclays, NatWest, and Crédit Suisse or Julius Bär to establish themselves in the market for private customers have proved fairly unsuccessful.

Can we sum all this up, therefore, and speak of an 'American challenge', as Jean-Jacques Servan-Schreiber claimed in his book published in 1967? Incidentally, West Germany experienced a similar debate about 'excessive foreign influence' or the 'Americanization of business'. This was triggered by the fact that roughly DM11.1 bn. of the aggregate nominal capital of all German industrial enterprises was in foreign hands. In 1964, this amounted to about 10 per cent . A breakdown of these participations by nationality reveals that the United States was to the fore, accounting for 34.1 per cent of the total, followed by the Netherlands, Switzerland, the United Kingdom, and France (with 17.4, 16, 9.8, and 7.1% respectively).[12] These figures undoubtedly show the strong expansion of the United States, yet at the same time they also indicate the international orientation and links between the world's developed economies.

Servan-Schreiber considered the battle 'over electronic data-processing equipment, computers' to represent the core of the approaching industrial war between Europe and the US.[13] If we consider the present position of Bill Gates and Microsoft, his fears have possibly been proved correct. But a look at banking produces different, rather mixed results. At the time, the sharp increase in foreign banks, especially those from the US, probably did seem to be 'an invasion of Continental Europe by banks from overseas, and in particular of the liberal ground of the Federal Republic'.[14] However, I think it remarkable that in the 1970s the American banks for the most part moved their foreign activities away from London to the offshore financial centres of the Bahamas and the Cayman Islands. The share of balance-sheet business handled via London contracted from 50.6 to 37.5 per cent between 1973 and 1976, whereas the Bahamas and the Cayman Islands raised their share from 19.5 to 30.6 per cent over this period. In addition, American banks turned to the financial centres of the Middle East, as they were attracting the lion's share of the surplus petrodollars which had to be invested.[15]

Subjectively, therefore, the Europeans may well have felt that they were facing an American challenge in banking. In global terms, however, West Germany and continental Europe were rather part of an American worldwide expansion. Perhaps the aggressive approach of the Americans and their claim at the time to be the only global players caused a temporary shock. US banks earned themselves the reputation of being 'financial cowboys'[16] and helped promote competition, above all with the major banks. Yet the shock cannot have been very profound. The Bundesbank, writing in 1972, voiced the opinion that 'foreign banks established in the Federal Republic and participations of foreigners in German banks are of relatively marginal, albeit increasing, significance'.[17] In fact, virtually parallel to this development or only a little later, German banks expanded their activities in the United States. What is more, US and German banks alike were primarily developing their presence in the emerging international financial markets and providing financial support for the efforts of industrial companies from their home countries to expand worldwide.

2. Why Germany's Big Three Developed International Operations

Within a short time, West Germany, whose external trade had entirely collapsed by 1945, became a 'world export champion'. With deliveries abroad

amounting to more than US$11 bn., the Federal Republic had already over-
taken the United Kingdom by 1960 to occupy second place to the United
States (US$21 bn.).[18] The export level of around US$40 bn. later attained
by the United States was already matched by the early 1970s. Between 1986
and 1988 as well as in 1990, West Germany even overtook the US to claim
first place.[19]

The strong expansion of external trade was followed by a steady increase
in German companies' foreign investment. New investment increased from
an average of DM300 m. per year during the 1950s to roughly DM5 bn.
by the mid-1970s and practically DM10 bn. in the early 1980s.[20] By 1980,
the aggregate volume of Foreign Direct Investment, at DM148 bn., was
exceeded only by that of the United States (equivalent to DM422 bn.) and
the United Kingdom (DM156 bn.), whose figures include sizeable amounts of
pre-war investment.[21] The greater part, namely 65 per cent, of the altogether
DM74 bn. of German direct investment during the 1952–80 period went to
manufacturing, but no less than a tenth was already channelled into banks.[22]

West Germany's political weakness in the arena of international relations, which contrasted sharply with its international economic strength—
according to a popular saying, the Federal Republic of Germany was
'economically a giant but politically a dwarf'—was the result of the Second
World War. Consequently, it went hand in hand with a special relationship
with the US and a peculiar role in the process of post-1945 European integration. The leading role of the United States was already a key element when the
West German state was being set up, as R.G. Livingston, a former top official
of the US state department, has noted:

Between 1947 and 1949, it was clearly the United States . . . that took the initiative to
erect a separate West German state. The British and French subsequently fell in line
behind United States occupation policies—they really had no choice—in supporting
the establishment of the Bizonal Economic Council, and subsequently, in 1949, the
United States forced a decision on the 'parliamentary' council, an assembly of German
politicians that drafted a provisional constitution for the Federal Republic.

In a collection of papers from a bilateral conference, Marion Gräfin Dönhoff
characterizes the German–American relationship and the special position
of the Federal Republic in Western Europe as follows: 'The Americans . . .
became accustomed to seeing the Federal Republic as sort of a little America:
economically strong, precise, reliable, achievement-oriented. And so the
Germans, who for years had been regarded with mistrust and suspicion,
gradually became accepted; they even took on a certain privileged position
among the Europeans.'[23]

Despite the manifest strength of the West German economy, the international expansion of the country's banks could only be pursued against this political background as a cautious, evolutionary process, and not in the form of mounting a challenge to strong foreign rivals. The first steps abroad, therefore, largely took the form of cooperation agreements with foreign partners. In view of the ever greater integration of the Western European market, including the creation of a single currency, the attitude of both politicians and the business sector in West Germany was frequently ambivalent.[24] On the one hand, they were keen to make a constructive contribution because of historical experience and the global challenges; but, on the other, they emphasized their own strength. This is underlined by the stony road to agreement at Maastricht in December 1991.[25] In West Germany, however, the major banks had assumed a prominent role among the advocates of European Monetary Union.[26] Commerzbank's chairman at the time, Walter Seipp, called for the establishment of a European central bank even before the EU governments began to negotiate.[27] At the end of the 1960s, a member of Commerzbank's management board had already stated: 'It seems to me that bank mergers are hardly feasible in the EEC without a single currency policy.'[28]

Rigid banking structures at home, characterized by the dominant market share of public-law and cooperative institutions, together with a high density of regulations, were further reasons for the large private-sector banks to become active abroad on a significant scale. Measured in terms of business volume, the market share of commercial banks contracted from 30.6 to 24.8 per cent between 1954 and 1970, while savings banks managed to raise their market share from 33.3 to 38.3 per cent and credit cooperatives from 8.0 to 11.5 per cent; specialist institutions and mortgage banks accounted for the remaining percentage shares. Within the group of commercial banks, the Big Three's share declined from 51 to 41 per cent (from 15.6% to 10.2%, if all banks are taken into consideration).[29] The degree of concentration expressed by the last-mentioned figure did not rise appreciably in subsequent decades[30] and is extremely low when compared with all the other Western European countries.[31]

Until the 1980s, when it was reduced, the density of regulation hampered the international activities of the Big Three German banks in particular, prompting them to move operations to so-called Eurocentres such as Luxembourg and London. At the 1979 annual German banking conference, the then president of the Bundesbank, Otmar Emminger, noted that 'One special problem is certainly the ever greater transfer of lending to subsidiaries abroad.'[32] The president of the federal banking supervisory authority, Inge Lore Bähre, added a further aspect, namely that banking in the meantime was no longer merely following trading activities. 'It is an established fact today that it is following the attractiveness of markets which have developed free from the influence of the central bank and state supervision and, in addition, are located around our globe such that it is now possible at last to conduct banking transactions right round the clock.'[33]

From the end of the 1970s onwards, banks cannot be said to have merely accompanied or followed companies abroad, as is revealed by the comment by the president of the German supervisory authority quoted above. However, it was not until the following decades that the financial sector largely 'became independent'. Reviewing the development of the German banking industry, Werner Ehrlicher writes:

In the lectures and textbooks of the fifties and sixties on 'money and credit', the monetary sector was presented as a service industry in the sense that it fulfils ancillary functions for the real economy. Accordingly, a highly parallel development was assumed—and could be observed in reality, too—between the development of the two sectors. Real turnover was thought to correspond to monetary transactions, monetary capital formation reflected real capital formation, and foreign-exchange transactions were seen as being closely related to the current and capital accounts. The change that has taken place in the meantime in the relationship between the real economy and the monetary sector can be summed up by saying that at both the national and the international level a monetary superstructure exists today which is created by effecting transactions on a grand scale that are exclusively restricted to the monetary sector. Put somewhat differently: only to a very limited extent does the monetary domain perform ancillary functions today; it has become independent and as such has turned into an autonomous area, which has its own objectives.[34]

With hindsight, it can be said that pointers to this development were already evident during the 1970s, for instance during the recycling of petrodollars, where German banks played a prominent role. However, by international standards, the leading banks frequently steered a distinctly cautious business policy, rejecting exaggerated expansion,[35] which ensured relative stability for the German financial sector.

3. The International Role of the Deutsch-mark

During the 1960s, the international business of German banks was already spurred by the growing esteem in which their currency was held abroad and its increasing use worldwide. 'The advance of the German banks on the international scene was favoured by the increasingly strong D-mark, which underwent its first modest revaluation in March 1961.'[36] In just over two decades, the West German currency, created in 1948, rose from nothing to become the world's second leading currency after the US dollar. Quite fittingly, a journalistically written economic history in the 1970s bears the title, 'The D-mark. The child of the occupying forces becomes an international star.'[37]

Initially, the rise of the D-mark was primarily at the expense of sterling, the once leading international currency which was relegated to second place during the 1920s by the US dollar, but which was still able to play an important subsidiary role for several decades. At the start of 1973, 6.7 per cent of the currency reserves of the central banks were already held in D-marks; sterling, in third place, accounted for 5.9 per cent and the dollar 84.5 per cent.[38] The D-mark's share expanded to over 10 per cent by the end of the 1970s and subsequently to about 15 per cent; this time, its rise was at the expense of the US dollar and despite the administrative obstacles imposed by the Bundesbank; however, 'excessive dollar creation and American "benign neglect" of the dollar as a store of value for private and official dollar holders have increasingly rendered such obstacles ineffective, or encouraged circumvention by various routes, especially that offered by the Euromarkets'.[39]

This increased the international business opportunities of banks with a D-mark basis, i.e. with access to the Bundesbank as a lender of last resort—which does not mean simply German banks, but also covers the foreign banks operative in Germany. As C. L. Holtfrerich argues,

The collapse of the Bretton Woods system of fixed exchange rates, the increasing role played by the D-mark in the Euromarket, the diversification of currency portfolios within a system of flexible exchange rates, the incipient demand for the D-mark as a reserve currency, the enormous expansion in international capital movements and other factors in which globalizing tendencies found expression at the time are the best explanations for the ever stronger trend for foreign banks to establish outlets in West Germany during the 1970s.[40]

In this connection, the occasionally voiced criticism that foreign banks suffered disadvantages in underwriting business[41] needs to be modified. The 'anchoring principle', introduced in 1968 and maintained until 1985, reserved the lead management of foreign issuers' D-mark bonds for German banks. The Bundesbank's main motive here was to control—and restrict—the use of the D-mark abroad. The competitive disadvantage for US investment houses, for example, which was the indirect outcome of this, is not as relevant as it may at first appear, since securities business in West Germany was still fairly weak during the first few decades after 1945; it did not become more significant until the 1980s and above all the 1990s.

Unlike the central banks, which were slow to diversify their currency reserves, the financial markets did not hesitate to use the D-mark to a considerable extent. By the 1960s, the German currency had already easily overtaken sterling in terms of the claims held by what were then known as

Eurobanks and had moved up to second place behind the dollar; towards the end of the 1970s, practically 20 per cent of these claims were denominated in D-marks.[42] A similar development was registered for international bonds as well as for longer-term Euroloans; if all currencies are taken into account, though, German banks as lead managers had a position roughly on a par with that of British and French banks.[43]

As an invoicing currency for world exports, the D-mark had achieved a share of almost 15 per cent by the end of the 1970s. This was largely due to the fact that for the most part—more than 80 per cent, in fact—German exporters could invoice in their national currency.[44] Only the US registered a higher share of its external trade invoiced in its own national currency, and Switzerland alone had similar ratios to Germany.

However, use of their own currency by German exporters removed the need for foreign-exchange and hedging transactions on the part of the banks. Above all, the imposition of such regulations as the minimum reserve requirement meant that Germany's foreign-exchange market remained fairly underdeveloped. In the 1980s and 1990s, it trailed far behind London and New York, and even ranked after such centres as Tokyo, Zurich, Singapore, and Hong Kong.[45] But the somewhat paradoxical constellation of a strong currency and a weak financial centre implied that German banks switched sizeable segments of their business abroad. All the same, even by the end of the 1970s, the international networks of outlets maintained by German banks were nothing like as extensive as those of their French or British rivals.

4. Cooperation versus Competition in European Banking

The international strategy of the leading German banks has been greatly influenced by Western European integration since the 1950s, much more strongly at any rate than by reactions to American competition. The focus here has always been on mutual cooperation agreements between European institutions. Frequently, though, these were limited in scope or duration, and in the final analysis they were overshadowed by the competition that continued to exist between members of the group.

In 1958, at the first German banking congress to be held after a gap of 20 years, international expansion had not yet become a topic, unlike the European Economic Community, launched at the start of that year. The idea that the new common market would ultimately lead to a common central bank and a single currency 'seems utopian to me', declared Hermann Josef Abs of Deutsche Bank.[46] At the 1963 banking congress, Abs stressed that all EEC countries had highly developed banking systems so that 'in none of the countries which we are looking at today is there any necessity nor even any sign of a need to establish additional banks from outside by setting up offshoots or affiliations'. For some time, however, there had been close European cooperation, said Abs.[47] 'There is neither any commercial need for an international expansion of banks' branch networks, nor would this be sensible or attractive from a private-enterprise angle.'[48] This was confirmed by his counterparts elsewhere in Europe, such as Peter Plantenga, general manager of Rotterdamsche Bank: 'It is much more practical to benefit through amicable business links with well-established correspondent bank partners from their knowledge of the business community and financing opportunities in their respective country than to attempt to operate independently in their market.'[49]

The necessity for banks to set up foreign outlets of their own was discussed to a greater extent at the 1968 banking congress. Will Marx, a member of Commerzbank's management board, pointed out that 'in this decade, the large American banks have gained a spectacular foothold in Europe; they even claim to be the only supranational banks in Europe ... German industry, which has built up a worldwide network of production and sales units, has long complained to us about how much better its competitors from the United States fare; in virtually every country in the world, they find that American banks offer their services.' However, this call to banks to establish foreign outlets of their own explicitly omitted Western Europe, where it was considered sensible for institutions to hold shares and participations in one another, but not to maintain branches in other Western European countries. Conversely, 'no institution from another European country has established a branch office here in the Federal Republic since the war.'[50] This situation did not alter until the 1970s. Before that happened, though, the first major wave of European banking cooperations occurred.

Practically all the larger German banks were involved during the early 1970s in the formation of banking clubs such as ABECOR (Dresdner Bank), EBIC (Deutsche Bank), Europartners (Commerzbank), and Orion (Westdeutsche Landesbank).[51] Most certainly, these steps can be seen in connection with a resurgence of European integration, which was reflected in the Werner plan of 1969—the first project for economic and monetary union—and in the enlargement of the European Economic Community as from 1973 to include Denmark, the United Kingdom, and Ireland.

Like their neighbours elsewhere in Western Europe, Germany's banks were confronted with the question of how to adjust to the larger market. They could either attempt to take on European dimensions or restrict themselves to their traditional home market, becoming no more than regional niche-players. For the first option, two approaches were possible. They could either create offshoots of their own or take over existing banks, or they could cooperate with similar institutions in other EEC countries. A strategy of going it alone is feasible for only a few very large banks, and even they soon find that they have reached the limits of their capital resources. Moreover, the more or less friendly takeover of banks can easily acquire a slightly imperialist character. One advantage of cooperation, on the other hand, is that less capital is tied up. Its drawback is possibly that co-ordination becomes more difficult. A mutual cross-shareholding may be useful for underpinning cooperation; at the same time, it offers protection against hostile takeovers.[52]

The banking clubs, which were too broad in conception and represented fairly loose arrangements, proved to be inadequate given the incompatible goals and development of their members.[53] They were later dissolved in order to make room for new forms of alliance. In retrospect, we can say that the banking cooperation agreements of the 1970s were over-ambitious ventures, lacking the necessary basis in reality. They shared this shortcoming with the Werner plan, the bold project for a European currency, for which also the time was not yet ripe.

Although it was 1992 before the Europartners cooperation was formally terminated, it had largely ground to a halt by the late 1980s. In Commerzbank's 1992 annual report, the brief statement appeared that 'After just over two decades of cooperation, the Europartners group has been dissolved, since the business goals and strategies of the individual members had become ever more difficult to reconcile with one another. Nevertheless, our good bilateral relations with these banks will remain intact.'[54]

At the start of 1988, Commerzbank's chairman, Walter Seipp, had reaffirmed the strategy of cooperation; however, he had also pointed out that

Loose constellations like the Europartners Group formed in the early 1970s no longer meet today's requirements. What would be needed, for example, is a deepening of cooperation through mutual cross-shareholdings. These can be seen as the preliminary step towards mergers in a distant future, and also as protection against hostile takeovers. Commerzbank took a step in this direction in 1984 with its 10 per cent interest in the major Spanish bank Banco Hispano Americano, which included representation on the bank's supervisory board.[55]

During the 1990s, this approach was maintained, backed by further equity participations, mostly in the form of cross-shareholdings.

5. German Banks in the United States of America

Foreign banks have had a significant presence in the United States only since the 1960s, after the state of New York granted permission for them to set up branches there. The combined balance-sheet totals of foreign banks in the

United States rose from US$7 bn. in 1965 to US$26 bn. in 1972 and roughly US$168 bn. by 1979. Banking groups from the United Kingdom, Canada, and Japan were the most prominently represented.[56]

After 1945, German banks tended to be slow to develop a network of operative units abroad. They mainly revived old correspondent banking relationships from the pre-war period and only gradually did they begin to build up their own international presence by opening representative offices. Commerzbank, for example, set up representative offices in Amsterdam, Madrid, and Rio de Janeiro in 1953. Perhaps German institutions still had too much internal reorganization to master during this phase—after all, the Big Three were re-merging and rebuilding their branch networks—and this made them reluctant to become involved in the international capital markets. Another factor which made them cautious was the experience of having twice lost their foreign assets in the first half of the century.

However, the general tendency towards a stronger international orientation in banking brought about a change of attitude in the 1960s. Five factors proved instrumental. The expansion of world trade, in which German exporters were prominent, made external trade finance increasingly important. In the Euromarket, the D-mark took its place alongside the US dollar as a major trading currency. The direct investments of German companies abroad caused banks to follow their clients. With an international presence, a US financing base could be developed by accepting customers' deposits. The foreign presence of American banks encouraged their German counterparts to establish offshoots of their own in other countries.[57] In retrospect, this strategic step proved to be correct for, even by the second half of the 1970s, foreign commercial business accounted for more than 30 per cent of the total earnings of Germany's Big Three banks.

In the US and worldwide, German banks adopted a mixed strategy for setting up their international networks of outlets. In addition to representative offices, they opened branches, acquired participations and established joint subsidiaries as part of cooperation agreements.

One of the first German banks to explore the US market was Commerzbank. In 1967 it opened a representative office in New York, which was transformed into a branch in 1971—the first operative unit of a German bank. In Commerzbank's annual report, the opening of the New York branch was described as 'a logical complement of our growing activity in the international financial markets'; 'at the same time, we are in a better position to provide financing for the growing interest of German industry in investing in the USA', and conversely the bank said it was now also able 'to offer US concerns with European offshoots a comprehensive service'.[58]

In 1972, EuroPartners Securities Corporation was founded in New York for investment banking activities as a joint venture under the cooperation agreement between the European banks Banco di Roma, Commerzbank, and Crédit Lyonnais. This institution was transformed into the wholly owned Commerzbank subsidiary Commerzbank Capital Markets Corporation (CCMC) in 1988. CCMC, a member of the New York Stock Exchange, looks after private and government investors worldwide, with particular emphasis on North America, in foreign-exchange dealings, investment banking, and corporate finance.[59]

Strategically, Deutsche Bank opted to go about things in a different order. Together with its partners in the EBIC Group, it founded the consortium bank European American Banking Corporation and European-American Bank & Trust Company in 1968. Both institutions primarily looked after European companies that were active in the US and American firms with European offshoots. After the financial burden incurred by the takeover of Franklin National Bank, which was intended to secure access to retail business, the two joint ventures were merged in 1977 to form a holding, European American Bankcorp. One year later, Deutsche Bank acquired from Union Bank of Switzerland the remaining shares of UBS-DB Corporation. The New York-based securities and new issues house, in which Deutsche Bank had acquired a stake in 1971, was renamed Atlantic Capital Corporation in 1978. The existence of these participations meant that Deutsche Bank did not establish a branch office in the United States until 1979, thus becoming the last of Germany's Big Three banks to take this step.[60]

Through its subsidiary German-American Securities Corporation (GASC), founded in Boston in 1968, Dresdner Bank became the first German credit institution to be directly represented on a US stock exchange. Business activities were expanded within the framework of the ABECOR group of European banks. In 1972, the wholly owned subsidiary GASC was integrated into the newly formed ABD Securities Corporation New York in a joint project with Bayerische Hypotheken- und Wechsel-Bank. Above all during the 1980s, Dresdner Bank steadily increased its shareholding in this investment bank. In September 1972, Dresdner Bank also opened a branch office in New York.[61]

German banks have continually stepped up their involvement in the US by opening further branch offices. By the start of the 1980s, 16 German institutions had a presence there, with a combined balance-sheet total of more than DM35 bn. In addition to the Big Three, regional banks and Landesbanks also became active in the United States; these included Bayerische Vereinsbank, Bank für Gemeinwirtschaft, BHF-Bank, DG Bank Deutsche Genossenschaftsbank and Westdeutsche Landesbank. Their preferred locations for banking operations even today are New York, Grand Cayman, Los Angeles, Chicago, and Atlanta, as well as San Francisco and Miami.[62]

In by far the majority of cases, foreign banks in the US have opted either to establish branch offices or to set up an agency or subsidiary; participations in investment houses have tended to be less common. Business is largely concentrated on wholesale operations, i.e. jumbo loans, export and import financing, and services such as international payments, swaps, options, and cash management. The outlets of German banks have rapidly gained a footing in the American market and have built up a set of regular domestic clients. In 1986, Klaas Peter Jacobs, branch manager of Commerzbank in New York at the time, reported that of his branch's overall business volume 60 per cent was generated by US companies and 20 per cent each by German customers and international transactions.[63]

6. The Herstatt Shock and the Debate on the 'US Model' of Banking

The collapse in June 1974 of Bankhaus I. D. Herstatt, a private bank largely unknown to the broader public outside Germany, not only led to a marked tightening-up of banking regulation and supervision, but also to a deposit insurance scheme that, by international comparison, is the most comprehensive of its kind. The bank's failure also triggered a structural debate that, in retrospect, can be seen as a confrontation on what was felt by the critics to be the 'advantages of the American system'. Whereas the Americans introduced the dual banking system into Japan after 1945, this did not happen in West Germany; moreover, the break-up of German major banks into regional units was also no more than temporary.

Through rapid expansion of its deposits and above all risky foreign-exchange transactions, Herstatt had grown into Germany's largest private banker;[64] however, its ultimate business volume of DM2 bn. corresponded to no more than 5 per cent of that of Commerzbank at the end of 1973. Nevertheless, the bank's failure sent shock waves through the system. Deposits were withdrawn from private banks on a large scale.

When the hysteria in the late summer [of 1974] began to revive the worst memories of the 1931 banking crisis, the Bundesbank intervened, first by setting up a liquidity consortium and then 'Liquiditäts-Konsortialbank' [to serve as the 'lifeboat' institution of the German banking industry], along the same lines as its predecessor at the time of the bank failures in the German Reich, more than forty years previously, which had been factors in preparing the ground for Nazi rule.[65]

Banking supervision was generally tightened up, for instance by means of principle 1a, resolved on 30 August 1974, which limited open positions in foreign-exchange business to 30 per cent of a bank's liable capital.[66]

Comparable or even far more serious banking crises in other industrial countries had far less serious repercussions. This holds true for the secondary banking crisis in the UK in 1973–5 and the collapse of Franklin National Bank[67] in the US in 1974, an institution which had been 102nd in the world league table at the end of 1972 with deposits of US$3.5 bn. (equal to DM11.2 bn.). It also holds true for the American Savings and Loan crisis during the 1980s. The last-mentioned crisis even gave rise to a moral-hazard debate in connection with the deposit insurance scheme, in which it was claimed that over-generous cover would prompt banks to adopt imprudent business policies, which could even make banking crises possible. The prevailing philosophy in Germany was very different. In the wake of the Herstatt crisis, the scope of deposit insurance was raised from the previous level of only DM20,000 to 30 per cent of a bank's liable funds. Even in the case of smaller institutions, this would imply virtually complete cover for all deposits and consequently more extensive insurance protection than in the other industrial states. However, this by no means appears to have promoted an irresponsible approach to business policy as the moral-hazard argument claims that it might. Rather, it has tended to produce a sound banking system[68] which has led to relatively cautious expansion at the international level and has largely managed to avoid asset bubbles.

In the structural debate triggered by the Herstatt crisis, the special features of the German universal bank system were called into question, with many aspects of the American system being held up as a positive alternative.[69] After four and a half years of investigation, the study commission set up by the federal finance minister in November 1974 presented a solid final report of more than 600 pages, in which a 'strong minority'[70] of experts submitted a critical assessment of various features of the German system and advocated changes along the lines of American structures.

Conflicts of interest were singled out for criticism, which—it was claimed—result from universal banks' double role as lenders and shareholders in individual companies, combined with their representation on the supervisory board. The latter aspect was thought to permit too strong a concentration of power and to impair competition. German universal banks were also suspected of having less interest in the development of securities markets because they preferred to make loans to companies. However, the alleged strengths of the dual banking system in this connection are not reflected in the final appraisal: '. . . the commission concludes that it is not recommendable to abandon the universal banking system; . . . on the whole, this [system] has proved its worth;

alleged or actual faults of the present banking system fail to provide suffi-cient reason for a change of system. The universal banking system is firmly integrated into our economic structure.'[71]

It is apparently an irony of history that dual banking systems which had either developed over time or had been decreed by law were dismantled over the next few decades. In the United Kingdom, this occurred in the wake of the Big Bang of 1986, when the leading commercial banks moved into investment banking through takeovers or by establishing subsidiaries. In the United States, this tendency spread during the 1990s, the most spectacular example being the merger of Citibank and Travelers Group to form an *Allfinanz* or *bancassurance* concern, while the trend was generally sanctioned in legal terms at the end of 1999. In Japan, too, this development is similarly well advanced. All the same, it is worth noting that the debate on the strengths and weaknesses of the American dual banking system compared with the continental European universal banking system, which was conducted on a broad scale for the first time after the Herstatt collapse, has continued right up to the present to exert a substantial intellectual influence; it recently resurfaced again in connection with the crisis of the Holzmann group at the end of 1999.

7. Conclusive Remarks

The response to the American challenge can be seen as very much a secondary reason for the strategy of international expansion pursued by Germany's Big Three banks. The momentum was provided by the resurgence of the West German economy and the worldwide activities of German firms, with the banks assuming a supporting function. At the same time, the banks had ground to make good because they had lost all their foreign outlets as a result of the war. The prospect of developing activities abroad was made more attractive by the limited business opportunities available to them in Germany due to the predominance of the public-law institutions and the restrictions imposed on banking by the supervisory authorities and the Bundesbank— above all in the form of the minimum reserve requirements. It is only with these qualifications that Bernd Rudolph's statement is valid that 'the close relationship between bank and client typical of the German banking system and the pressure of competition from American institutions virtually served as a stimulus for banks to accompany their corporate customers abroad. From the mid-1960s onwards, therefore, a trend for banks to establish a European presence can be noted'.[72]

Whereas the American challenge in the first decades after 1945 was no more than a secondary aspect among the factors determining the strategies of the leading German banks, it moved more into the limelight towards the end of the

1990s. Since the collapse of the Eastern bloc, we have inhabited a new world. This has been compounded by European Monetary Union, which has given rise for the first time to a financial area comparable in size to that of North America, with the euro a leading world currency taking its place alongside the US dollar. Even in the first year of its existence, the single European currency was used for roughly the same volume of international bond issues as the dollar. In other areas, it will take time for the dollar's prominent role to be challenged; when it happens, a bipolar world currency system will develop.

What we are experiencing to a greater extent, therefore, is the development of divergent interests on either side of the Atlantic. These relate to the major issues surrounding the World Trade Organization (WTO) and extend to the details of banking regulation through international capital-adequacy standards. The attempt to establish compatible accounting rules—International Accounting Standards (IAS) versus US practice (US GAAP)—is relevant for the whole of business and for global competition. The American challenge of the 1960s was only the prologue to the story.

NOTES

1. C.-L. Holtfrerich, *Finanzplatz Frankfurt: Von der mittelalterlichen Messestadt zum europäischen Bankenzentrum* (Munich: C. H. Beck, 1999), 225 ff.
2. H. Van der Wee, *Der gebremste Wohlstand: Wiederaufbau, Wachstum und Strukturwandel der Weltwirtschaft seit 1945*, Geschichte der Weltwirtschaft im 20. Jahrhundert, 6 (Munich: dtv Deutscher Taschenbuch Verlag, 1984), 532–3.
3. U. Steuber, *Internationale Banken: Auslandsaktivitäten von Banken bedeutender Industrieländer*, HWWA-Studien zur Außenwirtschaft und Entwicklungspolitik (Hamburg: Verlag Weltarchiv, 1974), 26 ff.
4. H. Wolf, *30 Jahre Nachkriegsentwicklung im Deutschen Bankwesen* (Mainz: Hase & Koehler, 1980), 123–5.
5. The business volume of the outlets of foreign banks amounted to roughly DM73 bn. in 1988; about 40% of this was generated by Japanese banks, practically 30% by US banks, and roughly 10% by Italian banks, see J. Stein, *The Banking System in Germany* (Cologne: Bank Verlag, 1990, 16th rev. edn.), 34.
6. Holtfrerich, *Finanzplatz Frankfurt*, 278.
7. See 'Deutsch-amerikanische Banken-Kooperation', *Zeitschrift für das gesamte Kreditwesen*, 19/3 (1996), 4–5; W. Scheele, 'Citibank', *Zeitschrift für das gesamte Kreditwesen*, 28 (1975), 589–92; S. Rometsch, 'Chase Manhattan Bank', ibid., 592–4; A. Knör, 'Chemical Bank', ibid., 594–6; W. Scheele, 'Die unterschiedlichen Strategien amerikanischer Banken im Ausland, insbesondere in der Bundesrepublik Deutschland', paper presented at Freie Universität Berlin, 16 January

1976 (mimeographed); Verlag Hoppenstedt GmbH (ed.), *Banken-Jahrbuch 1999* (Darmstadt: Hoppenstedt, 1998); C. Hartkopf, *Die Geschäftspolitik amerikanischer Banken in Deutschland, 1960–1995* (Frankfurt am Main: Peter Lang, 2000).

8. Institute of International Bankers, *Global Survey of Permissible Activities for Banking Organizations in Financial Centers Outside the U.S.* (n. p.: Institute of International Bankers, 1988), 23–8. The study also expressly emphasizes the efficiency of the universal banking system and its contribution towards the stability of Germany's financial system and its economy as a whole.

9. U. Steuber, *Internationale Banken: Auslandsaktivitäten bedeutender Industrieländer*, Veröffentlichungen des HWWA-Instituts für Wirtschaftsforschung, Hamburg, suppl. vols., 1976 and 1977 (Hamburg: Verlag Weltarchiv, 1977 and 1978), 36–7; G. Vosshall, 'Auslandsbanken als Wettbewerbsfaktor im deutschen Bankwesen', in B. Röper, (ed.), *Wettbewerbsprobleme im Kreditgewerbe*, Schriften des Vereins für Socialpolitik, NS, 87 (Berlin: Duncker & Humblot, 1976), 106–16.

10. The ratio of 'lending to banks' to 'lending to non-banks' was about 30:70 for all groups of banks in 1979, yet for foreign banks it was 60:40. The same picture emerges for the funding side. While the ratio of 'deposits from banks' to 'deposits from non-banks' stood at 33:67 for the banking industry as a whole, it was 82:18 for foreign banks; see Citibank AG, 'Der Marktanteil der ausländischen Banken in Deutschland' (Frankfurt am Main: unpublished, *c.* 1980).

11. Scheele, 'Citibank'; B. Morschhäuser, 'Auslandsbanken in Deutschland: Retail ist die Ausnahme', *Bank und Markt* (1993/2), 22–6.

12. G. Freiherr von Falkenhausen, 'Die US-Investitionen in der Bundesrepublik', *Zeitschrift für das gesamte Kreditwesen*, 18 (1965), 440–2; Deutsche Bundesbank, *Monthly Report*, May 1965.

13. J.-J. Servan-Schreiber, *Le Défi américain* (Paris: Denoël, 1967).

14. Wolf, *30 Jahre Nachkriegsentwicklung*, 89.

15. Steuber, *Internationale Banken*, suppl. vol. (1976), 11 ff and 16–17.

16. R. D. Hunter, 'American Banks in Europe: Deregulation and Competition', in: G. Bull (ed.), *International Banking Review-Europe* (London: Sterling Publications, 1986), 31; similarly in Scheele, 'Die unterschiedlichen Strategien'.

17. Deutsche Bundesbank, *Monthly Report*, April 1972, 21.

18. International Monetary Fund, *International Financial Statistics Yearbook* (Washington, DC: IMF, 1979), 62–3.

19. Ibid., (1996), 114–15.

20. Federal Ministry of Economics (ed.), *Leistung in Zahlen* (Bonn: Bundesministerium für Wirtschaft, 1975), 88; also ibid., (1988), 76.

21. H. Krägenau, *Internationale Direktinvestitionen* (Hamburg: Verlag Weltarchiv, 1987), 36.

22. Ibid., 241 ff.

23. M. Gräfin Dönhoff, 'The Ugly American from the German Perspective', in A. Theis and J. S. Toll (eds.), *German–American Interrelations* (Tübingen: Attempto Verlags GmbH University Press, 1985), 172.

24. F. Franzmeyer, 'Der Binnenmarkt als ordnungs- und wirtschaftspolitische Strategie', in M. Kreile (ed.), *Europa 1992-Konzeptionen, Strategien, Außenwirkungen* (Baden-Baden: Nomos, 1991), 29.

25. K. Dyson and K. Featherstone, *The Road to Maastricht* (Oxford: Oxford University Press, 1999), 449.

26. Ibid., 281. See also D. Marsh, *The Bundesbank* (London: William Heinemann, 1992), 206 ff.

27. *Handelsblatt*, 31 December 1987.

28. W. Marx, 'Zusammenarbeit der Banken über die Grenzen hinaus', in Bundesverband deutscher Banken (ed.), *XI. Deutscher Bankiertag 1968* (Frankfurt: Fritz Knapp, 1969), 146.

29. L. Mülhaupt, *Strukturwandlungen im westdeutschen Bankwesen* (Wiesbaden: Gabler, 1971), 17, 22.

30. At end of 1998: 11.0%; Deutsche Bundesbank, *Monthly Report*, February 1999, 20.

31. European Central Bank, *Possible Effects of EMU on the EU Banking System in the Medium and Long Term*, (Frankfurt am Main: European Central Bank, February 1999), Annexe 2, table 3.1.

32. Bundesverband deutscher Banken (ed.), *XIII. Deutscher Bankentag* (Cologne: Bank Verlag, 1979), 10.

33. Ibid., 21.

34. W. Ehrlicher, 'Von der "wirtschaftlichen Wende" zur Wiedervereinigung', in H. Pohl (ed.), *Geschichte der deutschen Kreditwirtschaft seit 1945* (Frankfurt am Main: Fritz Knapp, 1998), 327–8.

35. H. Schröder, 'Chancen und Risiken deutscher Banken im Europäischen Binnenmarkt', in T. Reichmann, and A. Voßschulte, *Europa ohne Grenzen: Chancen und Risiken der deutschen Wirtschaft* (Munich: dtv Deutscher Taschenbuch Verlag, 1992), 176.

36. H. Wolf, 'The Basis is Established: 1945–1975', in Commerzbank AG (ed.), *The Changing Face of Banking: Commerzbank at 125* (Frankfurt am Main: Fritz Knapp: 1995, abridged version), 10–13.

37. H. Roeper, *Die D-Mark: Vom Besatzungskind zum Weltstar* (Frankfurt am Main: Societäts-Verlag, 1978).

38. W. Rieke, 'The Deutschmark as a Reserve and Investment Currency', in Group of Thirty (ed.), *Reserve Currencies in Transition* (New York: The Group of Thirty, 1982), 57. The switch from sterling to D-mark investments occurred within the space of a few years, between 1970 and 1973: Bank for International Settlements, *Reserves and International Liquidity* (Basle: BIS, 1988), 8.

39. W. Rieke, 'The Development of the Deutschmark as a Reserve Currency', in Group of Thirty (ed.), *Reserve Currencies*, 17.

40. Holtfrerich, *Finanzplatz Frankfurt*, 281.

41. G. Franke, 'The Bundesbank and Financial Markets', in Deutsche Bundesbank (ed.), *Fifty years of the Deutsche Mark* (Oxford: Oxford University Press, 1999), 247–8; M. Kohlhaussen, 'Kreditwirtschaft und Bundesbank', *Zeitschrift für das*

gesamte Kreditwesen, 52 (1999), 922; Deutsche Bundesbank, *Monthly Report*, July 1985.

42. R. Klump, *Entstehung und Verwendung von Schlüsselwährungen* (Hamburg: Verlag Weltarchiv, 1986), 374.

43. Group of Thirty, *Risks in International Bank Lending* (New York: The Group of Thirty, 1982), 67.

44. Klump, *Entstehung und Verwendung*, 374–5; H.-E. Scharrer, D. Gehrmann, and W. Wetter, *Währungsrisiko und Währungsverhalten deutscher Unternehmen im Außenhandel* (Hamburg: Verlag Weltarchiv, 1978), 429, 432; P. B. Kenen, *The Role of the Dollar as an International Currency* (New York: Group of Thirty, 1983), 21.

45. Bank for International Settlements, *Central Bank Survey of Foreign Exchange and Derivative Market Activity* (Basle: BIS, 1996), 14.

46. Bundesverband deutscher Banken (ed.), *Verhandlungen des IX. Deutschen Bankiertages zu Köln am Rhein, 9. und 10. Oktober 1958* (Frankfurt: Fritz Knapp, 1959), 152.

47. Bundesverband deutscher Banken (ed.), *Verhandlungen des X. Deutschen Bankiertages, München, 14. und 15. Oktober 1963* (Frankfurt: Fritz Knapp, 1964), 94.

48. Ibid., 101.

49. Ibid., 103–4.

50. Marx, 'Zusammenarbeit der Banken', 143–6.

51. U. Steuber, *Internationale Bankenkooperation: Deutsche Banken in internationalen Gruppen* (Frankfurt am Main: Fritz Knapp, 1977), 173–89; H. E. Büschgen, 'Die Zusammenarbeit der Geldinstitute in Konsortien von 1945 bis zur Gegenwart', in H. Pohl (ed.), *Die Zusammenarbeit der Geldinstitute in Konsortien* (Frankfurt am Main: Fritz Knapp, 1989), 54 ff.

52. U. Ramm, 'National Banking: Strategies and Globalisation', paper given at meeting of European Association for Banking History (Amsterdam, 18 June 1999).

53. B. Rudolph, 'Die deutsche Kreditwirtschaft im europäischen Markt', in Pohl, *Geschichte der deutschen Kreditwirtschaft*, 473.

54. Commerzbank AG, *Annual Report 1992*, 21.

55. W. Seipp, 'Europa 1992—Herausforderungen für die Banken', in D. Duwendag (ed.), *Europa-Banking*, (Baden-Baden: Nomos, 1988), 258.

56. U. Steuber, *Internationale Banken*, Suppl. vol. (1976), 103; M. Morschbach, *Struktur des Bankwesens in den USA* (Frankfurt am Main: Fritz Knapp, 1981), 128 ff.

57. Marx, 'Zusammenarbeit der Banken', 141–9; M. Osthoff, 'Das Bankwesen in den USA', *Die Bank*, 8 (1980), 371–4.

58. Commerzbank AG, *Annual Report 1971*, 42–3.

59. U. Ramm, 'The Commerzbank Group Today', in Commerzbank, *The Changing Face*, 16.

60. H. E. Büschgen, 'Deutsche Bank from 1957 to the Present', in L. Gall, *et al.*, *The Deutsche Bank 1870–1995* (Munich: C. H. Beck, 1995, repr. 1999), 754–6; M. Pohl, 'Die Deutsche Bank in den Vereinigten Staaten 1870–1999', in M. Pohl (ed.), *Zur deutschen und amerikanischen Identität: Die Deutsche Bank in den USA* (Munich: Piper, 1999), 57–77.

61. H. G. Meyen, *120 Jahre Dresdner Bank, Unternehmens-Chronik 1872 bis 1992* (Frankfurt am Main: Frankfurter Societäts-Druckerei, 1992), 269.

62. Wolf, *30 Jahre Nachkriegsentwicklung*, 87–97; *Platow-Brief*, 11 July 1983.

63. K. P. Jacobs, 'European Banking in the USA', in G. Bull (ed.), *International Banking Review—Europe* (London: Sterling Publications, 1986), 29–30; see also Federal Reserve Bank, *An Overview of U.S. Financial Institutions* (New York: Federal Reserve Bank, 1988) 19–25.

64. I.-D. Herstatt, *Die Vernichtung. Glanz und Elend des Kölner Bankhauses I. D. Herstatt* (Berlin: Edition q, 1992), 75.

65. W. Reimann, '"Herstatt" auch 25 Jahre nach der Krise noch aktuell', *Börsenzeitung*, 122 (30 June 1999), 21.

66. Deutsche Bundesbank, *Report for the Year 1974* (Frankfurt am Main: Deutsche Bundesbank, 1975), 20, 28.

67. Bank for International Settlements, *Forty-Fifth Annual Report* (Basle: BIS, 1975), 34.

68. H. Schröder, 'Deposit Insurance and Moral Hazard', in International Monetary Fund (ed.), *Finance & Development*, June 1999, 56.

69. O. Hahn, 'Zwischen Energiekrise und wirtschaftlicher Wende (1973–1981)', in Pohl, *Geschichte der deutschen Kreditwirtschaft*, 255 ff.

70. Federal Finance Ministry (ed.), *Bericht der Studienkommission 'Grundsatzfragen der Kreditwirtschaft'* (Bonn: Stollfuss, 1979), 8.

71. Ibid., 244.

72. Rudolph, 'Die deutsche Kreditwirtschaft', 468.

9

Central Banks and the Process of Financial Internationalization: A Secular View

HAROLD JAMES

There have been two waves of internationalization, or—to use the currently fashionable world, 'globalization'—in the modern history of the world economy, the first lasting from the 1870s to the 1920s, the second since the end of the 1960s. Central banks played a prominent part in each, but more frequently they represented an attempt to erect protective devices rather than acting as a facilitator of international financial connectivity. Unlike earlier central banks, which were essentially private institutions that gradually evolved to meet a need for central bank functions such as clearing, the provision of liquidity, and the supervision of the banking system,[1] the central banks that were established in the nineteenth-century era of globalization were from the start charged with public functions. They were usually created at the initiative of governments or parliaments, rather than through private initiative; and their major function was seen as providing some form of defensive barrier against globalization. At this time, there began a dynamic of a competitive race of regulation and control against market-driven forces of innovation: a competition that persisted through the twentieth century, and which—one might think—central banks working on their own were bound to lose.

This chapter focuses on a particularly striking instance of this race. It explores the way in which international capital movements may interfere with and obstruct the primary task of a central bank, the provision of a stable means of exchange. It also examines a central area of conflict, the responsibility for financial regulation and stability, which has in most countries evolved outside the domain of the central bank: for some time in the United States and Germany, but in the United Kingdom only since 1998.

1. International Financial Crises and Central Banking: Germany and the USA under the Classic Gold Standard

The first wave of economic and financial internationalization began in the middle of the nineteenth century. The dramatic fall in transport prices produced an increase in goods shipments and financial flows, and a new degree of integration. Almost immediately a reaction set in.

Newly created central banks were supposed to limit the harmful effects of metallic flows, or in other cases to encourage inflows. Why was there a new rash of central bank foundations? The operation of the international gold standard did not require a central bank. The gold standard system is often treated in the literature as the high point of political and economic liberalism. In fact the debates about the gold standard and the institutions (notably central banks) that were believed necessary for its operation were about guiding and channelling capital to uses that were felt to be politically, militarily, and diplomatically desirable. Central banks had an important role to fill precisely because they could guide flows that would otherwise have been 'automatic'. The attraction of going on the gold standard to such countries as Russia or Argentina lay primarily in its confidence-inducing effects on foreign investors.

The two most important central bank creations (because they were in major industrial countries) occurred in Germany and the United States. Both reflected a calculation about the desirability and necessity of greater control as a response to financial crisis, the Reichsbank after the crash of 1873, the Federal Reserve System after 1907.

At the beginning of the 1870s, Germany faced general monetary and banking chaos. A multiplicity of private note-issuing banks in the German states made for a proliferation of monies of different degrees of solidity. The risks of financial instability, as well as its own fiscal interests, had led Prussia to restrict banking activity and in practice to attempt to concentrate business with the Prussian Bank established in 1846, which in practice exercised a near monopoly. After the political unification of 1871, the same questions were asked about Germany as a whole. One of the aims of the banking reform was to ensure that the note banks would give up their issuing activities. While in the first years after political unification, the central monetary problem had been the choice of a monetary standard, the debate thus shifted increasingly to the suitable institutional design of a mechanism for restraining speculative tendencies and banking abuses. This consideration became central after the boom and then the crash (*Gründerkrach*) of 1873. Many of the newly founded joint stock banks were created in order to launch industrial companies, and a speculative mania developed. In 1873, a number of banks failed, including one of the largest of the new banks, the Quistorpsche Vereinsbank. Karl Helfferich's influential study of the *Currency Reform* analysed the consequences of the unstable monetary situation and concluded: 'The consequence was that the boom was not constrained naturally, as it would have been in normal circumstances, by the quantity of money, and that growth was not kept in reasonable bounds by a noticeable increase in the cost of credit.'[2]

The second major issue facing Germany was a consequence of internationalization and the adoption of the gold standard. The international linkages created by gold required a new approach to monetary management. After 1874, a massive drain of gold from Germany began.[3] There was major public alarm as the brand-new gold coins disappeared from view (they were melted down for export), and exaggerated figures about the extent of the gold losses were widely quoted.[4] The drain corresponded to a large German trade imbalance that was the consequence of the very rapid growth of the early 1870s. The Reichstag discussion of whether a new central bank would be needed took place in the context of actual gold losses, and a fear of even greater outflows. In this way, it was far from being a simply academic debate about the relative advantages of different types of currency management. Explaining why circumstances had changed, the president of the Reich Chancellor's Office, Rudolf von Delbrück, said, 'This silver currency isolated us from fluctuations resulting from the in- and outflow of metallic money in international transactions.' Silver coins, with their uncertain quality and poor condition, had indeed been much less exposed to international movements. The proponents of a gold currency added that a double currency would lead to even greater movements of precious metals.[5] A central bank would, it was argued, be the best mechanism to orchestrate an appropriate response to a flow of precious metal. The first president of the Reichsbank, Hermann von Dechend, who never became a convinced adherent of mono-metallism, later characteristically defined the institution's 'principal task' as 'providing for the currency and sustaining monetary circulation in the country'.[6] It was in the context of protecting German gold from flowing out that the subsequently often-used phrase 'guardian of the currency' was first coined.

Like its German equivalent, the Federal Reserve System was born out of financial panic. In the first years of the century, a speculative frenzy drove the American stock market, and the economy. In retrospect, everyone believed that it had been 'plain to everyone that credit facilities were being granted too easily to the United States'.[7] But this is a familiar lament after every financial catastrophe. There had been a panic in March 1907, and share prices collapsed; then a recovery, and a much wider fall in October, which spread to many of the continental European exchanges, especially Amsterdam and Hamburg, and produced some banking collapses (notably the Società Bancaria Italiana). The most profitable and innovative but most vulnerable institution for speculation was the trust company (the analogy to the hedge funds of the 1990s). On 22 October, a run brought down the Knickerbocker Trust Company, and fuelled a general panic. The next day other Trust Companies experienced a run. As New York banks faced demands for the payment of deposits, they restricted payments, even though there was a simultaneous attempt to rescue bank liquidity through the device of issuing clearing house certificates. In retrospect, most commentators felt that the banks did not need to resort to the suspension of payments that rapidly hit business conditions across the country, and should not have done so. The author of the definitive study on the subject for the National Monetary Commission (who would later play a major role as adviser to governments and central banks during the depression), the Harvard economist Oliver Sprague, observed: 'Unfortunately there seems to be distinctly less unwillingness among bankers to resort to suspension than was the case twenty or thirty years ago. It may be attributed in part to the growing tendency since 1893 to look to changes in legislation alone as a remedy for financial ills.'[8] The consequence was that the lender of last resort function needed to be a public responsibility, which could not be left to the presumed benevolence of the large New York private banks. For the moment, the US had in practice depended on a foreign liquidity provider of last resort, in complete conformity with the logic of the gold standard regime.

The American and European crises cruelly exposed the weak position of the Bank of England, which lost gold reserves as Americans demanded more and more metallic money for payments. In effect, it was acting as a substitute for the then non-existent US central bank. Faced by a loss of its reserves, the Bank put its leading interest rate (Bank Rate) up to an unprecedented 7 per cent, before it could go back to a more comfortable and usual 3 per cent (March 1908).

Each crisis was followed by an attempt to draw lessons. The 1907 crisis highlighted a major weakness in the US banking system. The National Monetary Commission launched an extensive series of hearings, which included investigations of the currency and banking systems of other countries. Eventually it concluded that the US required its own central bank, rather than a proxy in London, in order to ensure financial stability. In consequence the Federal Reserve system came into being on the eve of the First World War. In Germany, the Reichsbank needed to control the expansion of bank lending more adequately. It was given greater powers, and its banknotes became legal tender for the first time. In general, then, national authorities tried to increase the extent of control, because they feared the destabilizing consequences of leaving finance to the vagaries of an international market.

In what sense did the new institutional innovations represent improvements that strengthened the international order? Or were they merely new sources of instability? It is often assumed that globalized economics requires corresponding far-sighted and benign institutions to manage it. Some commentators have discussed the evolution of the international economic order in this period as either one of enhanced cooperation between states, or a benign hegemony exercised by Britain (in monetary terms by the Bank of England). Keynes's oft-cited image depicted the Bank of England as the conductor of an international orchestra.[9] Neither of these views, although often repeated, is in reality supported by much more than retrospective wishful thinking induced by the miseries of the inter-war experience. Trade policy was becoming more nationalistic, central banks increasingly defined their tasks in national terms, often in explicitly military terms of building up a gold treasury to prepare for war. And the instances of cooperation in the face of a crisis are distinctly episodic. The spirit of Colbert appeared to triumph over that of Adam Smith.

The hegemonic interpretation suffers from the fact that Britain, apart from keeping goods markets open, did very little to stabilize the international economy. In part because it was a privately owned institution that had to show a profit, the Bank of England held very low gold reserves, which made it technically unsuited to any major international project of stabilization. This was the predicament that became apparent to every analyst after 1907. Unlike in later periods, it did nothing to help other countries make the transition to a stable currency standard.

This was not a very *well-managed* system then, but it was a system that worked well partly because attempts at management were not very effective. In that sense the contrast with the inter-war period, in which there were sustained and sincere attempts at cooperation that eventually proved eminently unsuccessful, or the rather patchy history of post-1945 international economic cooperation, is misplaced. Benign international institutions may be desirable, but they are very rare.

2. International Monetary Cooperation in the 1920s

The attempt to recreate an integrated international economy in the 1920s depended heavily on the idea of independent central banks as guarantors of monetary stability and facilitators of international cooperation. The doctrine of central banking held that monetary authorities should be independent of governments so that they did not need to respond to political pressures. They should run monetary policy in accordance, not with domestic priorities, but rather with the requirements of the international system.

The most forthright exponent of this theory, the long-serving Governor of the Bank of England, Montagu Norman, made quite explicit the political role that the central bank needed to play:

Central Banking is young and experimental and has no tradition: it may last and may develop, or its usefulness, to fill a short post-war need and no more, may soon come to an end. On the one hand its sphere is limited by the qualification that no Central Bank can be greater than its own State—the creature greater than the creator. On the other hand, a Central Bank should acquire by external help (as in some ex-enemy countries) or by internal recognition (as in France) a certain freedom or independence within, and perhaps without, its own State. By such means alone can real co-operation be made possible. I cannot define the position thus acquired but it should surely permit a Bank to 'nag' its own Government even in public and to decide on questions on other than political grounds.[10]

Central banks were to be established before a country stabilized on gold in order to prepare the institutional ground. The new institution should be independent of the government. As the Brussels Conference formulated it in 1920, 'Banks and especially Banks of Issue should be free from political pressure and should be conducted only on lines of prudent finance.'[11]

The constitutions of the new banks were thus framed with clear political objectives. Norman made the point quite explicit: 'It seems evident that the limitations imposed on new and reorganized [central] banks during the last few years arise more from the fear and mistrust of political interference than from the needs of central banking as such.'[12]

But it was not just *vis-à-vis* their governments that central banks needed independence: they were also threatened by the claims of their commercial banking systems. As Continental central banks fuelled inflation by cheap rediscounting of bills (the German Reichsbank raised its rate only in 1922, long after the inflation had become hyper-inflation), Norman declared in 1921: 'A Central Bank should protect its own traders from the rapacity of other banks in its own country.'[13]

The new central banks of the inter-war years included those associated with currency stabilization schemes in Austria, Hungary, and Germany; but the principle was extended throughout the world. In South America, Chile had a new bank in 1926, Argentina in 1936, and in Brazil commission after commission staffed with British or American advisers recommended the introduction of this institution. Canada started its bank in 1935.

The central bank governors now, in distinct contrast to the pre-1914 world, saw themselves as members of a club, engaging in friendly and intimate relationship with each other. 'You are a dear queer old duck and one of my duties seems to be to lecture you now and then,' wrote Benjamin Strong of the Federal

Reserve Bank of New York to Montagu Norman.[14] In particular Strong, Norman, and their German colleague Hjalmar Horace Greeley Schacht shared a similarity of outlook and behaviour. After Strong's death in 1928 from complications following tuberculosis, his successor George Harrison never succeeded in recapturing the imagination as well as the dedicated loyalty of his European colleagues. Five years after Strong's departure, Schacht wrote to Norman: 'I feel most strongly that, after the death of our American friend, you and I are the only two men who understood what had to be achieved.'[15] France, which stabilized relatively late, remained on the edge of the charmed circle of bankers.

This harmonious relationship, built up on the basis of close personal ties, came under strain because of US payments surpluses that were rapidly recycled as capital exports. With newly established confidence, and above all under the impact of US lending, commercial banking systems outside the United States expanded rapidly. In Austria, total bank deposits increased by 26.6 per cent between 1925 and 1929 (an annual rate of 6.1%); French deposit banks 63.9 per cent (13.2%); German Great Banks 143.9 per cent (25.0%); the principal Italian banks 28.2 per cent (28.2%); and Polish banks 222.6 per cent (34.0%). The growth outside Europe was slower, but still quite dramatic: Argentina had a growth in deposits between 1925 and 1929 of only 14.9 per cent (annual rate 3.5%); but Colombia 100 per cent (18.9%); Brazil 61.3 per cent (12.7%); and Mexico 49.3 per cent (10.5%). In Chile there was no substantial movement, and in Bolivia a contraction.

How rapid these expansions were may be judged by a comparison with the US and the UK. Over the corresponding period, all bank deposits in the US rose at an annual rate of 3.2 per cent; and in England and Wales by 1.3 per cent annually (the figures for Scotland and Northern Ireland are not substantially different). For the world as a whole, the League of Nations in 1934 calculated an increase of total deposits in commercial banks in 40 countries from $70 bn. at the end of 1925 to $82.5–84 bn. at the end of 1929. This represents a rise at an annual rate of 4–4.5 per cent, roughly in line with increases in world trade and world industrial activity in the same period.[16]

The expansions created the appearance of inflationary finance. They could not be controlled by orthodox means. If central banks attempted to tighten money by raising rates (the classical remedy under the gold standard for the restraint of over-rapid development), they would *increase* the incentives for hot money inflows, and thereby reduce their control of the market. The doctrine of central bank control and autonomy as a precondition for confidence and capital flows thus ran into the objection that any step the central bank might take on discount rates might be ineffective.

But apart from discount rates, the central banks had few weapons. In the US, Britain, and Japan they might engage in open market operations—the purchase or sale of securities to respectively increase or decrease liquidity—but elsewhere the statutes forbade such procedures because of the fear that they might be used as a mechanism for launching a new inflation. Even in the US, where there might have been thought to have existed a much greater room for manœuvre, the Federal Reserve system was in fact highly cautious in its open market policy until 1933, in other words until after the catastrophe of the Great Depression.

In central Europe, the conventional way of restraining development was by rationing credit at the central bank. 'The Central Bank is trying, primarily, to operate by fixing, not the price of the service which it renders, but the amount of the service which it will render.'[17] But it could only really be effective in this during a period of stringency or crisis: and central banks in central Europe thus needed crisis, institutionally, in order to be able to control the development of their markets.

The problem was widely noted at the time. In 1931, the League of Nations Financial Committee's Gold Delegation stated:

in certain countries during the last few years, the independence and power of commercial banks and other financial institutions has tended to increase, so that control by the central banking authorities has been rendered more difficult. In the ultimate analysis the control of the Central Banks over commercial banks is determined by the 'cash' reserves whether in notes or sight deposits with Central Banks which commercial banks have to maintain.[18]

But in practice, these non-interest-bearing reserves were extremely small: in Germany they amounted to less than 5 per cent of money in circulation, and less than 2 per cent of bank deposits; in Hungary there were indeed no sight deposits at the central bank.

Not surprisingly, within a few years after the first stabilizations central bankers became rather gloomy about the new world they had constructed. In March of the year in which US capital exports peaked, Benjamin Strong wrote: '1927 is going to be a barren and disappointing year for Europe . . . stabilization and reconstruction, which have been the vogue since the League first dealt with Austria, have for the time being passed out of fashion.'[19] The conditions for stabilization had become much looser: the operation no longer involved the imposition of a straitjacket.

France and the US were building up large gold reserves because of their claims to reparations (in the French case) or war debts (for the US). Only a solution to the political issue could solve the economic issue: but correspondingly, economic rationality demanded an end to war debts and reparations.

On the other hand, France and the US responded to the growing Anglo-German pressure to bear the strain of adjustment by reducing their rates. They also encouraged domestic expansion by publicizing doubts about the stability of the gold exchange standard system, and advocated a return to a pure gold standard, under which reserves could only be held in gold.

In the meantime, the US might support the depoliticization of reparations (so long as no link with wardebt was admitted); and this solution formed the basis of the Young Plan recommended by the Paris Experts' conference of spring 1929 and implemented at the two conferences in The Hague. The initial discussions had taken place as early as 1927, during the time in which the great boom in US lending kept European industries busy and European workers employed. The capital markets were buoyant, so that the French might be persuaded to commercialize German reparation debt and thus make it more secure. The Germans might benefit not only from a reduction in the total level of reparation obligations, but also because the depoliticization would send favourable signals to New York, and allow capital inflows to continue. The vigour of the 1920s capital markets effectively paralysed the central banks' capacity to act.

3. Managing International Capital Markets and Debt Crisis: Bretton Woods Institutions since the 1970s

With the financial panics of 1931 and subsequently, the system of international cooperation broke down, and central banks attracted a great deal of criticism as the major culprits of the Depression. For Keynes and his followers, Montagu Norman became the symbol of financial ignorance and dogmatism. Monetary reformers even tried to assassinate his German colleague, Hans Luther. The Federal Reserve System's ineffectiveness was pilloried by politicians and commentators, from every political and ideological angle. Both Hoover and Roosevelt agreed in their criticism, and economists as diverse as J. K. Galbraith, Milton Friedman, and Anna Schwartz provided solid justifications for this suspicion.

When international cooperation was resurrected, it was done as an issue of collaboration between finance ministries and treasuries. Thus the Tripartite Pact of 1936, with its very feeble arrangements for the stabilization of the dollar, the franc, and the pound, excluded the central banks and required the action of Treasury Stabilization Funds. The Bretton Woods resolution to wind up the Bank for International Settlements was more than a response to doubts about the wartime role of the BIS. It reflected the feeling that central banks and institutions designed to promote cooperation between them were ineffective and malign. The International Monetary Fund was owned by national governments, in practice by their ministers of finance, and not by their central banks.

In the 1930s and subsequently, central banks evolved a new bureaucratic role, as the administrators of exchange and capital controls. The post-war order, as designed at Bretton Woods in 1944, relied on the premise that capital flows would not take place in the foreseeable future. When large-scale capital movements resumed in the 1960s, most central banks conceived them as a threat to their management of the economy. Some, like the Bundesbank, began to see floating exchange rates as the only way of preserving the autonomy of domestic monetary policy.

The internationalization of capital markets in the 1970s appeared as an even greater challenge. Within a few years, the apparently enormous problems created by the oil price increases of 1973–4 began to appear surmountable, but only because commercial banks engaged once more in the international activities they had largely refrained from since the Depression era. The OPEC surpluses were recycled, mostly through credit markets rather than through multilateral institutions (despite the IMF Oil Facilities). Although drawings on the IMF increased, the rise of private international debt was much more dramatic. Correspondingly, the debts of developing countries rose. Most of the medium income developers found it easier and more attractive to borrow from banks than from international institutions. Many international civil servants remember being kept waiting outside Finance Ministries and central banks, while the (mostly American) investment bankers cut their own deals.

The Euromarkets proved to be an apparently easy institutional mechanism for recycling the petroleum revenues, mostly to governments, and mostly on a short-term basis. In 1974–5, loans to governments and public financial instit-utions accounted for over half of total Eurocredits. The maturity of the loans fell. While in 1974, two-thirds were still between seven and ten years, and one-tenth were over ten years, in 1975 two-thirds were dated between one and six years, and only 1 per cent was longer than ten years. The behaviour of the markets indicated that they expected the recycling phenomenon to be short-lived; and at first, banks found the exercise rather unfamiliar. In the summer of 1974, some of New York's leading bankers told the IMF's managing direc-tor of their worries over instability on the Euromarkets. David Rockefeller, chairman of Chase Manhattan Bank, believed that the banks could only cont-inue to recycle oil money for another six months at the maximum: 'Both the capital of the banks and the increasing lending risks', he argued, 'are serious constraints. . . Recently some of the incoming Arab money has already been moving to the Federal Reserve instead of to private banks. This may sharpen the scarcity of funds in the market.'[20]

The explosion of short-term lending also alarmed central banks and the IMF. Initially, in 1974, the Fund's *Annual Report* had asked whether private banks would be able to finance the recycling process.[21] By 1976, the *Report* noted the 'sudden escalation' of borrowing after 1973, and warned, 'Many borrowing countries, however, have become potentially vulnerable to any significant change in their access to external credit, or to any seriously adverse shift in their export earnings. This vulnerability is heightened by the eroding effects of inflation on the real value of external reserves, which are now quite low in relation to current and prospective imports.'[22] The Fund's then managing director, Johannes Witteveen, delivered his warnings both in public and in private. In spring 1976, he told a conference that: 'Competitive enlargement of this role of private banks might well foster a climate of all-too-easy borrowing by deficit countries, thus facilitating inflationary financing and delaying the adoption of needed adjustment policies ... In general, therefore, a very careful and balanced policy by the international banks is needed.'[23] Later in the year he told the Interim Committee at the Fund meeting in Manila that 'commercial bank lending should not be so easily available that it made the need for adjustment less clear, and hence caused the authorities to accumulate larger debts than were desirable'.[24]

In 1977 US officials continued to note Witteveen's concern about international bank lending: 'He is worried that incentives favoring bank lending abroad may be too attractive, that such lending is essentially uncontrolled, that it leads to international liquidity creation (as countries borrow foreign currency to add to their reserves), and that its continuation may permanently prevent another SDR allocation.'[25] The same theme appeared in statements in the Annual Meeting. Since there was a danger of resurgence of inflation, the world required 'more stress on the adjustment of external positions and less emphasis on the mere financing of deficits.'[26]

Central banks and banking regulatory authorities shared this concern. The chairman of the Federal Reserve Board, Arthur Burns, in 1977 proposed compiling a list of questions on the current indebtedness of borrowing countries, and on the content of bank lending. When the BIS discussed the Burns suggestion with individual banks, the response was largely hostile. Almost all the bigger banks opposed such intervention, and declared themselves fully 'satisfied with their present information on, and methods of assessing, country risk situations', while 'The recommendation of a checklist of questions would appear to reflect on their past lending policies and would therefore be resented by them.' Other banks believed simply that they should not provide information to regulators, but that the 'official' institutions such as IBRD, IMF, or BIS should have the 'job' of putting together information (although it was not clear from which sources such data could be compiled). As a result, the Burns and BIS discussions for the moment led nowhere.[27]

Such advice from national and international regulators was very unpopular with the intended subjects of regulation. Bankers did not see why they should not lend across frontiers, and some came to believe that the Fund's advice was obsolete, outmoded, and suitable for a past era when capital markets had not reached their current levels of sophistication and integration. In this view, it was the market, rather than multilateral institutions, that held out the best way of solving the world's problems.

Finance ministers in deficit countries felt equally strongly that warnings about financing and invocations to adjust were quite inappropriate. One of the attractions of the Euromarkets was that it allowed them to ignore the warnings of the IMF. Vast resources opened up that involved virtually no foreign control. As one astute comment noted, 'probably no international capital market in history has had a lower degree of political interference, to the dismay of "strategic minds" like that of Dr. Kissinger.'[28] In the Interim Committee, Mario Enrique Simonsen, the Finance Minister of Brazil, in 1976 said that 'he was rather disturbed by Mr. Witteveen's reference to commercial banking: banks should naturally be cautious in lending, but not only to foreign countries.'[29] In the following year, he was even more explicit in his insistence that the Fund should not give advice or attempt to influence the private sector: 'While they [the developing countries] would certainly welcome the technical assistance of the Fund and other institutions, in helping them to improve their own statistical and informational systems, the developing countries continued to feel that the Fund could play no useful role as a purveyor to the private sector of judgments, analyses, and forecasts.'[30]

In fact, judged in relative terms, the Fund's activity indeed diminished. In the course of the 1970s, the proportion of developing countries' current account deficits financed by the IMF was lower than it had been in the 1960s (5.1% rather than 7.5%).[31] On the other hand, it was hard to argue that Fund support should simply ignore the extent of commercial lending. Debt incurred through commercial banks clearly affected the outcome of Fund programmes, and the Fund needed to take private liabilities into account in judging the viability of member countries' external position. In 1979, the Fund decided that if the size or growth rate of external indebtedness might affect the design of a Fund-sponsored adjustment programme, performance criteria for the programme should include foreign loans with a maturity over one year (and in exceptional circumstances, non-trade-related loans under one year might be included).[32]

Bankers saw their own activities as quite separate from the IMF's sphere of influence. Irving Friedman explained confidently that 'because they depend upon full and prompt servicing of their loans for their financial profitability and viability, private banks (in contrast to the Fund and the Bank) understandably tend to focus their attention upon the best managed countries, and, within these countries, the best managed firms in the most advanced sectors of the economy'.[33] Another prominent banker, Rimmer de Vries of Morgan Guaranty, in April 1982 formulated the new consensus among the private sector in the following terms: 'in recent years Fund and commercial bank lending have evolved in different directions', they had distinct and separate spheres of operation, and 'thus the Fund must not be viewed as a protective umbrella under which the international banking community can find shelter in times of trouble.'[34] This view gained further support from politicians and commentators who feared that the private sector might at some time attempt to use international institutions to support their own operations. Already in 1978 the US House of Representatives had debated an 'anti-bail-out' amendment of Congressman Pattison, aimed at prohibiting the use of IMF loans to pay off arrears owed to private banks.[35]

The response to the 1982 debt crisis brought the IMF back into the centre of the international financial system. Its major contribution was not in blocking movements, but in linking banking regulation with systemic issues. 'Bail-ins' (alternately called 'concerted lending' or 'forced lending') involved pressure on commercial banks to put in new money to problem debt cases. In the Mexican package, which served as a model, US$8.3 bn. of new funds were required: of this only US$1.3 bn. came from the IMF, US$2 bn. from governments, and US$5 bn. from banks. In applying suasion to the banks, the IMF cooperated very closely with central banks. In effect, there was now a triangular conflation of the functions of an international arbiter, a domestic regulator, and the market. First, the IMF had become a part of the domestic regulatory mechanism of US banking. Linkage of loans with IMF programmes could offer a way of avoiding the consequences of non-accruing or non-performing loans. Or, to put it another way, the definitions of what constituted sound banking were being rewritten in accordance with the requirements of the world financial system as a whole. Secondly, the banks themselves became part of the IMF's international surveillance exercise. Their funds greatly enhanced the facilities that the IMF could hold out as the reward to a country for the successful completion of a programme—in effect for rejoining the international financial system. An IMF programme was supposed to have a catalytic effect on the private sector. And finally, the IMF would do the work that the banks had hitherto neglected to perform themselves: negotiate sound criteria for the use of funds, which would make economic stabilization and adjustment possible and would allow for banks to be repaid. In order to get this service, however, the banks would have to pay the price of putting up additional resources. By acting in this way, the IMF ensured that lending continued, and that the cutting off of external credit did not produce a world depression of the type experienced in the past.

The outbreak of the 1980s debt crisis encouraged a renewed interest in financial regulation across frontiers. One important US initiative extended the regulatory debates that had taken place in the course of the 1970s. It was now thought that banking supervision should be carried out internationally in a more systematized and open way than the tentative, informal, and secret co-ordination and exchange of regulatory experience carried out in the framework of the Basle Committee on Banking Regulation and Supervisory Practices (which had begun functioning in 1974). Part of the pressure came from domestic opinion in the US, and the widespread fear that a solution to the international debt problem would involve a bail-out of the banks. The consequent reluctance of the US Congress in 1983 to increase IMF quotas (as part of the Eighth General Review) could only be overcome through a legislative measure that extended control of banking. The International Lending Supervision Act (November 1983) gave US regulatory authorities the legal right and the obligation to 'cause banking institutions to achieve and to maintain adequate capital by establishing minimum levels of capital.' It also included a request for American regulators to pursue a convergence of international bank capital standards. Subsequent negotiations, first with the UK, then with Japan, produced a set of standards embodied as the Basle Accord of 1988.[36]

The Accord required an 8 per cent ratio of recognized capital to credit-weighted risk exposure by the end of 1992. Five different categories of relative risk were established, with loans to OECD/GAB official borrowers having a zero risk weight, and loans to non-OECD/GAB governments having a 100 per cent weight. Like any arbitrary categorization, this system encountered obvious objections. Would it not, for instance, act as a deterrent to developing country borrowing, and also of borrowing by industrial corporations? And would it not make lending to industrial country governments too attractive? The full absurdity of the categorization became apparent after Mexico and Korea's entry into the OECD—which in both cases temporarily lifted the credit ratings—was followed by a financial crash. There exists both a scope and a demand for the evolution of a more sophisticated and sensitive system of standards; and inevitably, it lags behind the reality of financial markets. One result has been the partial acceptance by regulators of banks' own systems of risk management.

In addition, by the early 1990s a new financial innovation came to play a part analogous to that of commercial bank lending in the later 1970s and early 1980s. At that time, the growth of financial intermediation had been neglected by national regulators, in part out of fear of affecting the competitive position of banks. Over a decade later, such lending constituted much less of a systemic risk, but the threat now came from the largely unregulated growth of newer financial innovations, especially from derivatives markets. They involve a separation and sale of various components of risk; in this way they lower individual risk, and have been an important cause of the major growth of international capital movements. At the same time they contain an increased systemic risk (it is possible to imagine a chain effect of defaults and bankruptcies). Unlike bank lending, this off-balance-sheet activity has not been the concern of the BIS. The IMF, as part of its surveillance mission, produced the first major account of the systemic dangers posed by derivative markets.[37] More effective action, however, depends on the willingness of national authorities to act together in concert in this area of supervision and regulation. The most recent G-7 initiative, the Tietmeyer proposals, envisages a 'financial stability forum' in which the activities of national regulators and international associations of regulators (the Basle Committee on Banking Supervision, the International Organization of Securities Commissions, the International Association of Insurance Supervisors) will be coordinated with the World Bank and the IMF. Unless a large secretariat is developed, and this forum takes over responsibilities from existing international institutions, it is hard to see this forum developing into an effective supervisor.

Obviously the question of international financial stability was raised very directly by the outbreak of the Asian crisis, and the contagion effects in Russia and Brazil. Unlike the 1930s, attempts at purely national control of capital movements are now, fortunately, almost unanimously rejected. Latin America had experimented with these controls in the 1980s, but learnt the lessons from the failures of that decade when it came to confronting the financial panics of 1997–8. Only Malaysia has experimented with the reintroduction of capital controls, but has eventually been forced to stage a partial retreat.

The threat of financial contagion which pushed the IMF into acting as a *de facto* lender of last resort in Mexico in 1995 and more widely after 1997 provoked an unprecedented amount of discussion and criticism. At the same time, there has been a greater suspicion of existing international institutions, and a greater willingness to contemplate radical redesigns of the 'international financial architecture'. In these debates, it is worth thinking of how slow and painful the process of the evolution of cross-national regulation of banks has been. On the basis of the historical evidence, the prospects for collaboration seem slim, outside extreme crisis situations such as 1982.

Another strategy might hold a greater prospect of success. If international regulation is to be effective, it will need to be supplemented and enforced by a better—more reliable and more prompt—flow of information that allows the participants in the market to be the ultimate source of judgement on financial soundness.

NOTES

1. C. A. E. Goodhart, *The Evolution of Central Banks* (Cambridge, Mass.: MIT Press, 1988).
2. K. T. Helfferich, *Die Reform des deutschen Geldwesens nach der Gründung des Reiches* (Leipzig: Duncker & Humblot, 1899), i. 356.
3. Helfferich, *Die Reform*, i. 378.
4. W. Lotz, *Geschichte und Kritik des deutschen Bankgesetzes* (Leipzig: Duncker & Humblot, 1888), 159.
5. *Verhandlungen des Deutschen Reichstages* (1874), 150, 156.
6. Ibid., (1889–90), 203.
7. *The Economist*, 24 August 1907, cited in J. H. Clapham, *The Bank of England* (Cambridge: Cambridge University Press, 1944), ii. 388.
8. O. M. W. Sprague, *History of Crises under the National Banking System* (Washington, DC: National Monetary Commission, Government Printing Office, 1910), 273.
9. For cooperation, see the classic statements of B. Eichengreen, *Golden Fetters: The Gold Standard and the Great Depression 1919–1939* (New York: Oxford University Press, 1992), and idem, *Globalizing Capital: A History of the International Monetary System* (Princeton, NJ: Princeton University Pres, 1996), 35: 'This kind of international cooperation, while not an everyday event, was critical in times of crisis. It belies the notion that the gold standard was an atomic system. Rather, its survival depended in collaboration among central banks and governments.' For benevolent hegemony, the canonical text is C. P. Kindleberger, *The World in Depression 1929–1939* (London: Allen Lane, 1973), 296–301.
10. Bank of England Historical Archive, G1/307, Norman to J. P. Morgan, 19 November 1927.
11. Bank of England Historical Archive, OV50/6, Per Jacobsson, 'Notes on a Conversation with Sir Otto Niemeyer', 13 December 1933.
12. Norman's Preface to C. H. Kisch and W. A. Elkin, *Central Banks: A Study of the Constitution of Banks of Issue* (London: Macmillan, 1928).
13. Bank of England Historical Archive, OV50/8, 1936 Compendium 'Principles of Central Banking'.
14. Bank of England Historical Archive, G1/421, Strong to Norman, 1 May 1927.
15. Bank of England Historical Archive, G1/415, Schacht to Norman, 6 November 1933.
16. League of Nations, *Commercial Banks 1925–1933* (Geneva: League of Nations, 1934), 5, 48–9.

17. *Banker*, 76 (1926), 445.
18. Second Interim Report, 20 January 1931, 14.
19. Bank of England Historical Archive, G1/421, Strong to Norman, 12 March 1927.
20. International Monetary Fund Central Files, C/US/820, Witteveen memorandum, 'Notes on discussions with New York bankers, 25 July 1974', 31 July 1976.
21. IMF, *Annual Report 1974*, 26; also Ibid., 1975, 19.
22. Ibid., 1976, 20, 22.
23. Witteveen address, 'The IMF and the International Banking Community', Financial Times Conference, New York, 29 April 1976, reproduced in IMF, *IMF Survey*, 3 May 1976, 139.
24. International Monetary Fund Central Files, G142.42, Interim Committee, 2 October 1976.
25. Gerald R. Ford Presidential Library, Burns Papers, B72, IMF, Witteveen facility, Ted Truman, background material for Witteveen luncheon, 2 November 1977.
26. IMF, *Summary Proceedings of the Annual Meetings of the Board of Governors* (1976), 16–17
27. Gerald R. Ford Presidential Library, Burns Papers, B3, B15, 1976–8, Lamfalussy cable to Burns, 27 October 1977.
28. E. Lisboa Bacha and C. F. Diaz-Alejandro, 'Topical Reflections on the History and Theory of International Financial Markets' in G. K. Helleiner (ed.), *For Good or Evil: Economic Theory and North-South Negotiations* (Toronto: University of Toronto Press, 1982), 140.
29. International Monetary Fund Central Files, G142.42, Interim Committee, 2 October 1976.
30. International Monetary Fund Central Files, G142.42, Interim Committee, 24 September 1977.
31. IMF calculations; see also H. James, *International Monetary Cooperation since Bretton Woods* (Washington, DC: IMF and Oxford: Oxford University Press, 1996), table 9–1, 232.
32. International Monetary Fund, EBM 79/106–7, 6 July 1979; EBM 79/121, 23 July 1979.
33. I. S. Friedman, 'Evolution of Risk in International Lending: A Lender's Perspective', in Federal Reserve Bank of Boston, *Key Issues in International Banking* (Boston: Federal Reserve Bank of Boston, 1971), 119.
34. R. de Vries, 'The Limited Role of IMF', *World Financial Markets*, April 1982, 10.
35. Gerald R. Ford Presidential Library, Burns papers, B72, Jay Brenneman memorandum, 23 January 1978.
36. See B. J. Cohen, *In Whose Interest? International Banking and American Foreign Policy* (New Haven: Yale University Press, 1986); J. Jude Norton, 'Capital Adequacy Standards: A Legitimate Regulatory Concern for Prudential Supervision of Banking Activities?', *Ohio State Law Journal*, 49 (1989), 1325; D. Granirer, 'A Great Power Concert: The Political Economy of International Financial Regulatory Cooperation', Ph.D. Thesis (Princeton, 1993); M. Goldstein, D. Folkerts-Landau, M. El-Erian, S. Fries, and L. Rojas-Suarez, *International*

Capital Markets: Developements, Prospects, and Policy Issues (Washington DC: International Monetary Fund, 1992), 10–15.

37. M. Goldstein, D. Folkerts-Landau, P. Garber, L. Rojas-Suarez, and M. Spencer, *International Capital Markets*, Part II, *Systemic Issues in International Finance* (Washington DC: International Monetary Fund, 1993), 28, note that 'Some of the recent products may not be well understood either by senior management of banks or by supervisors of securities firms'.

Index

Seipp, Walter 184, 189
Servan-Schreiber, Jean-Jacques 2, 181–182
SFIDI (Societe Franco-Italienne de
    Developpement Industriel) 162
S. G. Warburg 14, 18, 48
short-term loans 77, 81
  and recycling 209–210
Simonsen, Mario Enrique 211
Singapore 75
single European market *see* European
    integration
Smith Barney 18
Societa Bancaria Italiana 203
Societe Financiere Europeenne (SFE) 146,
    168
Societe Generale de Banque (Belgium) 112,
    149, 150, 167
Societe Generale (France) 38, 39, 40, 44, 46,
    47, 150
Special Drawing Rights 77
speculation 3, 12, 34n., 201–202
Sprague, Oliver 203
spread banking 60
Standard Bank of New York 138
Standard Bank of South Africa 38–39, 40, 43
Stanford Report (1974) 124, 125
sterling 78–79
  as currency reserve 186–187
  devaluation 30n., 97
  restrictions on use 91–92
Strange, S. 79
Strauss Turnbull 14
Strong, Benjamin 205–206, 207
subsidiaries
  'back door' 115–116
  and Eurodollar business 115
Suddeutsche Bank AG 37
Sudwestbank 37
Suez crisis 10
surplus countries, favourable treatment
    of 23
suspension of payments 203
swap transactions 3, 10, 24, 28n.
Switzerland 12, 13, 187
  banks and Eurobonds 18
  banks as intermediaries 17
  and Eurodollar market 86
syndicated loans 14–15, 68, 121, 125
syndicates 3, 6, 18
  see also banking clubs; consortium banks

tariffs 9, 22, 34n., 53
tax havens 16, 75, 182

technology transfer 108
term loans 57–58, 68, 112
  American-style 114, 116
Tietmeyer proposals 214
Tokyo, as financial centre 78
Toronto Dominion Bank 138
transaction costs 141, 142
Travelers Group 194
Tripartite Pact (1928) 208
trust companies 203
trust funds 112
Tschoegl, A. E. 136, 138
Tuke, Antony 46

UK
  balance of payments 11, 80
  bank deposits 206
  competition from US banks 16, 113–114,
    179
  debt crisis (1982) 212, 213
  dual banking system 194
  and Eurodollar market 85
  government lending 37
  innovative capacity of banks 47–49
  merchant banks 38
  nationalization of banks 38
  overseas banks 38–39, 42–43
  pre-war banking dominance 27
  regulation of banks 88, 89, 96, 200
  'special relationship' with US 24, 62
  see also London
UK Treasury 89–90
underwriting, by foreign banks 186
Union Bank of Switzerland (UBS) 18, 145,
    191
Unit of Account loans 88
unit trusts, EEC shares 84
United Dominion Trust 48
universal banking system 117, 132n.,
    193–194, 196n.
Urban, S. 137
US
  balance of payments deficit 23, 77, 86,
    91–92, 179
  favourable treatment under Bretton
    Woods 22–23
  foreign direct investment 152, 179
  and Germany 183, 189–192
  multinational strategies 23, 53–55
  post-war financial dominance 26–27
  'special relationship' with UK 24, 62
  State Department 8
  welfare programmes 24